Physics in Outline

MAIDSTONE SCHOOL
FOR GIRLS
Huntsman Lane Maidstone

Also available from Stanley Thornes (Publishers) Ltd

PHYSICS FOR ALL by J. J. Wellington
A-LEVEL PHYSICS by R. Muncaster

Teachers who would like a free booklet giving answers to the tests should send a *large* stamped addressed envelope to Stanley Thornes (Publishers) Ltd., Educa House, Old Station Drive, Leckhampton Road, Cheltenham, GL53 0DN.

Physics in Outline

A Concise O-level Text

R Candlin MA

Stanley Thornes (Publishers) Ltd

© text R Candlin 1983
© diagrams ST(P) Ltd 1983

All rights reserved. No part of this publication may be reproduced, stored in a retrieval system or transmitted in any form or by any means, electronic, mechanical, photocopying, recording or otherwise, without the prior written consent of the copyright holders. Applications for such permission should be addressed to the publishers: Stanley Thornes (Publishers) Ltd, Educa House, Old Station Drive, Leckhampton Road, CHELTENHAM GL53 0DN, UK.

First published 1983 by
Stanley Thornes (Publishers) Ltd,
Educa House,
Old Station Drive,
Leckhampton Road,
CHELTENHAM GL53 0DN

British Library Cataloguing in Publication Data

Candlin, R.
  Physics in outline.
  I. Title
  530   QA23

ISBN 0-85950-366-6

Typeset by Tech-Set, Gateshead, Tyne and Wear.
Printed in Great Britain at The Pitman Press, Bath.

Contents

		Preface	vii
		Acknowledgements	ix
		Photocredits	x
		A note on units	xi
Section A		**MECHANICS**	1
Chapter	1	Measurements and density	3
	2	Speed, velocity and acceleration	12
	3	Force	23
	4	Moments	35
	5	Momentum and Newton's laws	41
	6	Energy and power	46
	7	Machines	53
	8	Pressure and pumps	57
	9	Archimedes' principle	65
Section B		**HEAT**	69
Chapter	10	Temperature	71
	11	Thermal expansion	76
	12	Gases	80
	13	The kinetic theory	88
	14	Heat capacity	92
	15	Change of state	98
	16	Heat transfer	105
Section C		**LIGHT**	111
Chapter	17	Properties of light	113
	18	Reflection and refraction	117
	19	Lenses	128
	20	Optical instruments	136

Section D		**WAVES**	141
Chapter	21	Oscillations and waves	143
	22	Sound	149
	23	Stationary waves	154
	24	Wave patterns	159
	25	Light waves	164
	26	Colour	172
Section E		**ELECTRICITY AND MAGNETISM**	175
Chapter	27	Charge	177
	28	Current and voltage	183
	29	Resistance	189
	30	Cells, circuits and energy	197
	31	AC, rectifiers and oscilloscopes	204
	32	Magnetism	210
	33	Motors and dynamos	217
	34	Transformers	227
	35	Electrical safety and domestic wiring	230
Section F		**NUCLEAR PHYSICS**	233
Chapter	36	Atoms and nuclei	235
	37	Radioactivity	237
	38	Waves and particles	244

APPENDIX/INDEX 245

SI units 247

Index 249

Preface

There are some excellent O-level physics textbooks on the market, but in the author's opinion many of them are too long and seem to be trying to do the teacher's job as well as their own. This concise text aims to cover all the topics in the syllabuses of the various examination boards with a sufficient amount of explanation while keeping the book small enough for convenience in use and not too long to be suitable for revising.

Any attempt to include a full range of class experiments and demonstration experiments would have made the book unwieldy. It was felt that it is better to leave to the individual teacher the selection of supporting demonstrations and of class experiments additional to the ones mentioned in the text, bearing in mind the apparatus available and the requirements of the particular syllabus being aimed at.

The descriptions of experiments in the text are intended to show the principles and the methods and also to be suitable for revision; they are not intended as work-sheets. The teacher is in a better position than the author is to provide instructions for the experiments, either in the form of work-sheets or else on the chalkboard or o.h.p., because he knows the particular apparatus that the class will use and also what skills the class has already acquired.

A selection of questions is provided at the ends of the chapters and these are aimed at developing understanding. Past examination questions, or parts of them, are included only when they seemed to provide suitable practice for candidates of all examination boards. It is left to the teacher or the school to obtain past papers of the appropriate board so as to give pupils practice in answering questions similar to those that they will meet in the actual examination.

R Candlin
1983

Acknowledgements

I wish to express my thanks to Mr J C Siddons for his careful checking of the script and for many valuable comments and suggestions that he made, and also Mr D J Haynes for his most helpful discussion and ideas. I thank Stanley Thornes (the publishers) for their patience and helpfulness.

I am grateful to the following examination boards for permission to reproduce questions from past papers (abbreviations used are shown in brackets; an asterisk in the text denotes a part question):

Associated Examining Board (AEB)
University of Cambridge Local Examinations Syndicate (C)
Joint Matriculation Board (JMB)
University of London School Examinations Department (L)
Oxford Delegacy of Local Examinations (O)
Oxford and Cambridge Schools Examination Board (O & C)
Southern Universities' Joint Board (SUJB)
Welsh Joint Education Committee (W)

RC

Photocredits

The author and publisher are grateful to the following who provided photographs and gave permission for reproduction:

p. 69 Heat: Barnaby's Picture Library
p. 141 Waves: Paul Brierley
p. 175 Electricity: Science Photo Library
p. 233 Nuclear: Pergamon Press Ltd (from *Cloud Chamber Photographs of the Cosmic Radiation* by G D Rochester and J G Wilson; photographs by W M Powell and E Hayward)

A Note on Units

With a few exceptions SI units have been used throughout.

At O-level the style m/s is currently used by all examination boards except the SUJB which uses the style m s^{-1}. The former style has therefore been adopted in this book.

On graphical axes the style v(m/s) has been used in preference to v/(m/s) or v/m s^{-1}.

Section A:
MECHANICS

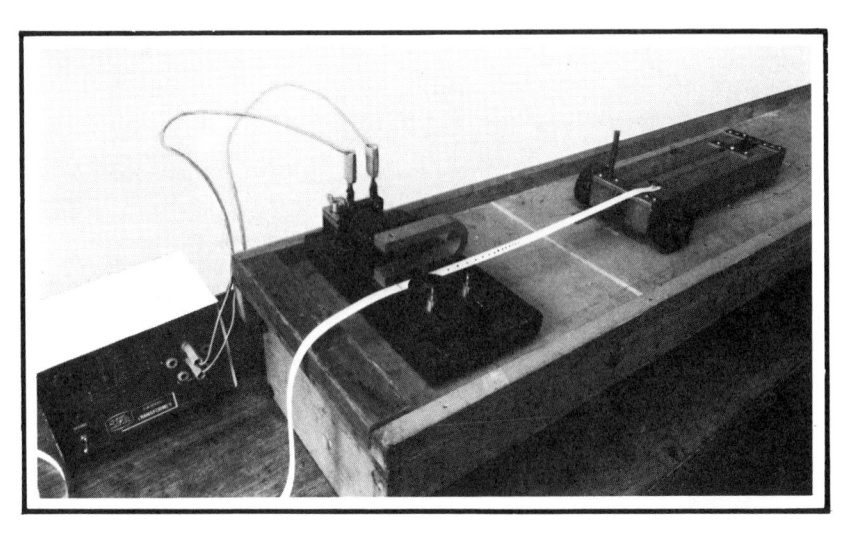

A ticker timer.
The trolley is accelerating down a slope. The ticker timer prints dots on the paper tape to measure the acceleration.

Chapter 1

Measurements and Density

Units of Measurement

If we are to understand the world around us we need to make measurements, and before we can make measurements which are meaningful to other scientists we need a system of units which is universally recognised. The agreed system is called the Système International, or SI for short. The three most basic units in this system are:

for length, the **metre** (abbreviated to m),
for mass, the **kilogram** (kg),
for time, the **second** (s).

The kilogram is defined as a mass equal to that of a lump of metal alloy which is kept in a laboratory near Paris. The metre and the second are defined in terms of the wavelength and the frequency of certain kinds of light.

Other units are derived from these. For example, if a rectangle is 3 m long and 2 m wide its area is:

$$3 \, m \times 2 \, m = 6 \, m \times m$$

and so 'metre times metre' is a unit of area. It is called 'square metre' and written m^2 for short. Similarly, the unit of volume is the cubic metre (m^3).

Units can be divided as well as multiplied. If a car travels a distance of 100 m in a time of 5 s, its average speed during that time is:

$$\frac{100 \, m}{5 \, s} = 20 \frac{m}{s}$$

This unit of speed is called 'metre per second' and we will write it as m/s, though in more advanced work it is $m \, s^{-1}$.

A list of SI units, complete enough for an O-level course, is given on pp. 247 and 248.

Measurement of Length

The commonest instruments for measuring length in a school physics laboratory are the metre rule and the half-metre rule. They can be used to measure to an accuracy of one millimetre, but this will not be accurate enough for some of the experiments which are mentioned in the next part of this chapter.

■ **Vernier callipers** (Figure 1.1) can measure lengths up to 100 mm or so to an accuracy of $\frac{1}{10}$ mm. The method of reading the scale is:

(i) look at the zero of the vernier scale and read where this comes on the main scale, estimating the figure for tenths of a millimetre;

(ii) look along the vernier scale to see which vernier division coincides with one of the divisions on the main scale — this gives the correct figure for tenths of a millimetre.

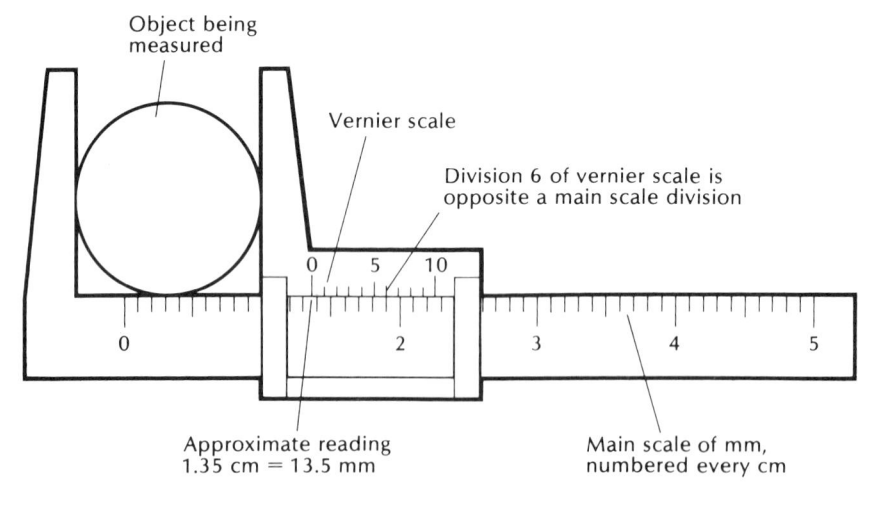

Fig. 1.1

For example, in Figure 1.1 the zero of the vernier scale is about half-way between 13 mm and 14 mm on the main scale, giving an estimated reading of 13.5 mm. Division number 6 of the vernier scale coincides with one of the main scale divisions, and so the correct reading is 13.6 mm.

Quick Question 1

If the zero of the vernier scale almost exactly coincides with the 2 cm mark on the main scale, and division number 9 of the vernier scale exactly coincides with a main scale division, what is the true reading? Give the answer in millimetres.

Measurements and Density

■ The micrometer screw gauge (Figure 1.2) can measure lengths up to 20 mm or so to an accuracy of $\frac{1}{100}$ mm. To use it, close the jaws with nothing between them by screwing up the sleeve, but do this by turning the ratchet so as to avoid applying too much force. If you hold the sleeve itself to screw it up, you could damage the gauge by straining it. The scale should read zero if the gauge is correctly adjusted, but if it does not, you should note the zero reading. Next open the jaws, and screw them up on the object to be measured — again, this must be done by turning the ratchet. Then read the scale, and subtract the zero reading.

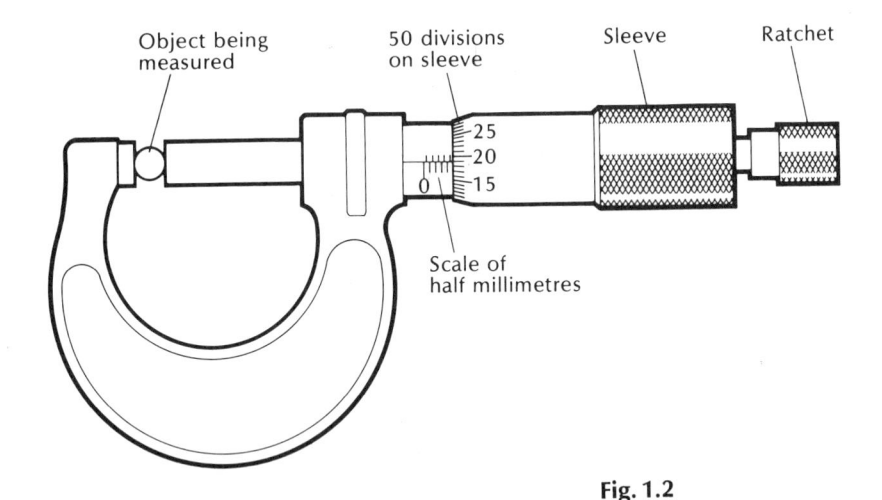

Fig. 1.2

The method of reading the scale is:

(i) read the main scale, estimating the figure for tenths of a millimetre. In Figure 1.2 there are four millimetre divisions uncovered and a half millimetre and a little more, so your estimate might be 4.6 or 4.7 or 4.8 mm;

(ii) read the scale on the sleeve. In Figure 1.2 this reading is 19, but since the sleeve rotates twice for each millimetre of travel this could mean either 19 or 69 hundredths of a millimetre. So the reading is 4.69 mm.

Quick Question 2

What is the diameter of the ball bearing being measured by a micrometer in Figure 1.3?

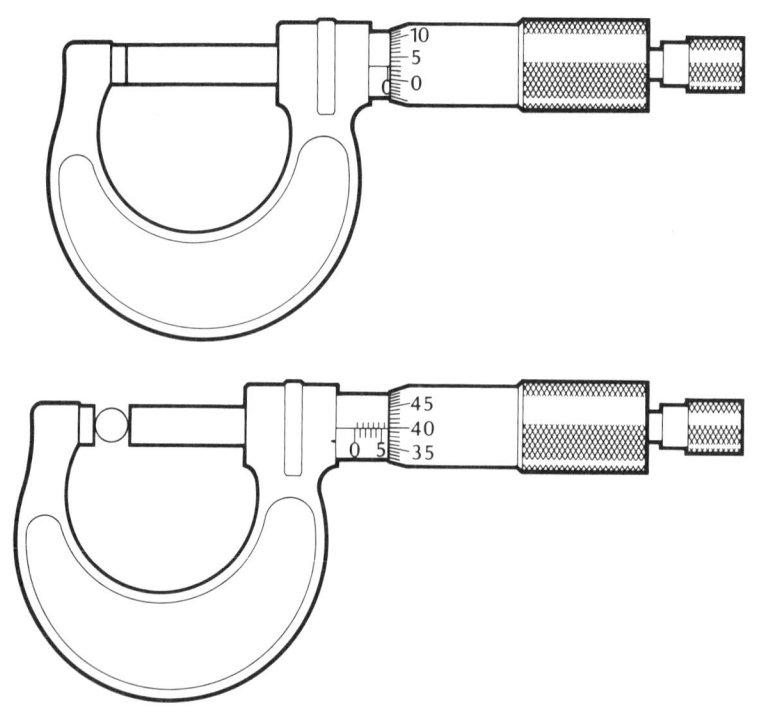

Fig. 1.3

Density

If we divide the mass of a body by its volume, we obtain a useful quantity which is the same for any one material – for example, it is the same for a small steel bolt as it is for a large girder made of the same kind of steel – but it is different for different materials. This quantity is called 'density'.

■ The **density** of a body is its mass divided by its volume:

$$\rho = \frac{M}{V}$$

where ρ (the Greek letter 'rho') is the density.

The SI unit of density is the kilogram per cubic metre (kg/m³). Here are some values:

iron	8000 kg/m³
water	1000 kg/m³
air at standard temperature and pressure	1.3 kg/m³

The value given for water is exact when the temperature is 4 °C and is near enough for most purposes at other temperatures. The other two values are approximate.

Quick Question 3

What is the mass of water in a rectangular swimming bath 8 m long, 5 m wide and 1.5 m in average depth? Give the answer in tonnes. (1 tonne = 1000 kg)

A cubic metre is an inconveniently large volume for laboratory experiments, and so it is a good idea to work in thousandths of this amount. Since a thousandth of a kilogram is a gram, and a thousandth of a cubic metre is a cubic decimetre (often called a litre), it follows that a kg/m³ can equally well be called a g/dm³ or 'gram per litre'. So:

$$\text{Density of water} = 1000 \text{ kg/m}^3$$
$$= 1000 \text{ g/dm}^3$$
$$= 1 \text{ g/cm}^3$$

■ The relative density of a body is its density divided by the density of water. It has no units. For example, the density of iron is 8000 kg/m³ = 8 g/cm³, and so its relative density is 8.

Methods of Measuring Density

For a body of regular shape the method is to weigh it to find its mass, then to find its volume by measuring it with a rule or with vernier callipers or with a micrometer screw gauge, and then to divide the mass by the volume.

Quick Question 4

A rectangular wooden plank 2.0 m long, 100 mm wide and 20 mm thick is weighed and found to have a mass of 3.0 kg. What is its density?

For a body of irregular shape a displacement method may be used or, for greater accuracy, a method based on Archimedes' principle as described on p. 66. The next two experiments are versions of the displacement method.

Use of a Displacement Can

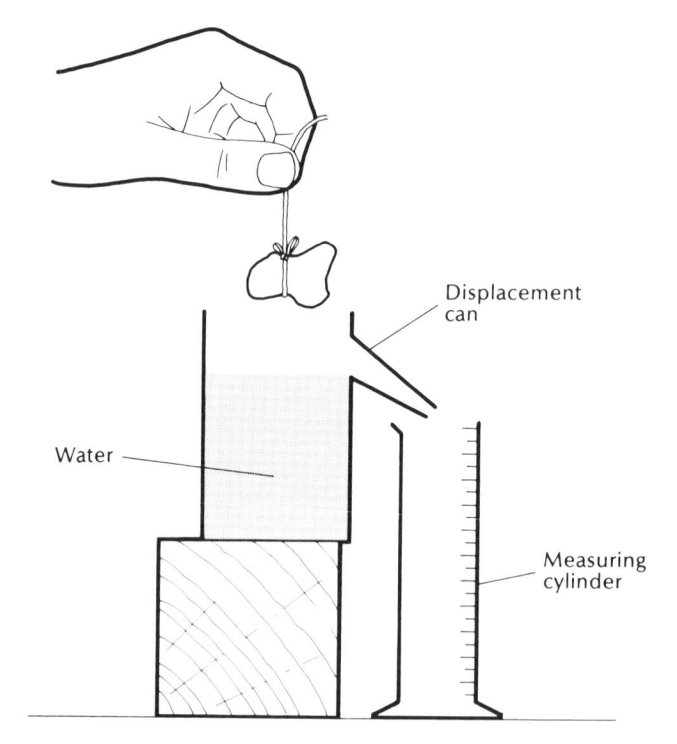

Fig. 1.4

Weigh the object whose density is to be found. Over-fill the displacement can with water and wait until the excess water has drained out. Place a measuring cylinder under the spout. Lower the object gently into the can. Wait until the displaced water has finished overflowing into the measuring cylinder and then read its volume. Divide the mass by the volume to find the density.

Displacement in a Measuring Cylinder

Fig. 1.5

Measurements and Density

Weigh the object. Read the volume of some water in a measuring cylinder. Put the object into the measuring cylinder so that it is completely submerged in the water and read the total volume. Subtract one volume reading from the other to find the volume of displaced water, which is also the volume of the object. Divide the mass by the volume to find the density.

This experiment can be done with objects which float in water, by holding the object below the water surface with a stiff piece of wire. The experiment can also be done with sand. In this case the result is not the density of the sand as a whole, but the density of the material of which each grain is composed.

Comparison of Densities by U-tube

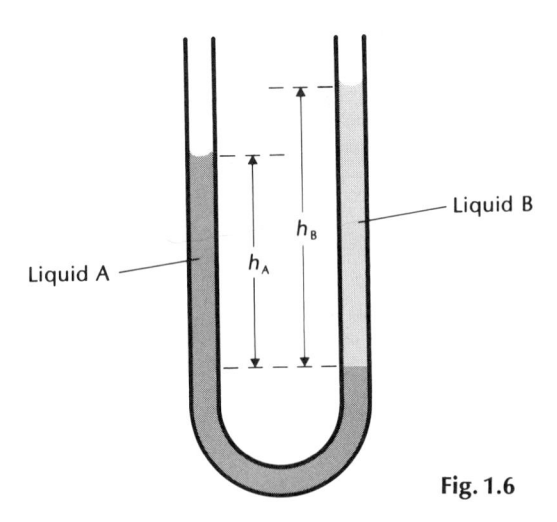

Fig. 1.6

This method is suitable for liquids which do not mix, such as oil and water. In Figure 1.6:

$$\frac{\text{Density of A}}{\text{Density of B}} = \frac{h_B}{h_A}$$

The reason for the truth of this equation will become clear later; it follows from the equation at the bottom of p. 58.

Quick Question 5

If liquid A is water and liquid B is oil, and the heights are $h_A = 160$ mm and $h_B = 200$ mm, what is the density of the oil?

Questions on Chapter 1

1 Read the vernier shown in Figure 1.7.

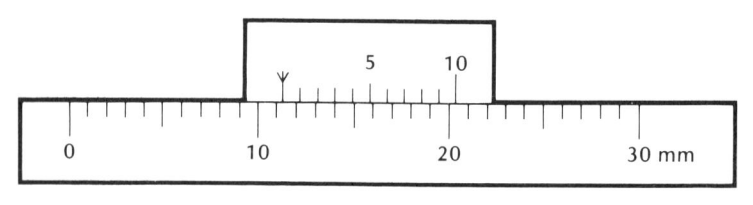

Fig. 1.7

2 Read the micrometer screw gauge shown in Figure 1.8.

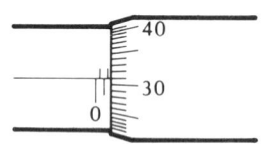

Fig. 1.8

3 Figure 1.9 shows a micrometer being used to measure the diameter of a wire. What are *a)* the zero error and *b)* the diameter of the wire?

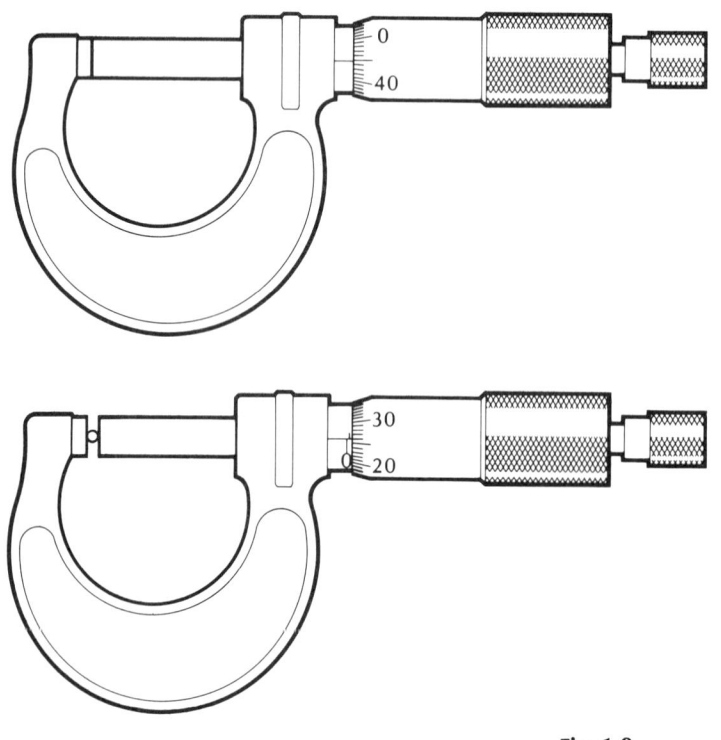

Fig. 1.9

4 An aluminium cube measuring 50 mm along each edge has a mass of 340 g. *a)* What is its density? *b)* What is its relative density?

5   What is the mass of a concrete paving slab 1 m long, 0.6 m wide and 50 mm thick? The density of concrete is 2500 kg/m³.

6   A sailing boat requires a keel of mass 1 tonne. If the keel is made of iron, what volume of iron is needed? (Density of iron = 8000 kg/m³. For the meaning of a tonne, see p. 248.)

7   A 10 litre container has a mass of 0.5 kg. What will its total mass be when it is full of paraffin which has a relative density of 0.8?

8   A room measures 6 m long, 5 m wide and 3 m high. The air in it has a density of 1.2 kg/m³. What is the mass of the air in the room?

9   A measuring cylinder is filled to the 100 cm³ mark with oil at a temperature of 0°C. The oil has a density low enough to ensure that ice will sink in it. When some ice is put into the oil, the oil level rises to the 150 cm³ mark, and when all the ice has melted the oil level is at the 146 cm³ mark. Find the density of ice. (Density of water = 1000 kg/m³)

10 An irregularly shaped lump of lead is lowered into water in a displacement can (see Figure 1.4) and the displaced water overflows into a beaker. The following readings are taken:

Mass of lead	560 g
Mass of empty beaker	40 g
Mass of beaker + displaced water	90 g

What are a) the density of lead and b) its relative density?

11 A 100 cm³ measuring cylinder has a mass of 60 g. When it is filled with dry sand up to the 50 cm³ mark its total mass is 140 g. a) What is the density of the sand?

The sand is now poured out and the measuring cylinder is filled with water up to the 50 cm³ mark. When the sand is poured back in, the water rises to the 82 cm³ mark. b) What is the density of the material of which the sand grains are composed?

12 A U-tube similar to the one shown in Figure 1.6 is set up on a bench. Liquid A is water and liquid B is toluene.

The heights of the surfaces measured from the level of the top of the bench are:

Water surface	315 mm
Toluene surface	350 mm
Water–toluene interface	100 mm

What are a) the density of toluene and b) its relative density?

Chapter 2

Speed, Velocity and Acceleration

- The speed of a body is the distance it moves divided by the time taken. The equation is written as:

$$v = \frac{s}{t}$$

because the letter v is used for speed as well as for velocity and the usual letter to represent distance travelled is s.

- The velocity of a body is its speed and direction of movement. For example, 20 metres per second due north and 20 metres per second due east are the same speed but not the same velocity. A train moving along a curved track, or a satellite in orbit round the Earth, may each be moving at a constant speed, but their velocities are not constant because the direction of motion changes.

s–t and v–t Diagrams

These are graphs of distance against time and of speed against time respectively. Figure 2.1 shows the s–t and v–t diagrams for four bodies.

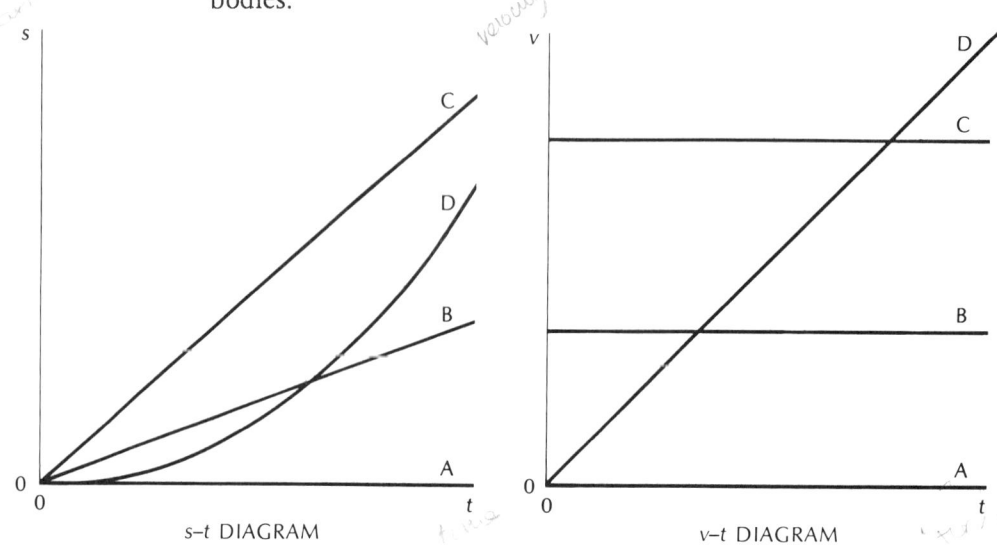

Fig. 2.1

Speed, Velocity and Acceleration

- Body A is at rest.
- Body B is moving at constant speed.
- Body C is moving at constant speed faster than B.
- Body D is accelerating.

Figure 2.2 shows both diagrams for a ferry-boat travelling across a river, waiting for a time, and then returning. The time taken to accelerate is ignored. Notice that in the *v–t* diagram the speed is counted as positive when the boat is going in one direction and negative when it is going the other way.

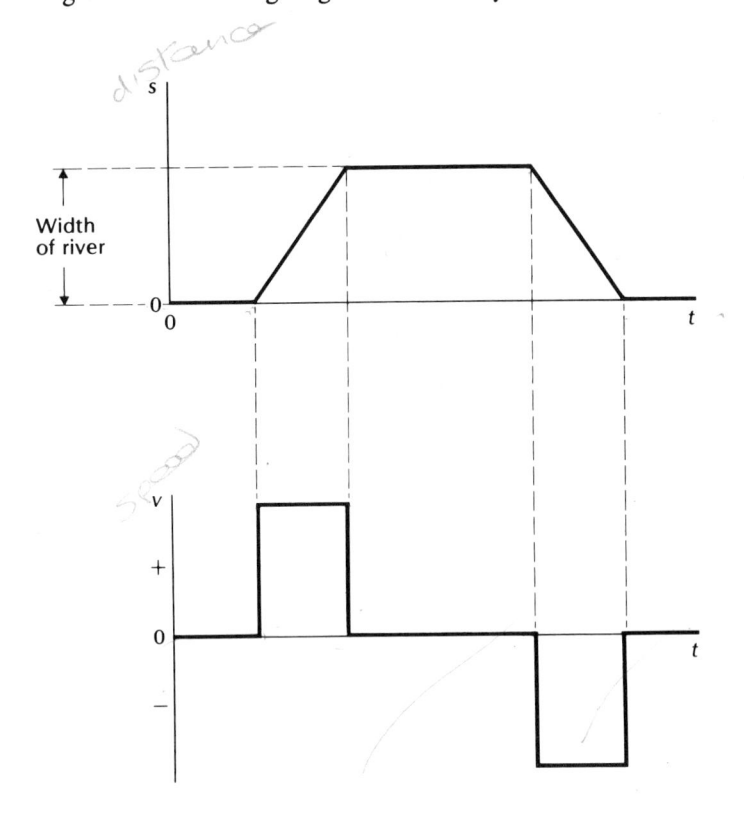

Fig. 2.2

Figure 2.3 shows a stone falling to the ground without bouncing.

The *v–t* diagram is the more useful of the two because it shows the distance travelled and the speed and the acceleration all on the same diagram.

> The distance travelled, *s*, is represented by the area under the line, as explained overleaf.
>
> The speed, *v*, is represented by the vertical coordinate.
>
> The acceleration, *a*, is represented by the gradient, as explained on p. 15.

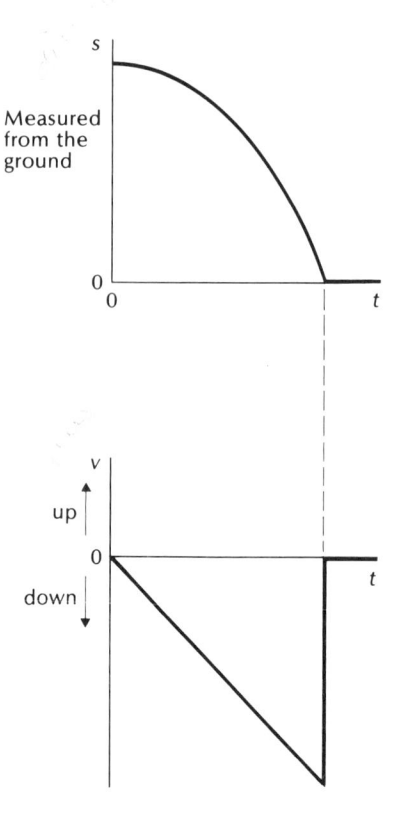

Fig. 2.3

To see how the area under the line on the graph represents the distance travelled, consider Figure 2.4. The dark shaded area represents a speed of one metre per second continuing for one second, which works out to one metre of distance travelled. The whole shaded area is 12 times as big, representing a distance of 12 m travelled in the whole three seconds.

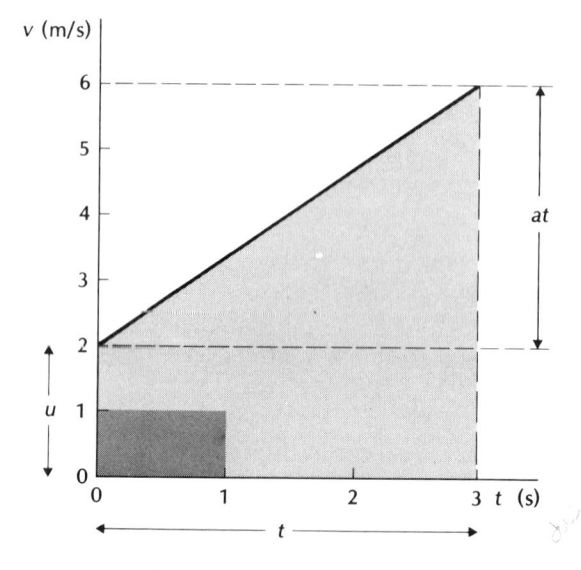

Fig. 2.4

Speed, Velocity and Acceleration

Acceleration

■ The **acceleration** of a body is the change of its velocity divided by the time taken to change. Written in the form of an equation, this definition is:

$$a = \frac{v-u}{t}$$

In this equation and in the other equations in this section:

a is the acceleration,
u is the initial velocity,
v is the final velocity,
t is the time taken,
s is the distance travelled.

The SI unit of acceleration is written m/s^2, since it is m/s divided by s. It is called 'metre per second per second' or 'metre per second squared'.

Quick Question 6

A racing car takes five seconds to accelerate from 40 m/s to 60 m/s. What is its average acceleration?

Since the gradient of a graph is the increase in the vertical coordinate divided by the increase in the horizontal one, it follows that acceleration is represented by the gradient of the v–t graph. In Figure 2.4 the gradient of the sloping line is:

$$\frac{6 \text{ m/s} - 2 \text{ m/s}}{3 \text{ s}} = 1\tfrac{1}{3} \text{ m/s}^2$$

and this is the acceleration.

Gravitational Acceleration

■ The **acceleration due to gravity** is the acceleration of any body which is falling freely, without appreciable air resistance. It does not depend on the mass of the body. It is called g, and at the Earth's surface:

$g = 10 \text{ m/s}^2$ in calculations in which a 2% error does not matter

or

$g = 9.8 \text{ m/s}^2$ more accurately.

The value of g at a point in space near to the Earth or to some other planet depends on two things: the mass of the planet, and the distance of the point from the centre of the planet. At the top of a mountain g is slightly less than at sea level because of the greater distance away from the centre of the Earth, and since a satellite in orbit round the Earth is further away still, the value of g which affects it is smaller still.

A method of measuring g is given on p. 18.

Uniform Acceleration Formulas

When the speed, v, is constant, the distance travelled is given by $s = vt$. When the speed is changing, it is the mean speed which must be used. If the acceleration is constant, the mean speed is $\dfrac{u+v}{2}$; therefore:

$$s = \frac{u+v}{2}t \qquad \text{(the equation without } a\text{)}$$

The definition of acceleration gives a second equation:

$$a = \frac{v-u}{t} \qquad \text{(the equation without } s\text{)}$$

Problems on uniformly accelerating bodies can be solved by using these two equations.

Example 2.1 A stone dropped down a well takes 2.0 s to reach the bottom. How deep is the well? ($g = 10 \text{ m/s}^2$)

Solution Start by using the definition of acceleration to find the final speed, v:

$$a = \frac{v-u}{t} \qquad \therefore v = u + at = 0 + 10 \times 2 = 20 \text{ m/s}$$

Then the other equation gives the answer:

$$s = \frac{u+v}{2}t = \frac{0+20}{2} \times 2 = 20 \text{ m}$$

Example 2.2 A train is travelling at a speed of 10 m/s and starts to accelerate with a uniform acceleration of 0.20 m/s². How far does it travel during the first half-minute after it starts to accelerate?

Speed, Velocity and Acceleration

Solution A sketch graph is useful in this question (Figure 2.5).

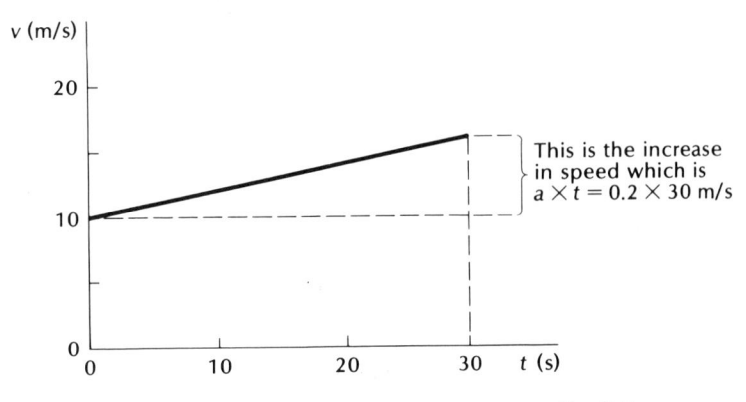

Fig. 2.5

(Annotation on graph: This is the increase in speed which is $a \times t = 0.2 \times 30$ m/s)

$$
\begin{aligned}
s &= \text{Area under the graph} \\
&= \text{Area of rectangle} + \text{Area of triangle} \\
&= \text{Length} \times \text{Width} + \tfrac{1}{2} \times \text{Base} \times \text{Height} \\
&= 30 \times 10 \quad + \tfrac{1}{2} \times 30 \times (0.2 \times 30) \\
&= 300 + 90 = 390 \text{ m}
\end{aligned}
$$

Additional Formulas

By combining the first two acceleration equations it is possible to obtain three more*:

$$s = ut + \tfrac{1}{2}at^2 \quad \text{(the equation without } v\text{)}$$
$$s = vt - \tfrac{1}{2}at^2 \quad \text{(the equation without } u\text{)}$$
$$v^2 - u^2 = 2as \quad \text{(the equation without } t\text{)}$$

If you don't learn these three equations, it may still be worth remembering that:

$$s = \tfrac{1}{2}at^2 \quad \text{when } u = 0$$

as this is useful in calculations about falling bodies. It is easily proved from the v-t diagram (Figure 2.6), because the distance travelled is the area of the triangle, which is:

$$\tfrac{1}{2} \times \text{Base} \times \text{Height} = \tfrac{1}{2} \times t \times at = \tfrac{1}{2}at^2$$

*Not generally required by examination boards.

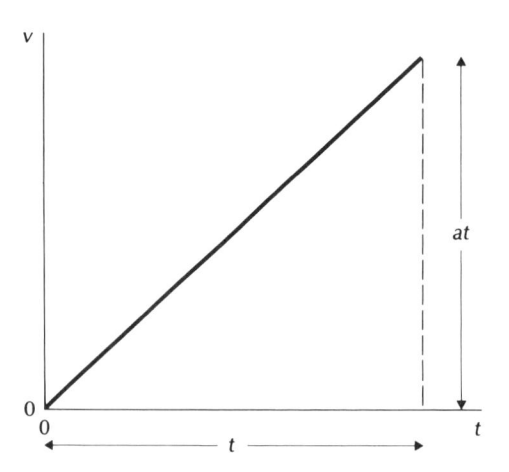

Fig. 2.6

Measurement of Acceleration

1 A Free-fall Experiment

This is a way of measuring the acceleration of a freely falling ball bearing.

Since the air resistance of the ball bearing is negligible, this is a measurement of the acceleration due to gravity. Figure 2.7 shows the apparatus. When the double switch is moved across, the electromagnet is switched off and the ball bearing starts to fall. At the same moment the other half of the switch completes the control circuit of the electric timer so that it starts timing. The trap door, made of iron or steel, is held in the closed position by a magnet until the ball bearing hits it and knocks it open; this breaks the timer control circuit and stops the timer. (You may meet a different circuit for this experiment — there are many ways of doing it.)

To calculate the result, first measure the height, s, and read the time of fall, t, from the timer. Divide s by t to find the average speed. This average speed is half of the final speed, because:

$$\text{Average speed} = \frac{u+v}{2} \quad \text{and} \quad u = 0$$

Therefore doubling the average speed gives the final speed, v. Then divide v by t to find the acceleration.

The calculation is simpler if you remember the equation:

$$s = \tfrac{1}{2}at^2$$

which gives $$a = \frac{2s}{t^2}$$

Speed, Velocity and Acceleration

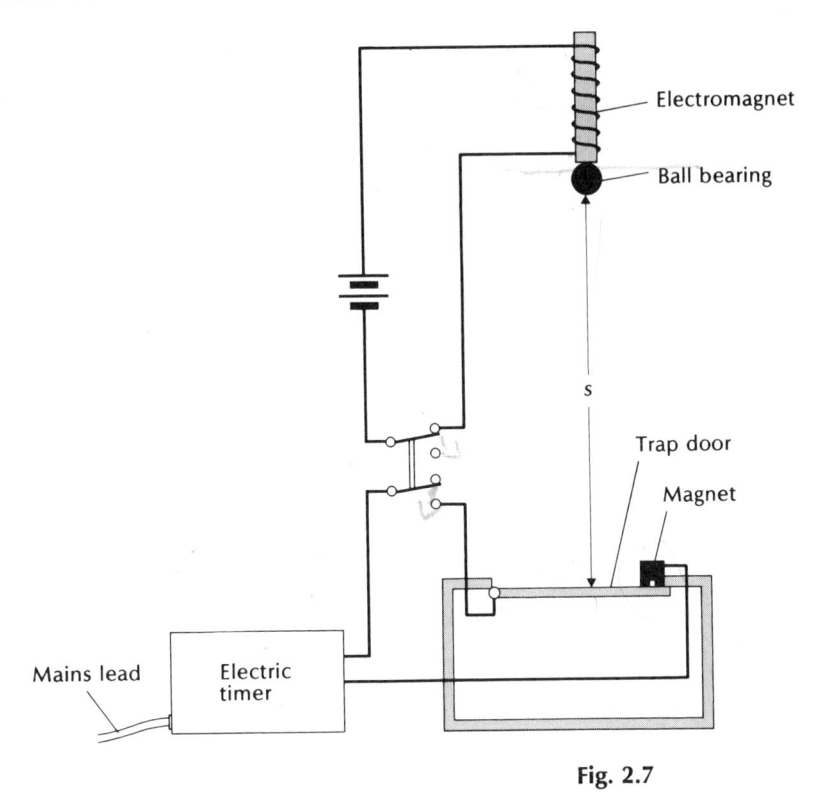

Fig. 2.7

Quick Question 7

If a ball bearing is timed to fall 0.80 m in 0.40 s, what value does this give for g?

2 The Use of a Ticker Timer

Figure 2.8 shows a ticker timer being used to measure the acceleration of a trolley caused by a stretched elastic cord. This is an outline of the method.

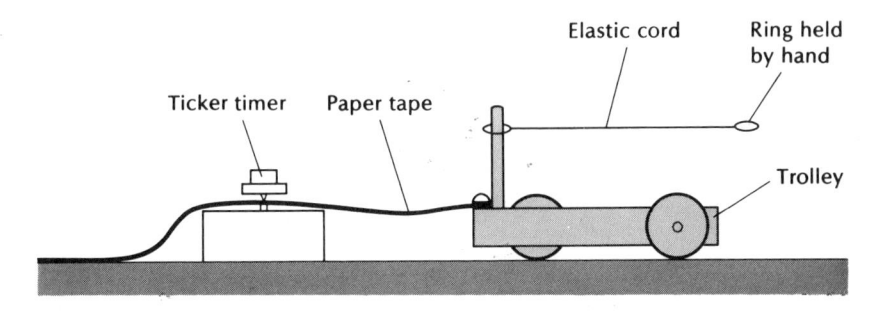

Fig. 2.8

Accelerate the trolley so that the tape is pulled through the ticker timer. The ticker timer prints a dot on the tape once every fiftieth of a second. Cut the tape into sections, cutting through every tenth dot. The time which each of these sections took to pass through the timer was ten fiftieths of a second, which is 0.2 s, sometimes called a 'ten-tick'.

Next stick the strips of tape on a sheet of paper to form a graph as shown in Figure 2.9. Draw a straight line as nearly as possible through the ends of all the pieces of tape.

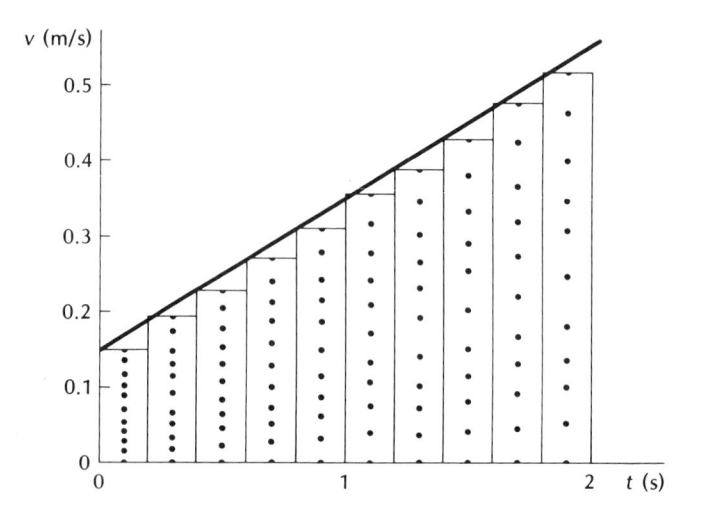

Fig. 2.9

Mark the graph scales like this:

- *Vertical scale.* Since each section of tape represents 0.2 s, it would be 0.2 m long if the speed was 1 m/s. Therefore the 1 m/s mark must be 0.2 m (20 cm) up from the origin of the graph.

- *Horizontal scale.* Each section of tape represents one-fifth of a second and so five tape-widths correspond to one second.

Find the acceleration from the gradient of the graph.

For example, in Figure 2.9:

$$a = \frac{v-u}{t} = \frac{0.55-0.15}{2} = 0.2 \text{ m/s}^2$$

The use of a 'friction-compensated slope' in this experiment is described in the next chapter.

Speed, Velocity and Acceleration

Questions on Chapter 2

1. A car is able to accelerate from rest up to 60 miles per hour in 9 s. Assuming that 60 m.p.h. equals 27 m/s, what is the car's mean acceleration, expressed in SI units?

2. How far does the car of Question 1 travel during its nine seconds of acceleration? Assume that the acceleration is uniform.

3. How far does the car of Question 1 travel during the next nine seconds if it maintains a steady sixty miles per hour?

4. A car travels at a constant speed of 20 m/s for 30 s and then brakes so as to come to a stop after a further 10 s. The retardation (negative acceleration) is constant during this last ten second period. Find:
   a) the total distance travelled by the car during the whole forty seconds, and
   b) the retardation during the braking.

5. A car is travelling at 18 m/s (about 40 miles per hour). What is the least distance in which the car can stop after the driver sees an obstruction on the road in front of him, if the driver takes 0.5 s to react before applying the brakes, and the brakes then cause a retardation of 6 m/s^2?

6. A stone is dropped from a high window and takes exactly 2 s to reach the ground. Air resistance is negligible and the acceleration due to gravity may be taken to be 10 m/s^2.
   a) How fast is the stone moving 1 s after being released?
   b) How fast is the stone moving 2 s after being released?
   c) What is the mean speed of the stone during the whole 2 s?
   d) How far did the stone fall?

7. A ball bearing is dropped in a laboratory and timed by an automatic device which registers a time of fall of exactly half a second when the ball drops through a vertical distance of 1.20 m. What value does this give for g?

8. A cricketer throws the ball vertically upwards into the air and then catches it as it falls. If the ball rises ten metres above his hands, for how long is it in the air? ($g = 10$ m/s^2)

9. A juggler throws a ball into the air and catches it 1.6 s later. How high above his hands did it rise?

10 Figure 2.10 is a full-scale diagram of a piece of ticker tape that has been used to measure the acceleration of a trolley on a laboratory bench. A line has been drawn through every tenth dot. By making measurements on the figure, find *a)* the mean speed between A and B, *b)* the mean speed between B and C, and *c)* the acceleration of the trolley.

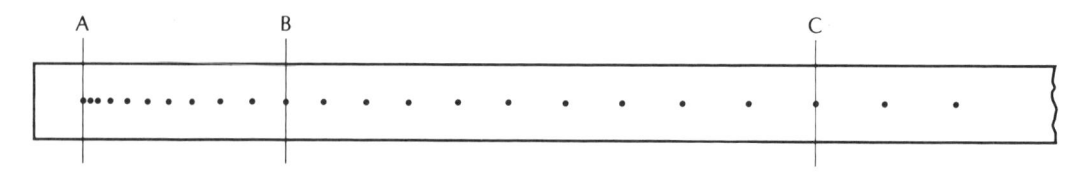

Fig. 2.10

11 An iron mass falls freely, pulling a length of ticker tape behind it. A ticker timer marks the paper every $\frac{1}{50}$ s. The distance of each dot from the first dot is measured and the readings are:

Dot number: 1 2 3 4 5 6 7 8 9 10 11 12

Distance from first dot (mm): 0 2 8 18 32 50 72 98 128 162 200 242

a) Find the average speed during the first $\frac{1}{10}$ s.
b) Find the average speed during the second $\frac{1}{10}$ s.
c) From your answers to *a)* and *b)*, find the acceleration.

12 One end of a piece of ticker tape is stuck on to a stone. When the stone is dropped, the tape is pulled through a ticker timer and the measurements of five-dot lengths of tape are:

first five dots	0.050 m
second five dots	0.140 m
third five dots	0.230 m
fourth five dots	0.320 m

What was the acceleration of the falling stone?

Chapter 3

Force

A force is a pull or a push. Its effect may be to accelerate a body or to slow it down or, in combination with other forces, to stretch it, bend it or turn it.

■ A **newton** (N) is the force which gives to a mass of one kilogram an acceleration of one metre per second per second.

If only one force acts on a body, then:

$$F = ma$$

where F is the force   (in N)

  m is the mass   (in kg)

  a is the acceleration produced   (in m/s²)

This equation may be tested experimentally by using a ticker timer (see p. 19). The slope of the runway in Figure 3.1 is altered until the trolley, once it has started, will run down at constant speed without being pulled by the elastic cord; the slope is then 'friction compensated'. The trolley is next accelerated by using the

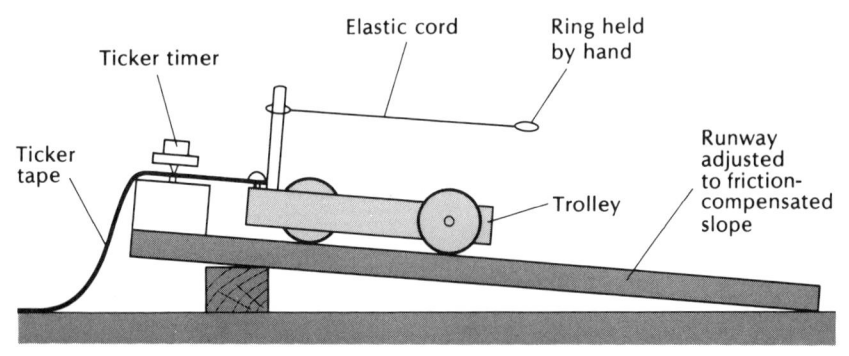

Fig. 3.1

elastic cord and the acceleration is measured by the method described on p. 19. The elastic cord should be stretched so that it just reaches the end of the trolley; using the length of the trolley as a gauge makes it possible, after a little practice, to apply the same force each time. This is repeated with different forces (by using two or three elastic cords together) and also with different masses (by adding more mass to the trolley). Although the results are not likely to be accurate they should be good enough to show that:

- the acceleration is proportional to the force, and
- the acceleration is inversely proportional to the mass being accelerated.

Putting these two results together, the experiment shows that:

$$F \text{ is proportional to } m \times a$$

Example 3.1 What is the force required to accelerate a car of mass 1000 kg to a speed of 10 m/s in 20 s, starting from rest?

Solution

$$a = \frac{v-u}{t} = \frac{10-0}{20} = 0.5 \text{ m/s}^2$$

$$F = ma = 1000 \times 0.5 = 500 \text{ N}$$

(The force required will actually be more than this as there will be some air resistance, and also the non-driven wheels will cause some frictional drag.) The other forces acting on the car — W and N in Figure 3.12(b) on p. 31 — do not affect the problem as they are equal in magnitude and opposite in direction and so they cancel each other out exactly.

Mass and Weight

These two quantities are confused in everyday speech but they are quite different things to a scientist. Weight is a force, and it is caused by the Earth pulling a body downwards. Mass is a measure of the quantity of matter in a body and therefore of its reluctance to accelerate.

For a body on the Moon, it is the Moon pulling it downwards which causes its weight. Since the Moon is both smaller and less dense than the Earth, the weight of a body on the Moon is less than the weight which the same body would have if it was on Earth. If an astronaut were to visit several planets in turn, his weight would be different on each one, but his mass would remain the same (unless he were growing fatter or thinner).

This table shows the difference between mass and weight.

	Unit	Direction	Value on the Moon for a given body
Mass	kg	none	same as on Earth
Weight	N	downwards	$\frac{1}{6}$ of Earth value

The equation connecting the mass of a body and its weight is:

$$\text{Weight} = mg$$

where g is the acceleration due to gravity. This means that a kilogram mass weighs about 10 N, as long as it is at the Earth's surface where $g = 10$ m/s^2.

Quick Question 8

> A lump of metal has a weight of 500 newtons. What is its mass?

There is another way of looking at this.* Since weight (in newton) equals mass (in kilogram) multiplied by g, the unit of g must be newton per kilogram. The name for g when it is looked at in this way is 'gravitational field strength'. It is equal to the gravitational acceleration and can be regarded as another name for the same thing.

Elasticity

■ Hooke's law states that the tension (stretching force) in a spring is proportional to the extension (length minus unstretched length). This is not an exact law, but it is true to a high degree of accuracy for most springs up to the maximum extensions for which they were designed.

Metal wires obey Hooke's law up to a certain extension called the **elastic limit**. When stretched beyond this, they stretch more than Hooke's law would predict and some of the stretch is permanent, so that they do not return to their previous length when the tension is removed.

Rubber bands do not obey Hooke's law.

Resultants

■ The **resultant** of two (or more) forces is the single force which, when acting alone, has the same effect as the two (or more) forces acting together. For example, if the force R in Figure 3.2 slides the packing case along the ground just the same as A and B do

---

*Not required by most examination boards.

when they are acting together, then R is the resultant of A and B. In Figure 3.2 and in the following diagrams the directions of the arrows represent the directions of forces — or, in Figure 3.4, of velocities — and the lengths of the arrows represent the magnitudes of the forces or velocities to some suitable scale.

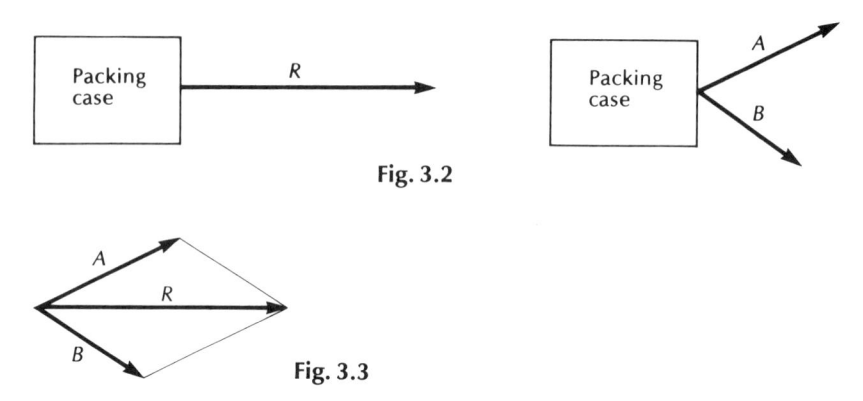

Fig. 3.2

Fig. 3.3

- The **parallelogram of forces**, shown in Figure 3.3, combines the forces A, B and R of Figure 3.2. The resultant of two forces can be found by drawing the parallelogram.

- The **parallelogram of velocities** is similar and is used to find the resultant of two relative velocities. (An example of relative velocity: if you walk along the corridor of a train you may go at 2 m/s relative to the train while the train may be doing 40 m/s relative to the track.) Figure 3.4 gives an example of the parallelogram of velocities.

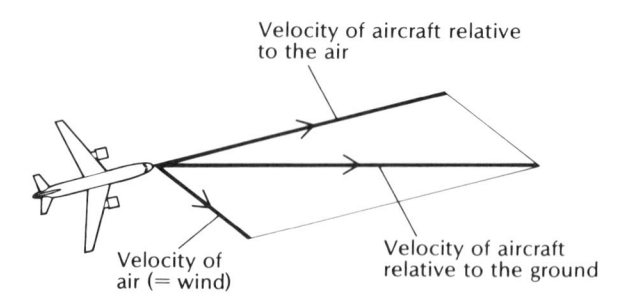

Fig. 3.4

Vectors and Scalars

- A **vector** quantity is one which has direction as well as magnitude. The parallelogram construction applies to any vector quantity, and not only to force and velocity. Examples of vectors are:

    displacement   force
    velocity   momentum
    acceleration   magnetic field strength

Force

■ A **scalar** is a quantity which does not have a direction, but can be fully specified by a number and a unit. Examples of scalars are:

    mass   energy
    density   pressure

This gives us another way of expressing one of the differences between mass and weight which are listed in the table on p. 24: mass is a scalar but weight is a vector.

The Triangle of Forces

> If a body is in equilibrium when three forces are acting on it, then those three forces can be represented by the three sides of a triangle taken in order.

Figure 3.5 shows a triangle of forces.

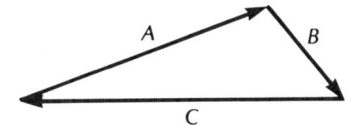

Fig. 3.5

The apparatus shown in Figure 3.6 can be used to test this statement. We know the magnitude and direction of each of the three forces acting on the knot:

- the magnitude — by counting the masses,
- the direction — by measuring with a protractor.

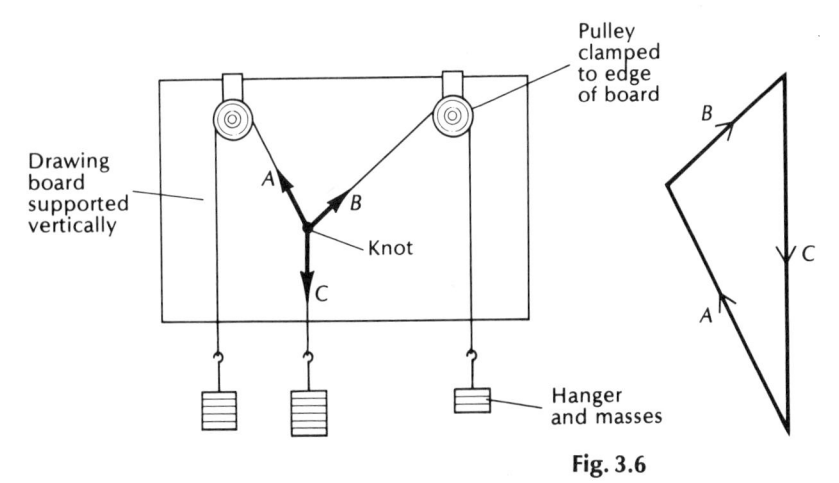

Fig. 3.6

The principle of the triangle of forces can be tested by drawing the forces to scale to see how accurately they will fit together, as shown on the right of the diagram.

The same apparatus can be used to test the parallelogram construction. To do this, draw the parallelogram with two of the forces and see how accurately the resultant found in this way is equal (in magnitude) and opposite (in direction) to the third force.

Notice that the triangle of forces (Figure 3.5) is not the same as half of the parallelogram of forces (Figure 3.7), because C in one diagram and R in the other one are in opposite directions. R is the resultant of A and B; C is called the 'equilibrant' of A and B, that is, the force that must be added to A and B to produce equilibrium.

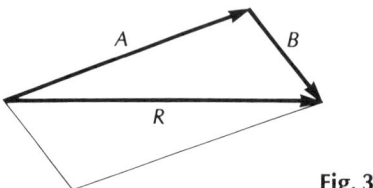

Fig. 3.7

Components

In Figure 3.8 the vertical force, V, and the horizontal force, H, have P as their resultant.

H is called the 'horizontal component' of P.
V is called the 'vertical component' of P.

The process of finding components is called **resolving** (or 'resolution'). It can be done by scale drawing but it is often better to use trigonometry:

$$H = P \cos \theta$$
$$V = P \sin \theta$$

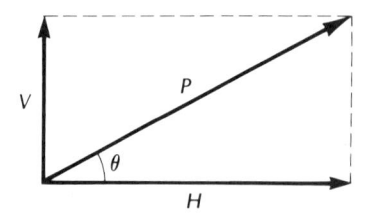

Fig. 3.8

Force

Quick Question 9 What are the vertical and horizontal components of a force of 100 N which acts at 30° from the vertical?

Example 3.2 A crane lifts a 500 kg mass. What horizontal force must be applied to the mass to keep the crane rope at an angle of 20° away from the vertical?

Solution Call the required force F and the tension in the crane rope T (Figure 3.9), and resolve vertically:

$$mg = T \cos 20°$$
$$500 \times 10 = T \cos 20° \quad \therefore T = 5320 \text{ N}$$

But F balances the horizontal component of T, and so it can now be found by resolving horizontally:

$$F = T \sin 20°$$
$$F = 5320 \sin 20° = 1820 \text{ N} = 1.8 \text{ kN}$$

(You may spot a shorter way of doing this, using the tangent of the angle.)

The abbreviation kN means 'kilonewton', which is a thousand newtons just as a kilometre is a thousand metres. This and other prefixes are given on p. 248.

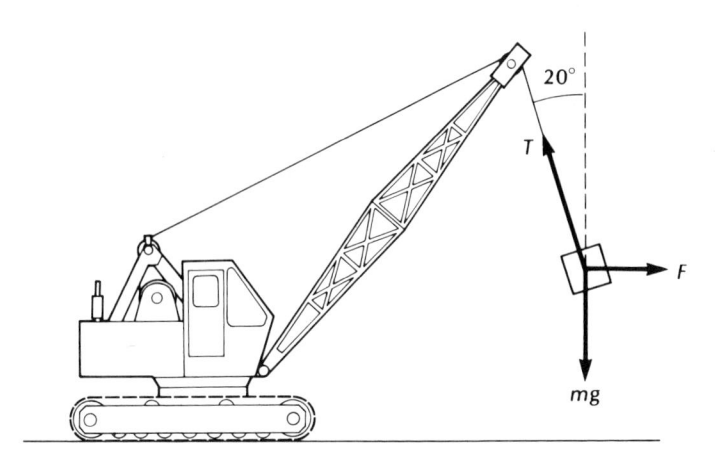

Fig. 3.9

Friction

Consider a sledge being pulled along over level ground by a horizontal rope. The three forces acting on the sledge are shown in Figure 3.10. They are:

W, the weight of the sledge,

T, the tension in the rope, and

C, the force which the ground exerts on the sledge, called the 'contact force'.

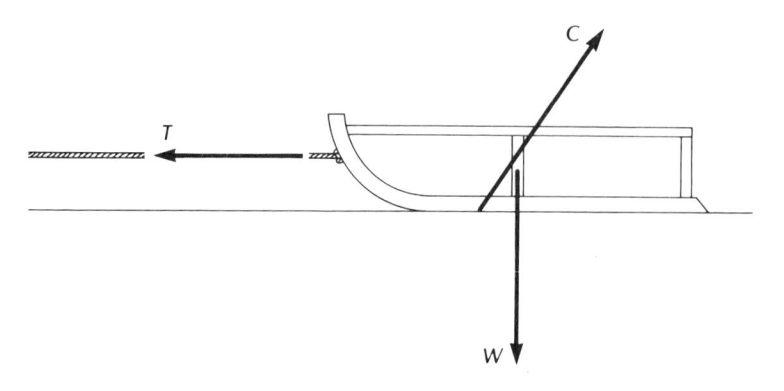

Fig. 3.10

If the sledge is moving at constant velocity and not accelerating or slowing down or turning, then the resultant force acting on it is zero, and the contact force, C, must exactly balance the resultant of the other two forces.

It is usually better to split C into two components, one normal (that is, at right angles) to the surface and the other parallel to the surface. These are shown in Figure 3.11 as:

N, the normal contact force, and

F, the friction.

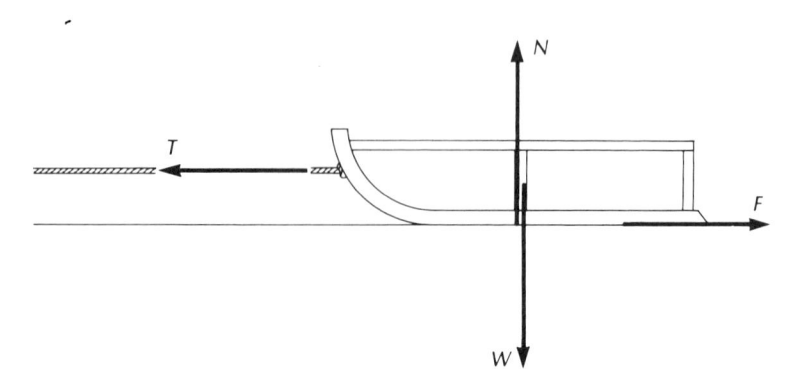

Fig. 3.11

Force

The friction is the force which opposes the motion. In most cases the maximum static friction (the friction which acts when there is no movement) is greater than the dynamic friction (or 'sliding' friction — the friction which acts when movement is taking place). This means that it usually needs more force to start a body moving against friction than it does to keep it moving once it has started.

Whenever a movement takes place against friction, heat is produced. This is why brake shoes get hot. Friction in the bearings of machinery is reduced by lubrication so as to avoid overheating, wear and waste of energy.

Force Diagrams

Figure 3.12 shows the forces acting on several bodies which have zero acceleration. The resultant force acting on each body is zero, and the body is said to be 'in equilibrium'.

(a) CAR PARKED ON A SLOPE

(b) CAR MOVING AT CONSTANT SPEED
It has rear wheel drive and so it is the friction of the rear wheels which drives the car forward. The friction of the front wheels is included in arrow D.

(c) PARACHUTE DESCENDING AT CONSTANT SPEED

Key
W = weight
F = friction
N = normal contact force
D = drag or air resistance

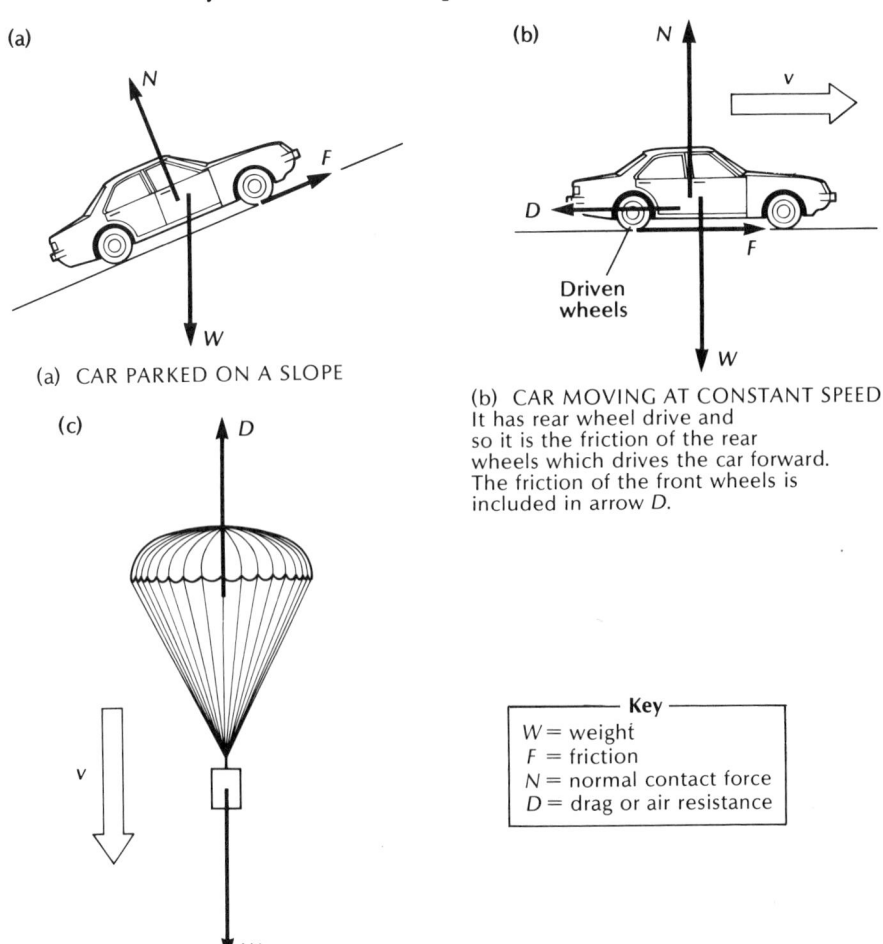

Fig. 3.12

Figure 3.13 shows uniformly accelerated bodies. The resultant force acting on these bodies is in the direction of the acceleration — that is, upwards in the case of the rocket and backwards for the puck which is slowing down. Note that although the puck is not speeding up, it still has an acceleration — it can be called a negative acceleration, or a retardation — and if this is constant the puck can be called a 'uniformly accelerated body'.

The satellite in Figure 3.14 is moving with uniform circular motion — that is, it is going at a constant speed in a circular path. The acceleration and the force acting on the satellite are both towards the centre of the circular path, which is the centre of the Earth.

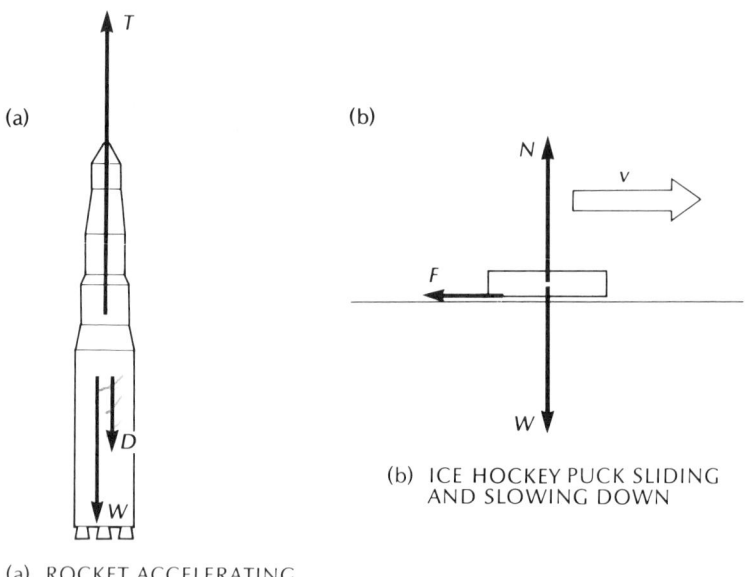

(a) ROCKET ACCELERATING UPWARDS

(b) ICE HOCKEY PUCK SLIDING AND SLOWING DOWN

Fig. 3.13

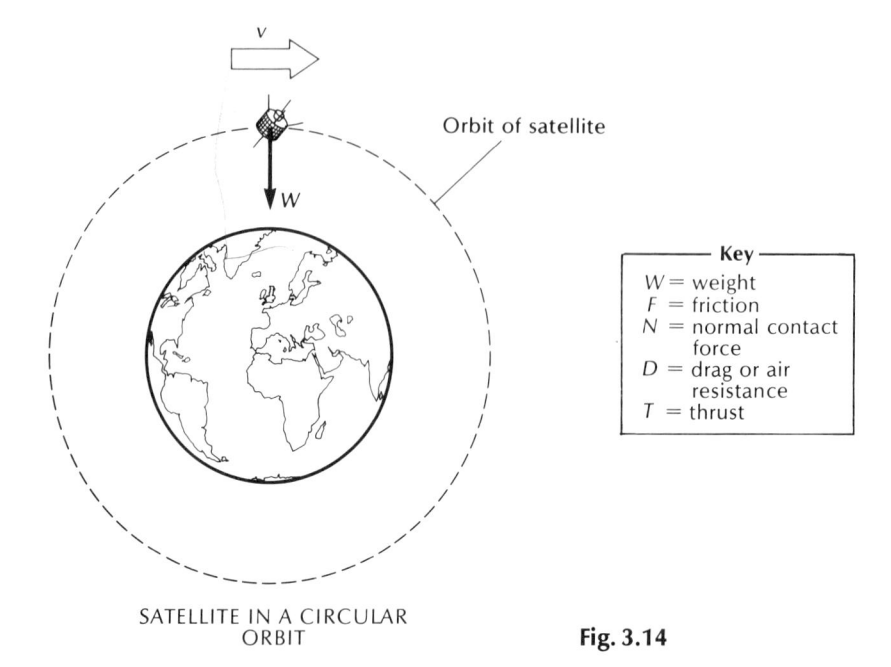

SATELLITE IN A CIRCULAR ORBIT

Key
W = weight
F = friction
N = normal contact force
D = drag or air resistance
T = thrust

Fig. 3.14

Questions on Chapter 3

1. What force is needed *a*) to give a 2 kg mass an acceleration of 3 m/s^2; *b*) to give a 100 g mass an acceleration of 60 m/s^2?

2. A trolley on a laboratory bench has a mass of 2 kg. What is its acceleration when a force of 5 N acts on it?

3. A space capsule has a mass of 10 t. What is its acceleration when it fires a rocket motor which causes a force of 2 kN? (t is the abbreviation of tonne; 1 t = 1000 kg)

4. A rocket of mass 100 kg has two forces acting on it as it moves vertically upwards just after lift-off: its weight, and the thrust of the rocket motor which is 3000 N. Ignore air resistance. Find *a*) the resultant force acting on the rocket and *b*) its acceleration. ($g = 10$ m/s^2)

5. A light spring which obeys Hooke's law hangs from a rigid support. When a load weighing 5 N is hung from the spring, the length of the spring is 160 mm; increasing the load to 10 N extends the spring to a length of 200 mm.
    a) How long is the spring with no load?
    b) What load extends the spring by 1 mm?
    c) How long is the spring with a load of 6 N?
    d) Draw a graph of extension against load for the spring.

6. Either by scale drawing or by calculation, find the resultants of these pairs of forces. In each case give the direction of the resultant as well as its magnitude.
    a) 10 N due east and 10 N due south
    b) 4 N north and 3 N east
    c) 2 kN vertically upwards and 1 kN horizontally
    d) 5 N due north and 3 N due south-east
    e) 20 N in a direction 060° and 20 N in a direction 180°, the directions being measured clockwise from north.

7. An aircraft steers due west at a speed of 120 knots. The wind is due south (that is, from the south) and its speed is 19 knots. In what direction is the aircraft travelling relative to the ground?

8. A kite of mass 500 g is flying steadily, remaining stationary. Three forces act on it: its weight, the pull of the string, and the force caused by the air moving past the kite. The pull of the string is 10 N in a direction at 40° from the vertical. *a*) Find the weight of the kite in newtons. *b*) Either by calculation or by scale drawing, find the magnitude and direction of the force on the kite caused by the air.

9 The force of the wind on the sails of a yacht is 2000 N in a direction 60° from the direction in which the yacht is pointing. Find *a*) the forward component of this force, which moves the yacht through the water, and *b*) the sideways component of the force.

10 An aircraft flies at 200 m/s in a direction 10° above the horizontal. At what rate is its height increasing? How long will it take, at this rate, to climb 1000 m?

11 *a*) State, with a brief explanation, whether it is possible, given forces of 3 N and 8 N, to produce a resultant force of
   (i) 5 N,   (ii) 15 N,   (iii) 8 N.
  b) An elephant is dragging a tree trunk along a horizontal surface by means of an attached rope which makes an angle of 30° with the horizontal. The tension in the rope is 4000 N.
   (i) By scale drawing, or otherwise, determine the horizontal force exerted by the rope on the tree trunk.
   (ii) Determine also the vertical component of the force exerted by the rope on the tree trunk. Explain why it serves a useful purpose.
   (iii) Name the other forces which act on the tree trunk and show clearly the directions in which they act. (L)

12 A man who swims at 2 m/s relative to the water sets out at right angles to the bank of a river 12 m wide. The river is flowing at 1.5 m/s so that it carries him downstream as he swims.
  a) How long would the crossing take in still water?
  b) How long does the crossing take in the moving water? Explain.
  c) How far downstream does he land?
  d) What is his speed relative to the bank?
  e) Show on a scale diagram the direction in which he should set out to be able to reach the point on the far bank which is directly opposite his starting point. (O)

Chapter 4

Moments

■ The moment (or turning effect) of a force is the magnitude of the force multiplied by the distance from the line of action of the force to the pivot, or to the point round which turning would take place. This distance is called the 'arm' (see Figure 4.1).

$$\text{Moment} = \text{Force} \times \text{Arm}$$

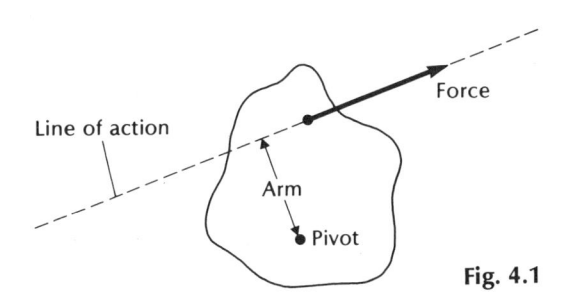

Fig. 4.1

■ A couple is a system of two forces which are equal in magnitude and opposite in direction, but not acting along the same line (see Figure 4.2). A couple has zero resultant but it has a moment, and the moment is:

$$\begin{pmatrix}\text{Moment of}\\\text{couple}\end{pmatrix} = \begin{pmatrix}\text{Magnitude of}\\\text{one force}\end{pmatrix} \times \begin{pmatrix}\text{Distance apart}\\\text{of forces}\end{pmatrix}$$

For example, the moment of the couple shown in Figure 4.2(b) is:

$$500\,\text{N} \times 2\,\text{m} = 1000\,\text{N m}$$

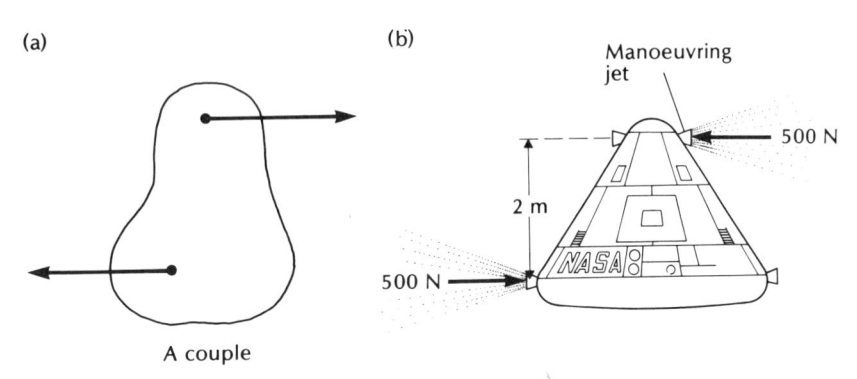

Fig. 4.2

The **principle of moments** states that:

> When a body is in equilibrium, the sum of all the clockwise moments acting on it around any point equals the sum of all the anticlockwise moments around the same point.

It is usually convenient, when applying the principle of moments, to choose a pivot or a support or the centre of gravity as the point round which moments are calculated, though any point could be chosen.

■ The **centre of gravity** of a body is the point through which the line of action of the body's weight passes, no matter which way up the body is. (Of course, the weight acts on all parts of the body, but the resultant of all these contributions acts through the centre of gravity.)

Example 4.1 A metre rule balances horizontally when it is supported at its 40 cm mark and an object whose weight is 0.50 N is hung from its 20 cm mark. What is the weight of the rule?

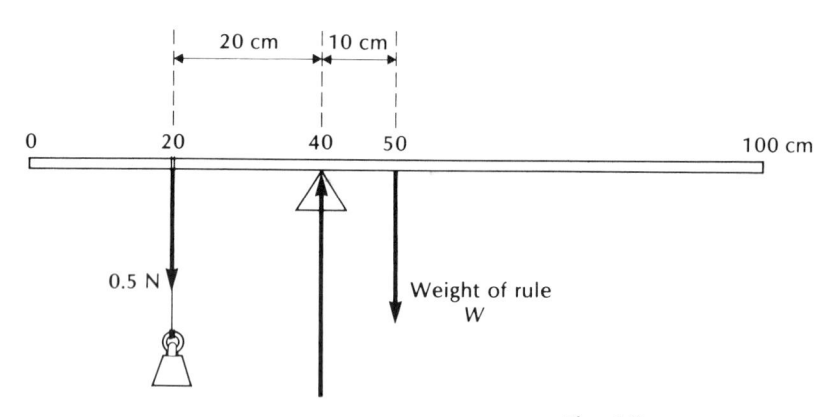

Fig. 4.3

Solution From Figure 4.3:

$$\text{Clockwise moment} = \text{Anticlockwise moment}$$
$$W \times 10 = 0.50 \times 20 \quad \therefore \quad W = 1.0\,\text{N}$$

Example 4.2 In Example 4.1, what is the reaction at the fulcrum? (This means the supporting force provided by the fulcrum.)

Solution Since the rule is in equilibrium the resultant force acting on it is zero, and the single upward force must equal the sum of the two downward forces.

$$\text{Reaction at fulcrum} = 0.5\,\text{N} + W$$
$$= 0.5\,\text{N} + 1.0\,\text{N} = 1.5\,\text{N}$$

Stability

If a body is in equilibrium, then the equilibrium is:

- **stable** if the body will return after a small displacement;
- **neutral** if the body is still in equilibrium after a small displacement;
- **unstable** if, after a small displacement, it tends to move further from its equilibrium position.

Notice, by looking at the examples in Figure 4.4, that a small displacement will cause the centre of gravity to:

- **rise** if the equilibrium is stable, or
- **fall** if the equilibrium is unstable.

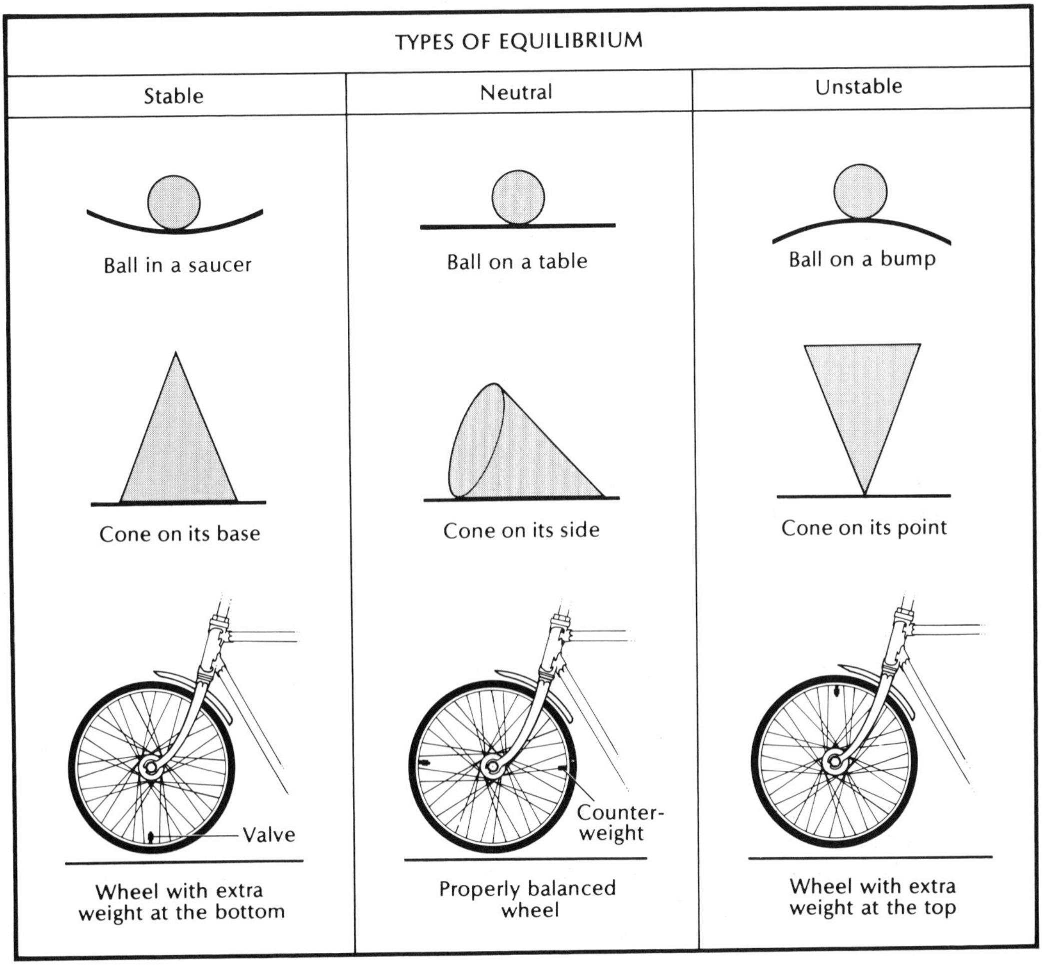

TYPES OF EQUILIBRIUM		
Stable	Neutral	Unstable
Ball in a saucer	Ball on a table	Ball on a bump
Cone on its base	Cone on its side	Cone on its point
Wheel with extra weight at the bottom (Valve)	Properly balanced wheel (Counterweight)	Wheel with extra weight at the top

Fig. 4.4

If two bodies are both in stable equilibrium, the more stable one is the one that can be tipped further before toppling. For greater stability, keep the base wide and the centre of gravity low. (See Figure 4.5.)

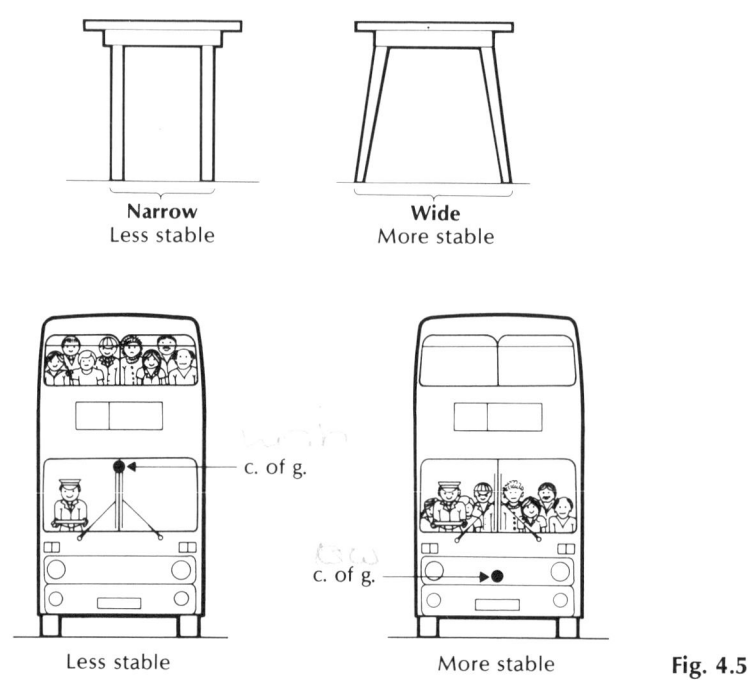

Fig. 4.5

Questions on Chapter 4

1 A man can exert a force of 200 N on the end of a spanner. What moment can he apply to a nut *a)* if the spanner is 0.1 m long and *b)* if it is 0.3 m long?

2 A nut needs a moment of 2 N m to turn it. What force is required when using a spanner of length *a)* 100 mm, *b)* 200 mm?

3 A screw picket — like a big corkscrew — is being driven into the ground to hold one of the guy-ropes of a flag-pole. If it needs a moment of 2000 N m to turn the screw, how long a lever is needed for one man to be able to turn it? Assume that a man can push the end of the lever with a force of 1 kN.

Moments

4 A boy weighing 150 N and his mother whose weight is 600 N sit on a see-saw 4 m long which is pivoted at its centre. If the boy sits right at one end, how far from the other end must the mother sit to make the see-saw balance?

5 To reach a high wall a painter stands on a uniform plank AB which is 3 m long and weighs 100 N (see Figure 4.6). One end A of the plank rests on one step of a staircase and the other end B is held by the painter's mate. The painter weighs 600 N and is standing 1 m from A. Find:
  a) the moment about A of the painter's weight,
  b) the moment about A of the weight of the plank,
  c) the total clockwise moment about A, and
  d) the force with which the painter's mate must support the end B of the plank.

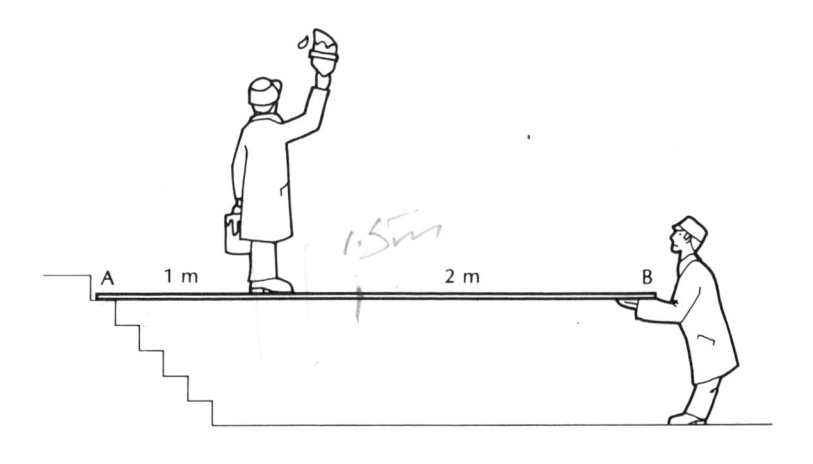

Fig. 4.6

6 A metre rule rests horizontally on a support placed at the 0.30 m mark and a downward force of 0.80 N acting at the end of the rule, as shown in Figure 4.7, keeps the rule from tipping. The rule is uniform, so that its centre of gravity is at its 0.50 m mark. Find the weight of the rule.

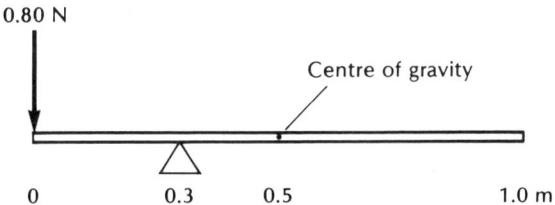

Fig. 4.7

7 In order to find the mass of the flag-pole shown in Figure 4.8, it is first balanced on a trestle to locate its centre of gravity. It balances when the trestle is 4.5 m from the thick end. A girl who knows that her mass is 50 kg sits on the thick end and the pole then balances when the trestle is 2.5 m from that end. a) What is the weight of the girl? Find b) the weight of the flag-pole and c) its mass.

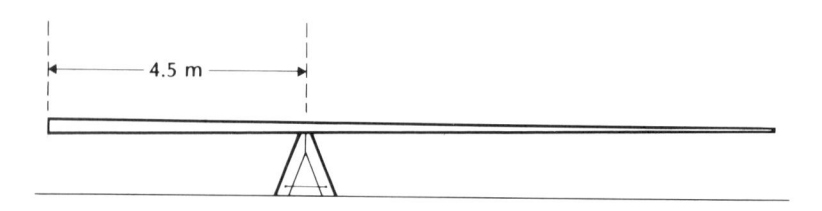

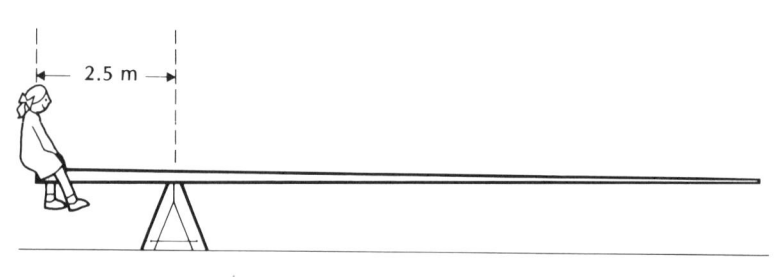

Fig. 4.8

8 To weigh a retort stand it is balanced horizontally on a bar, as shown in Figure 4.9. It is found that with nothing hanging from the stand the bar must be placed 300 cm from the top (A) of the stand, and when a one kilogram mass is hung from A the supporting bar must be 200 mm from A. Find the mass of the retort stand.

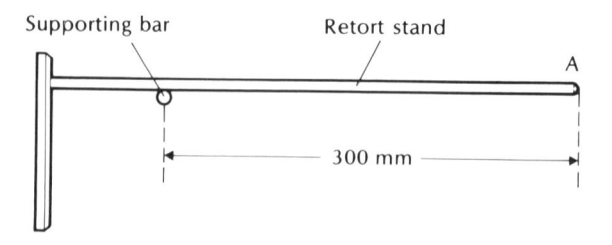

Fig. 4.9

Chapter 5

Momentum and Newton's Laws

■ The momentum of a body is its mass multiplied by its velocity:

$$\text{Momentum} = mv$$

The SI unit of momentum is the kilogram metre per second (kg m/s).

An important feature of momentum is that it is *conserved*, that is, the momentum of a body cannot change without an exactly equal and opposite change taking place in the momentum of some other body (or bodies) so that the resultant momentum remains constant. The applications of this that concern us are collisions and explosions. Here is an example of a collision problem.

Example 5.1 99 g of Plasticine is stuck on to a trolley of mass 700 g. An airgun fires a slug of mass 1.0 g so that the slug remains embedded in the Plasticine. It is found that the trolley recoils at a speed of 0.25 m/s. What was the speed of the slug?

Solution Figure 5.1 shows the situation.

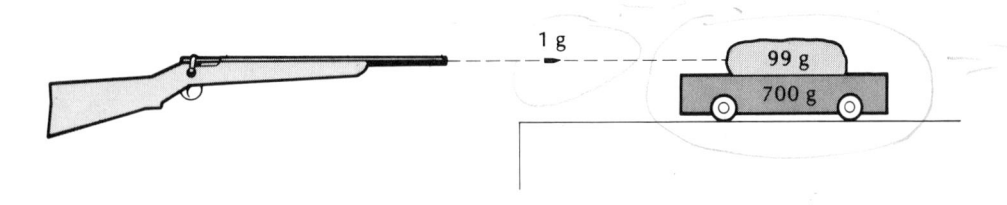

Fig. 5.1

$$\begin{pmatrix}\text{Momentum of slug}\\\text{before impact}\end{pmatrix} = \begin{pmatrix}\text{Momentum of trolley, Plasticine and}\\\text{slug after impact}\end{pmatrix}$$

$$m_1 v_1 = m_2 v_2$$
$$1.0 \times v_1 = (700 + 99 + 1) \times 0.25$$
$$\therefore \qquad v_1 = 200 \text{ m/s}$$

Explosions are similar, from the point of view of momentum changes, to bodies being driven apart by springs or by compressed air. Here is an example of this.

Example 5.2 If the airgun of Example 5.1 has a mass of 2 kg, and if it is held so lightly when it is fired that it is perfectly free to recoil, at what speed will it recoil?

Solution Backward momentum of recoil = Forward momentum of slug

$$2000 \text{ g} \times v_{recoil} = 1.0 \text{ g} \times 200 \text{ m/s}$$

∴ $$v_{recoil} = 0.1 \text{ m/s}$$

The Relation Between Momentum and Force

If no resultant force acts on a body (either no force at all or else a balanced set of forces), then its momentum remains constant. If it is still, it will remain so, but if it has already been set moving, it will continue to move with constant momentum. Now if a force starts to act on it, the momentum starts to change, and the rate at which the momentum changes is equal to the force:

$$\frac{\text{Change of momentum (in kg m/s)}}{\text{Time taken to change (in s)}} = \text{Force (in N)}$$

Sir Isaac Newton lived long before SI units were developed, and so to him these two things were not equal but proportional, as he stated in his second law.

Newton's Laws of Motion

1 If no resultant force acts on a body, it will continue in a state of rest or of uniform motion in a straight line.
2 If a force acts on a body, it will change its momentum and the rate of change of momentum will be proportional to the applied force.
3 If a body A exerts a force on another body B, then B will exert an exactly equal and opposite force on A.

Example 5.3 A rocket motor ejects 5 kg of gas at a speed of 800 m/s during a 20 s burn. What propelling force does this produce?

Solution

(Momentum of gas) $= mv = 5 \times 800$ kg m/s

$$\left(\begin{array}{c}\text{Rate of change} \\ \text{of momentum}\end{array}\right) = \frac{mv}{t} = \frac{5 \times 800}{20} \text{ kg m/s}^2$$

$$= 200 \text{ kg m/s}^2$$

Therefore the force acting on the gases is 200 N and, by Newton's third law, the force which the gases exert on the rocket — the propelling force — is also 200 N.

Impulse

The impulse of a force is the change of momentum that it produces. It is equal to the force multiplied by the time during which the force acts.

Questions on Chapter 5

1 What is the momentum of:
a) a shell of mass 2 kg moving at a speed of 800 m/s;
b) a car of mass 800 kg moving at a speed of 2 m/s;
c) an airgun slug of mass 1 g moving at 180 m/s;
d) a billiard ball of mass 120 g moving at 1.5 m/s?

2 An empty railway truck of mass 5000 kg moving at a speed of 0.5 m/s hits a stationary truck which is loaded and has a mass of 15 000 kg. At the moment of impact the coupling is done up so that the two trucks move together. Find:
a) the momentum of the empty truck before impact;
b) the total momentum of the two trucks after impact;
c) the speed of the trucks after impact.

3 A man of mass 80 kg runs at 4 m/s on to a raft of mass 320 kg which is close to the bank of a lake. The raft is not tied up, and so as the man stops running the raft and the man move together away from the bank. Find the speed with which the raft moves before the resistance of the water has slowed it down.

4 A man of mass 60 kg is standing on a stationary boat of mass 600 kg near to the bank of a lake. The man then jumps for the bank with a horizontal velocity of 5 m/s. What is the speed of recoil of the boat?

5 An aircraft of mass 20 000 kg fires a stream of forty projectiles from a forward-facing cannon. Each projectile has a mass of $\frac{1}{8}$ kg and moves at 800 m/s relative to the aircraft. Find:
a) the amount of momentum given to each projectile as it is fired;
b) the total momentum given to all forty projectiles;
c) the change in the aircraft's speed caused by firing the cannon.

6 A water pump delivers 20 kg of water each second to a fire hose. The water leaves the nozzle of the hose at a speed of 25 m/s. Find
a) the amount of momentum given to the water in one second and
b) the force needed to hold the nozzle.

7 A space-craft of mass 10 000 kg fires a rocket motor so that 10 kg of gas is emitted per second at a speed of 800 m/s. Find a) the momentum given to the gas in each second, b) the thrust of the rocket motor and c) the acceleration of the space-craft.

8 A rocket ejects 20 kg of gas during a burn lasting one minute, the velocity of the gas being 750 m/s. What force does the rocket exert?

9 A rubber ball of mass 100 g is thrown so that it hits one end of a trolley in a laboratory, as shown in Figure 5.2. The mass of the trolley is 800 g. The speed of the ball just before impact is measured by a photographic method and found to be 10 m/s. As a result of the impact the trolley starts to move along the bench and the ball rebounds with a speed which is measured as 6 m/s. Find:
a) the momentum of the ball just before impact;
b) the momentum of the ball after impact;
c) the change in momentum of the ball;
d) the speed of the trolley.

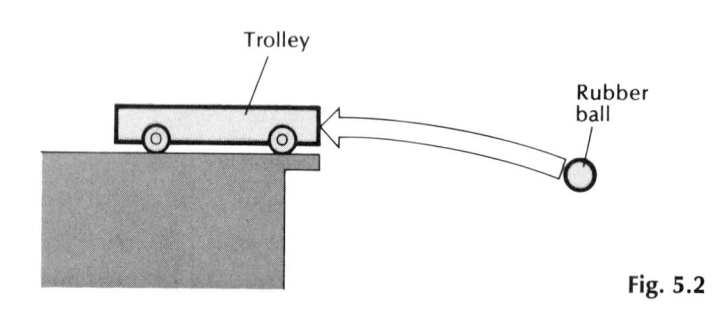

Fig. 5.2

10 Figure 5.3 illustrates an experiment with trolleys and a ticker timer. Trolley A is given a slight push and collides with trolley B. The pin penetrates the cork so that both trolleys stick together and move as one. The tape obtained is shown, full size, alongside a millimetre grid below. The time interval between each dot is 0.02 s.

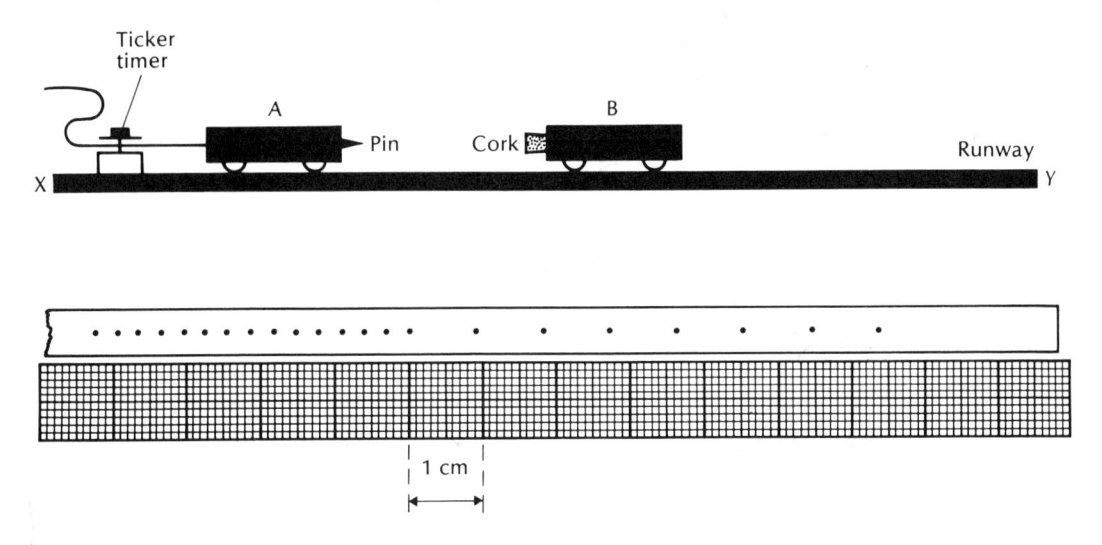

Fig. 5.3

a) Before carrying out the experiment, it is usual to make an adjustment which results in end X of the runway being slightly higher than end Y.
   (i) What is the purpose of this adjustment and why is it necessary?
   (ii) Has the adjustment been carried out in this case? Give a reason for your answer.
b) Using the tape, determine
   (i) the average speed, in cm/s, of trolley A before the collision,
   (ii) the time which has elapsed before the collision takes place, and
   (iii) the average speed, in cm/s, of the two trolleys A and B after the collision. (L)

Chapter 6

Energy and Power

Energy

If you want to raise a weight, three ways of doing it are by human muscles, or by burning fuel (for example, in a diesel-powered crane), or by using the electric mains (as in an electric lift). The same three methods may be used if you want to get something moving. Two of the methods — burning fuel and electric mains — can be used for the purpose of heating up something such as a kettle full of water; muscle power is not much use in this case, though rubbing would produce a certain amount of heat.

What is needed in these cases is energy, and so energy may be thought of as the quantity which is available from fuel, from electric mains or from human muscles, and which may be used:

for lifting things, giving them 'potential' energy,
for setting things moving, giving them 'kinetic' energy,
for heating things, giving them 'internal' energy.

> Energy cannot appear or disappear but can only change from one form to another. This principle is called the conservation of energy.*

The table shows a selection of forms of energy.

Form of energy		Example
potential	gravitational	a raised weight
	elastic	a stretched spring
kinetic		a moving bullet or a spinning flywheel
internal (heat)		a hot water bottle
chemical		fuel + oxygen, or a torch battery
radiant		infra-red rays
electrical		a charged capacitor

*We will meet an exception to this on p. 242.

Energy and Power

The term 'electrical energy' is also used to mean energy which is being transferred from one place to another by an electric current, as in Example 6.2 below, but if you want an example of something that *stores* energy as electrical energy a capacitor is the answer.

Quick Question 10 What energy change takes place when a car uses its brakes to slow down?   *potential → kinetic*

Example 6.1 What energy changes take place when a rubber ball is dropped on a hard floor?

Solution The answer to this question can conveniently be expressed diagrammatically like this:

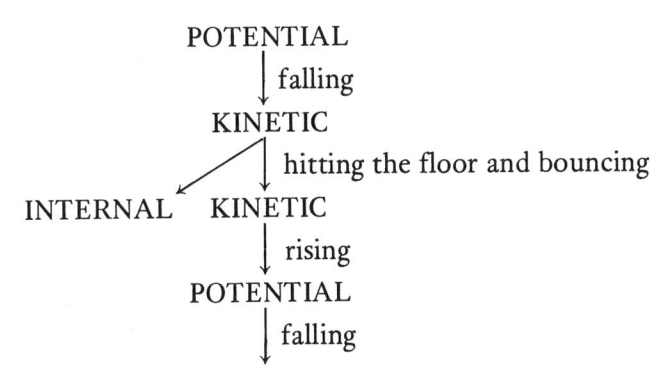

POTENTIAL
↓ falling
KINETIC
↓ hitting the floor and bouncing
INTERNAL   KINETIC
↓ rising
POTENTIAL
↓ falling

The process repeats with each bounce and eventually when the ball comes to rest on the floor all its original potential energy has turned to internal energy.

Example 6.2 What energy changes take place in an electric torch when it is in use?

Solution CHEMICAL → ELECTRICAL → HEAT → LIGHT
                                    ↘ some remains as HEAT

Notice that in this case light is not produced directly from electrical energy.

Energy has a tendency to change from other forms into internal energy. Both the examples given on this page illustrate this. The change from internal energy into other forms of energy cannot be done so easily, and much of it is invariably wasted. Devices for producing this change are called 'engines' and examples of these are petrol engines, diesel engines and rocket engines.

The Relation Between Energy and Force

Note the difference between energy and force. Supporting a picture on the wall needs a force, provided by the hook and cord, but it does *not* need a supply of energy. Raising it up to the hook from the floor needs energy.

A force supplies no energy when the body on which it acts is stationary. When energy is supplied, the amount of energy depends on:

- the strength of the force,
- the distance moved by the body,
- the angle between the directions of the force and the movement.

■ A joule (J) is the *energy supplied* by a force of one newton when it moves a body through a distance of one metre, if the force and the movement are in the same direction.

■ The **work** done by a force is the amount of energy transformed by it; therefore a joule can just as well be defined as the *work done* when a force of one newton moves a distance of one metre in the direction of the force.

The work done by a force is given by the equation:

$$W = F \times s$$

where W is the work done   (in J)
       F is the force   (in N)
       s is the distance moved (in m)

provided that F and s are in the same direction. If they are not in the same direction, the same equation can be used if s means the component of the distance moved, resolved in the direction of the force. For example, if the crane in Figure 6.1 moves its load diagonally as shown, the work done on the load is the weight multiplied by the *vertical* distance, h, because the force is vertical.

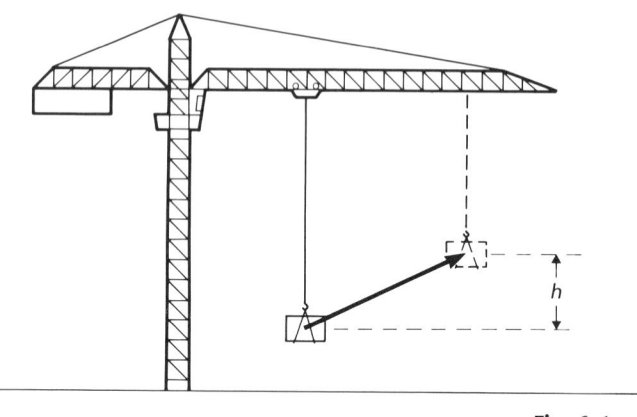

Fig. 6.1

Energy Formulas

$$\text{Gravitational potential energy} = mgh$$

where m is the mass
 g is the gravitational acceleration
 h is the height

Note that this is really the same formula as $W = Fs$, because the force needed to lift a body is equal to its weight which is mg, and h is the vertical distance moved.

Quick Question 11

> How much energy is used by a boy of mass 50 kg in going up a staircase 5 m high?

$$\text{Kinetic energy} = \tfrac{1}{2}mv^2$$

The proof of this does not concern us but we can test it by comparing the next example with Example 2.1 on p. 16.

Example 6.3 A stone is dropped down a well 20 m deep. If air resistance is negligible, how fast is it travelling when it reaches the bottom? (Assume $g = 10 \text{ m/s}^2$.)

Solution

$$\text{Kinetic energy gained} = \text{Potential energy lost}$$

(since there is no air resistance to cause energy to turn into heat)

$$\tfrac{1}{2}mv^2 = mgh$$
$$\tfrac{1}{2}\not{m}v^2 = \not{m} \times 10 \times 20$$
$$v^2 = 400$$
$$v = 20 \text{ m/s}$$

Quick Question 12

> If a boy of mass 50 kg could run at a rate of 100 m in 10 s, what would his kinetic energy be? Ignore the extra kinetic energy of his arm and leg movements.

Power

■ Power means the rate at which energy is supplied or used or transformed from one form to another:

$$\text{Power} = \frac{\text{Energy used}}{\text{Time taken}}$$

■ A watt (W) is a joule per second. It is the SI unit of power.

Quick Question 13
If the boy of Quick Question 11 takes 4 s to go up the staircase, what power is he developing?

Example 6.4 A crane lifts a 500 kg load through a vertical distance of 4.0 m in 10 s. What useful power does it develop? If its efficiency is 50%, what power does it use? What happens to the wasted energy? ($g = 10$ m/s^2)

Solution

$$\text{Power} = \frac{\text{Potential energy gained by load}}{\text{Time taken}}$$

$$= \frac{mgh}{t} = \frac{500 \times 10 \times 4.0}{10} = 2000 \text{ W} = 2.0 \text{ kW}$$

This is the useful power developed. Since half of the power is wasted, it uses twice this, that is, 4 kW.

The wasted energy becomes partly internal energy by means of friction and partly potential energy of the crane hook and other parts of the crane.

(For efficiency, see p. 54.)

Questions on Chapter 6

1 Calculate the amount of work done by:
   a) a crane in lifting a load weighing 2500 N through a vertical distance of 2 m;

Energy and Power 51

b) a man pushing a mower ten times across the width of a lawn 10 m wide, if the man is exerting a horizontal force of 50 N on the handles of the mower.

2 Calculate the amount of work done by:
a) a hotel porter in lifting a case weighing 100 N to a height of $\frac{1}{4}$ m off the floor;
b) a hotel porter carrying the same case up a staircase 10 m high.

3 How much energy is needed to raise:
a) a brick of mass 4 kg to a height of 10 m?
b) a girder of mass 400 kg to a height of 2 m?
Assume that $g = 10$ m/s^2.

4 A tractor pulls a plough with a force of 5 kN across a field 120 m wide in 80 s. Find a) the work done by the tractor and b) its power output.

5 What happens to the energy produced by the tractor of Question 4?

6 A cyclist maintains a steady speed of 5 m/s. a) If he is working at a power of 100 W when travelling along a level road, what is the resistance to his motion? b) The cyclist and his bicycle together have a weight of 800 N. What is his power output when he is going up a hill with a gradient of 1 in 40, assuming that his speed and the resistance to his motion are both the same as before?

7 A child slides down a slide with dimensions as shown in Figure 6.2. The force of friction, both on the sloping section AB and on the horizontal section BC, is equal to one-third of the weight of the child. How far along the horizontal section BC will the child slide before coming to rest?

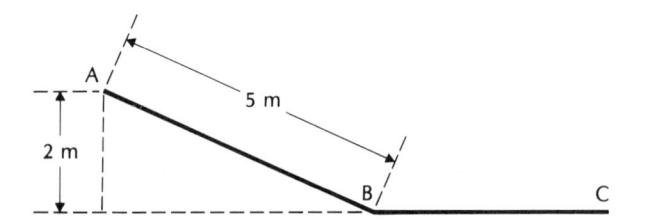

Fig. 6.2

(Hint: decrease of potential energy = work done against friction in moving from A to the stopping place.)

8 Calculate the kinetic energy of a) a bullet of mass 50 g travelling at 600 m/s and b) a car of mass 500 kg travelling at 6 m/s.

9

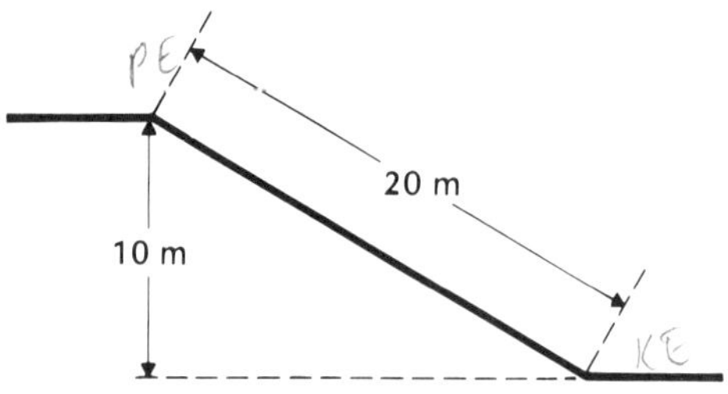

Fig. 6.3

A tobogganist and his toboggan together have a mass of 60 kg. He slides down a snow slope 20 m long and 10 m high, as shown in Figure 6.3. At the top of the slope his velocity is zero, and the force of friction as he slides down is equal to one-quarter of the total weight. Assuming that $g = 10$ m/s^2, calculate:
a) the decrease of gravitational potential energy;
b) the work done against friction;
c) the kinetic energy when he reaches the bottom of the slope;
d) his speed when he reaches the bottom of the slope.

10 A railway truck of mass 2000 kg moving at 1 m/s hits another truck of mass 3000 kg which is stationary. The two trucks couple together automatically and move together. Find:
a) the speed of the two trucks as they move together;
b) the kinetic energy of the first truck just before the impact;
c) the total kinetic energy of the two trucks after impact;
d) the amount of heat produced in the collision.

11 A machine pumps 9 m^3 of water every hour from a lake to a storage tank 30 m above the water level in the lake.
Calculate
(i) the work done by the machine every hour,
(ii) the power output of the machine.   (AEB)

Chapter 7

Machines

The work done by a force is:

Work = Force × Distance moved

if the directions are the same. If the force is doubled and the distance is halved, the amount of work is unchanged. A device for altering forces and distances moved like this is called a 'machine'. Examples of machines are levers, pulley systems, the inclined plane, the screw, the gear-box, the wheels and chain of a bicycle, and the hydraulic jack.

- The **effort** is the force applied to a machine and the **load** is the force exerted by the machine. The load also means the thing that the machine lifts.

- The **mechanical advantage** is the ratio in which the machine increases the force:

$$MA = \frac{Load}{Effort}$$

- The **velocity ratio** is the ratio in which the machine decreases the distance moved:

$$VR = \frac{Distance\ moved\ by\ effort}{Distance\ moved\ by\ load}$$

Notice that these two fractions are opposite ways up: the word 'load' occurs in the top of one but in the bottom of the other.

Quick Question 14

If a bicycle moves 30 cm along the road while the pedal is pushed down 10 cm, what is its velocity ratio?

These two ratios would be equal if the machine did not waste energy by friction and perhaps also by raising part of itself. For real machines, however, the mechanical advantage is less than the velocity ratio.

■ The **efficiency** of a machine is the energy given out by it expressed as a fraction or percentage of the energy put into it:

$$\text{Efficiency} = \frac{\text{Energy out}}{\text{Energy in}}$$

or $$\text{Efficiency} = 100 \times \frac{\text{Energy out}}{\text{Energy in}}\%$$

From this definition it is possible to prove that:

$$\text{Efficiency} = \frac{\text{MA}}{\text{VR}}$$

Proof:
$$\begin{aligned}\text{Efficiency} &= \frac{\text{Energy out}}{\text{Energy in}} \\ &= \frac{\text{Work done on load}}{\text{Work done by effort}} \\ &= \frac{\text{Load} \times \text{Distance moved by load}}{\text{Effort} \times \text{Distance moved by effort}} \\ &= \frac{\text{Load}}{\text{Effort}} \div \frac{\text{Distance moved by effort}}{\text{Distance moved by load}} \\ &= \text{MA} \div \text{VR}\end{aligned}$$

Quick Question 15

A car is jacked up to change a wheel. The gravitational potential energy of the car increases by 1 kJ, and 4 kJ of energy is wasted by turning into heat because of friction in the jack. What is the efficiency of the jack?

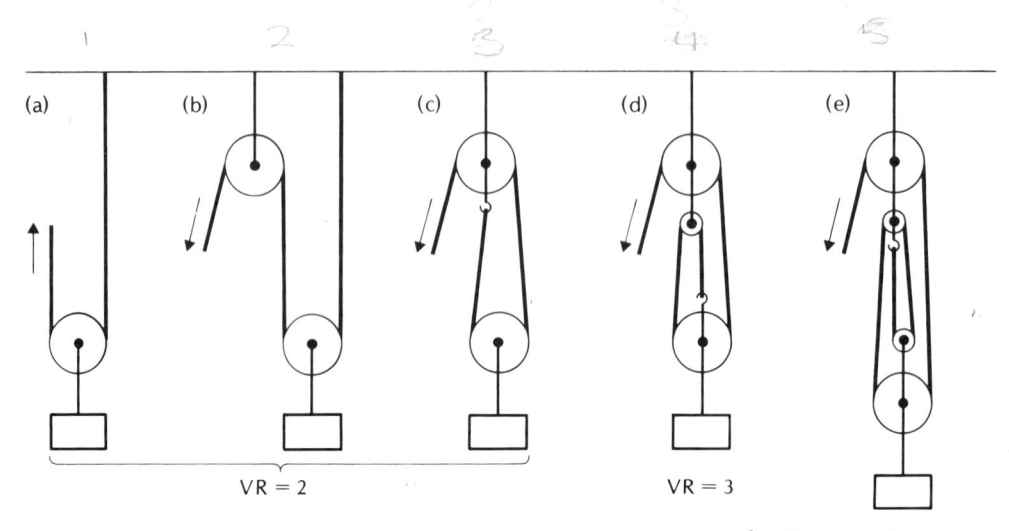

(a)   (b)   (c)   (d)   (e)

VR = 2   VR = 3

Fig. 7.1   VR = 4

Machines

■ A pulley system, if it is of the simple, single-string type shown in Figure 7.1, has a velocity ratio equal to the number of lengths of string which are shortened when the load is moved. Notice that in Figure 7.1(a) the effort string must be included in the count; this applies whenever the effort is pulling in the same direction in which the load moves.

VR = no. of pulleys

■ In the inclined plane of Figure 7.2 the load rises a distance h when the effort moves the length of the slope, l. So the velocity ratio is given by:

$$VR = \frac{\text{Slant distance}}{\text{Height}} = \frac{l}{h}$$

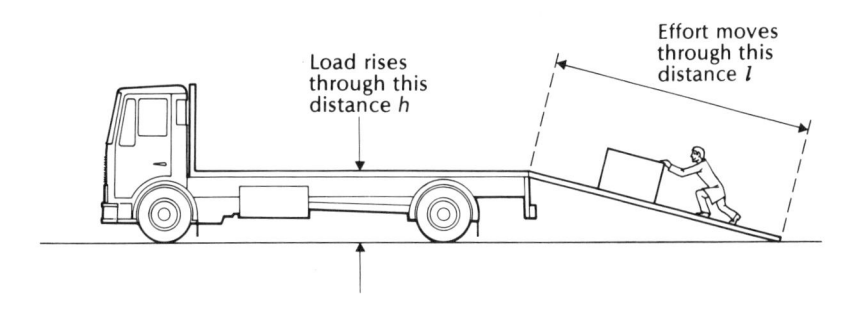

Fig. 7.2

■ In one revolution of the screw jack (Figure 7.3) the effort moves round a circle of circumference $2\pi \times$ radius and the load rises a distance equal to the pitch of the screw. Therefore:

$$VR = \frac{2\pi \times \text{Radius}}{\text{Pitch of screw}}$$

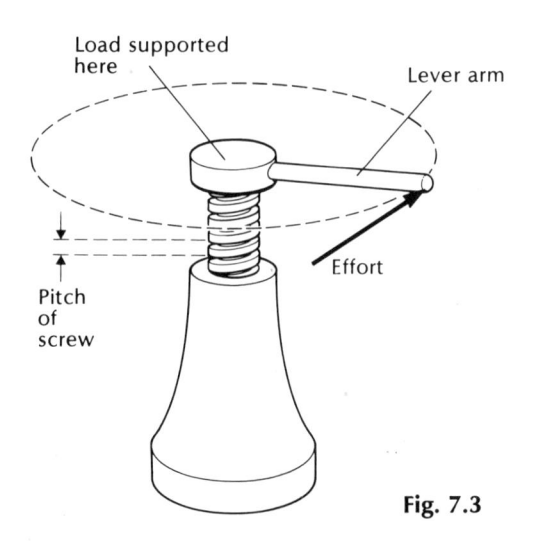

Fig. 7.3

Quick Question 16

The efficiency of a screw jack is quite low, as Quick Question 15 showed. Why would it not be an advantage if the friction could be reduced so much that the efficiency was nearly 100%?

- For a pair of **gear wheels** the velocity ratio equals the number of teeth on the driven wheel divided by the number of teeth on the driving wheel. To find the velocity ratio of a longer train of gear wheels, multiply together the velocity ratios of the separate pairs of wheels.
- The **hydraulic jack** is included in the next chapter.

Questions on Chapter 7

1. To lift a mass weighing 1000 N through a height of 2 m using a pulley system, a man pulls in 12 m of rope, pulling with a force of 250 N. What are *a*) the mechanical advantage, *b*) the velocity ratio and *c*) the efficiency of the pulley system?

2. If the pulley system of Figure 7.1(e) needs an effort of 40 N to lift a load of 120 N, what are *a*) its mechanical advantage and *b*) its efficiency?

3. In the pulley system shown in Figure 7.1(e), the lower block has a weight of 10 N and friction is negligible. *a*) What effort is needed to lift a load of 50 N? *b*) How much work must be done by the effort to raise this load through a distance of 0.50 m?

4. A screw jack has a screw of pitch 4 mm turned by means of a lever 140 mm long. If the efficiency is 25%, what are *a*) the velocity ratio and *b*) the mechanical advantage?

Chapter 8

Pressure and Pumps

- **Pressure** is the force pressing on a surface divided by the area on which it presses:

$$p = \frac{F}{A}$$

- The **pascal** (Pa) is the SI unit of pressure. A pascal is a newton per square metre. Other pressure units are:

  the millimetre of mercury (mmHg),
  the standard atmosphere.
  1 atmosphere = 760 mmHg = 100 kPa (approximately).

Quick Question 17

A man has a weight of 500 N. As he stands, his shoes touch the ground over an area of $\frac{1}{20}$ m². What pressure does he exert on the ground? Give the answer in pascals and also in atmospheres.

25 Pa or 0.25 atmospheres

In a liquid or a gas the pressure acts equally in all directions. It is a scalar quantity, not a vector one.

- The principle of the hydraulic jack is illustrated in Figure 8.1. The pressures in the two cylinders can be taken to be equal, since any

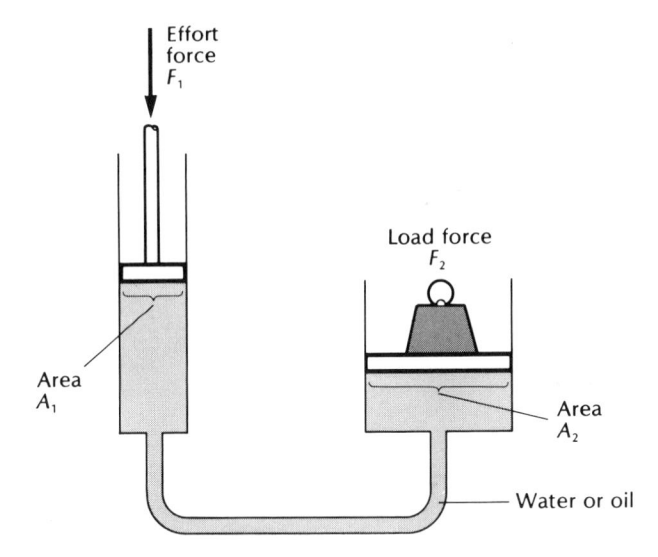

Fig. 8.1

differences of pressure caused by the cylinders being on different levels or by the liquid being in motion along the tube will usually be small enough to ignore. Therefore:

$$\frac{F_1}{A_1} = \frac{F_2}{A_2}$$

and so the mechanical advantage is equal to the ratio of the areas of the two cylinders, apart from the effect of friction.

Quick Question 18
If the load cylinder of a hydraulic jack has a diameter five times bigger than the diameter of the effort cylinder, and if friction is negligible, what is the mechanical advantage? If there is an appreciable amount of friction, what can then be said about the mechanical advantage?

A practical version of this also has a reservoir and non-return valves to allow repeated strokes, and also a bypass valve to allow liquid to return to the reservoir to let the load down again. The hydraulic brake system of a car is like Figure 8.1 but it has four driven cylinders instead of only one.

Pressure in a Fluid

■ In a liquid the pressure at a point depends on:
(i) the pressure acting on the liquid surface,
(ii) the depth of the point below the surface,
(iii) the density of the liquid, ρ,
(iv) the gravitational acceleration, g.

The pressure is equal at points on the same horizontal level (if the liquid is not flowing). Between two levels differing by a vertical height h there is a pressure difference:

$$\text{Pressure difference} = \rho g h$$

SI units should be used: Pa, kg/m³, m/s² and m.

Quick Question 19
How much does the pressure increase as you swim down to the bottom of a swimming bath 3 m deep?

Pressure and Pumps

- In a gas the same is true as long as the difference of height is not too big, but it is not true (for example) for the first ten kilometres of the atmosphere because the density changes with height.

Measurement of Pressure

A barometer is an instrument for measuring the atmospheric pressure.

- A simple **mercury barometer** (Figure 8.2) is used by measuring the distance h, which is called the 'height of the barometer'. Since this distance is on average 760 mm, the tube needs to be not much less than a metre long.

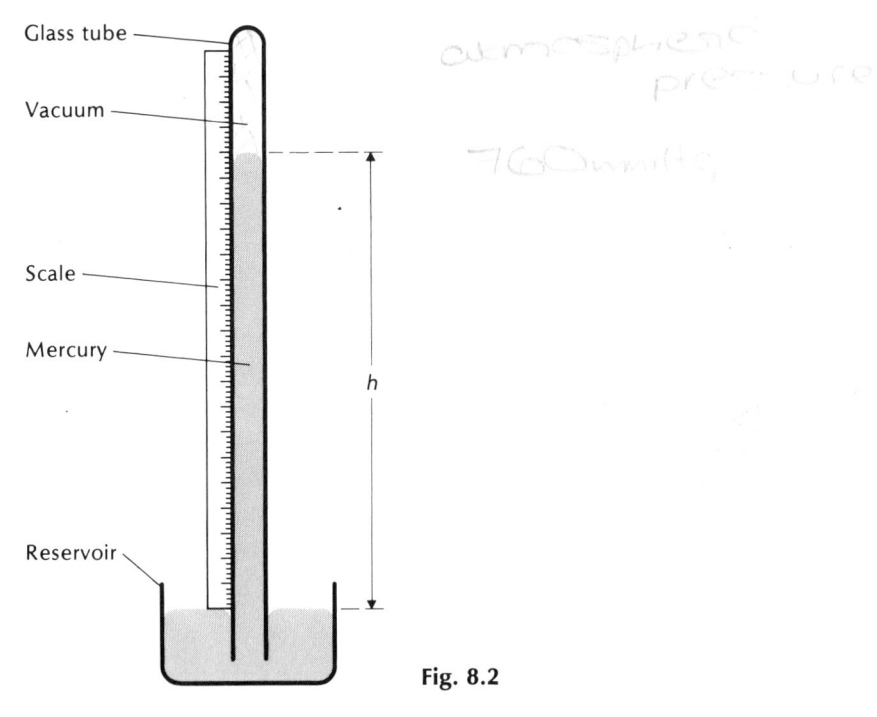

Fig. 8.2

- An aneroid barometer (Figure 8.3) is cheaper than a mercury one and has the advantage that it is not sensitive to acceleration and so

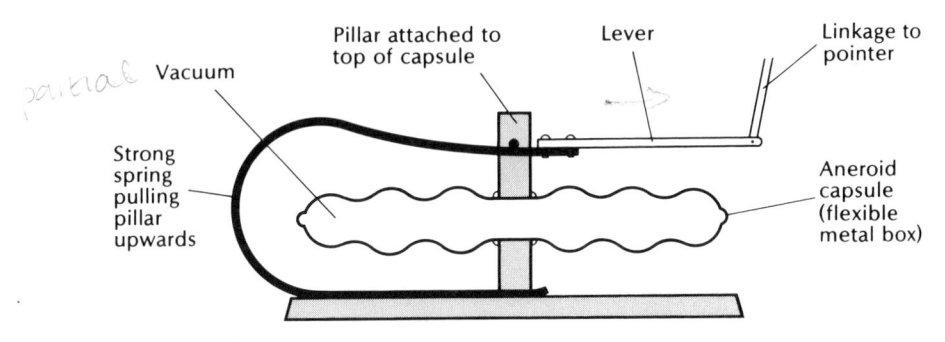

Fig. 8.3

can be used in a moving ship or aircraft. Atmospheric pressure tends to squash the capsule flat but the spring opposes this, and therefore a change in the atmospheric pressure causes the pillar to move up or down. This movement is magnified by levers which drive the pointer.

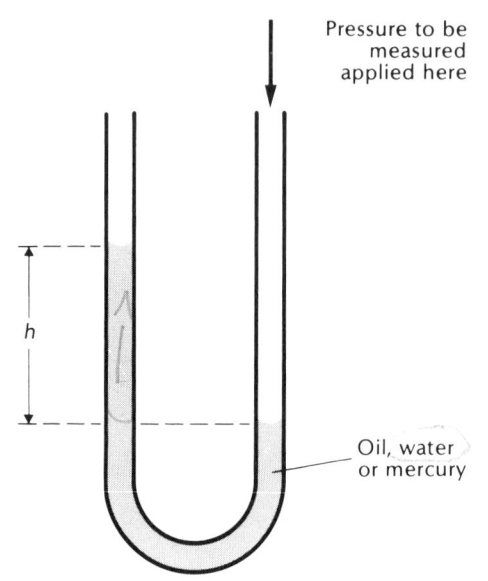

Fig. 8.4

■ A **U-tube manometer** measures pressure differences from atmospheric pressure if the left-hand side (in Figure 8.4) is left open, but if that side is connected to a vacuum pump then it measures actual pressure. (If a vacuum pump is used in this way, care is needed to ensure that no liquid can enter the pump.) In the application of this method to measuring the pressure of the gas supply shown in Figure 8.5, the excess pressure of the gas is:

$$p = \rho g h = 1000 \text{ kg/m}^3 \times 10 \text{ m/s}^2 \times h$$

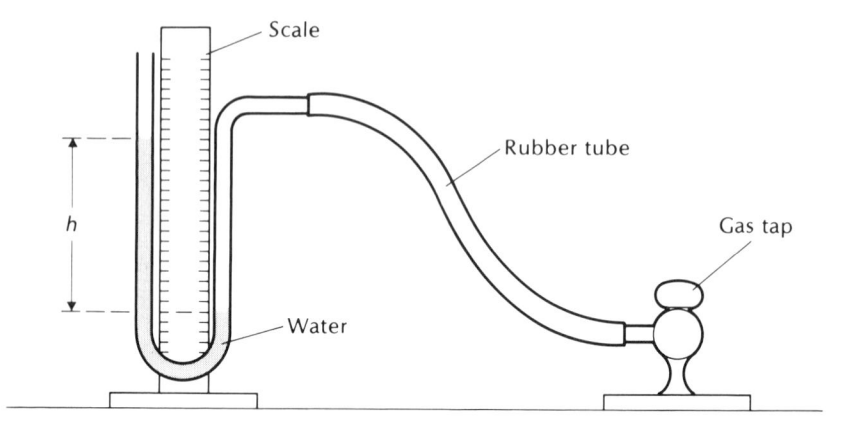

Fig. 8.5

If the total pressure of the gas is required, add atmospheric pressure to this.

To measure larger pressure differences a taller U-tube is needed, perhaps filled with mercury instead of water.

Pumps

A pump is a device for moving a liquid or a gas against a pressure difference. There are many different kinds, some working by rotation and some by a jet of water or of vapour. The principle of a piston pump is shown in Figure 8.6; a practical version of this is the bicycle pump (Figure 8.7). In the bicycle pump the cup-shaped leather washer acts as the intake valve because it lets air leak past it during the upward stroke; the delivery valve is the one attached to the tyre.

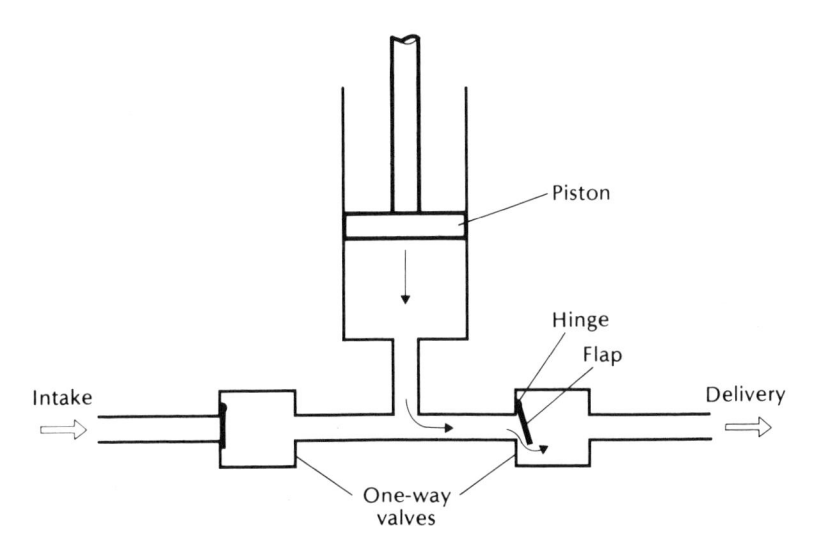

Fig. 8.6

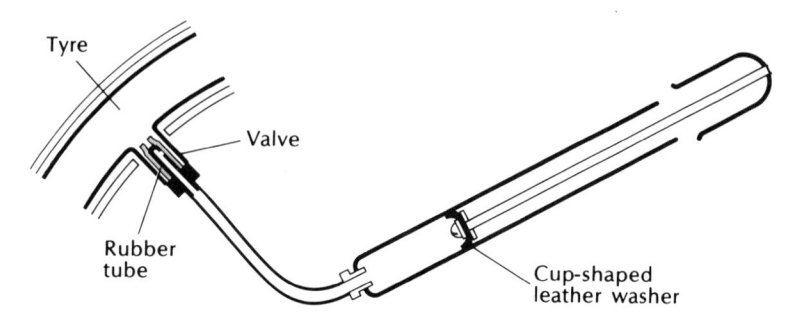

Fig. 8.7

Viscosity

The **viscosity** of a liquid or gas is its resistance to flow. Thick oil takes longer to flow through a funnel than water does, because of its higher viscosity.

Air resistance and water resistance are caused partly by the viscosity of air or water (energy being turned into heat) and partly by the formation of eddies and waves (energy being given to the air or water as kinetic energy).

Air resistance and water resistance, unlike friction between solid surfaces, depend on speed. As the speed of a falling body increases, the resistance increases and eventually becomes equal to the weight when the 'terminal velocity' is reached. The speed then remains constant (see Figure 3.12(c)).

Surface Tension

Liquids behave as if they had stretched skins over their surfaces. This 'surface tension' causes drops to be spherical and liquids to rise up narrow tubes if they can wet the surface — for example, water in a glass tube (see Figure 8.8). If a liquid cannot wet the surface, it tends to keep out of narrow places. An example of this is mercury which tends to keep out of the constriction of a clinical thermometer (see p. 74), because mercury does not wet glass.

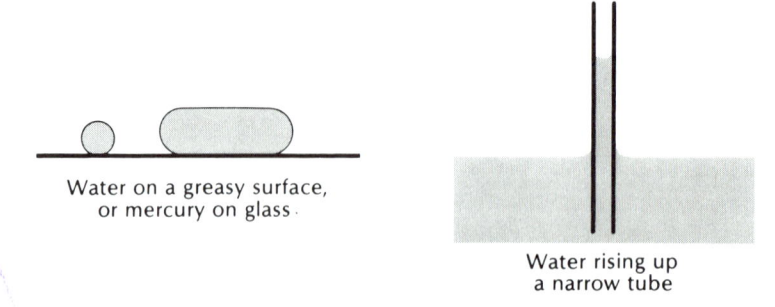

Water on a greasy surface, or mercury on glass

Water rising up a narrow tube

Fig. 8.8

Questions on Chapter 8

1   A man stands on snow wearing skis. If each ski rests on the snow over an area 3 m long and 0.1 m wide, and the weight of the man

together with his equipment is 900 N, what pressure do the skis exert on the snow?

If he takes off his skis and carries them, what pressure will his boots exert on the snow as he stands? Assume that each boot rests on the snow over an area equal to a rectangle 0.2 m by 0.1 m.

2 A car has a weight of 10 kN and each of its four tyres touches the ground over an area of $\frac{1}{100}$ m². A caterpillar tractor has a weight of 40 kN and each of its two tracks touches the ground over an area 2.5 m long and 0.2 m wide. Find the average pressure exerted on the ground by each vehicle. Which would be more likely to sink into soft ground?

3 A stone sculpture has a mass of 5000 kg. Its base which rests on the ground is 0.50 m square. What pressure does it exert on the ground? Give the answer both in pascals and in atmospheres, assuming that $g = 10$ m/s² and using the value of atmospheric pressure given on p. 57.

4 Using the value of atmospheric pressure given on p. 57, find the force which the atmosphere exerts on each of the two surfaces of a shop window measuring 3 m high and 4 m wide. Give the answer both in newtons and in tonne-force. (A tonne-force is the weight of a tonne mass when it is at the Earth's surface; it equals 10 000 N.)

5 A diver is working at a depth of 10 m below the surface of a fresh-water lake. Find a) the pressure difference due to the depth of water and b) the pressure acting on the diver. (Assume $g = 10$ m/s². For the density of water see p. 7. For atmospheric pressure see p. 57.)

If one item of the diver's equipment will not stand pressures greater than 4 atmospheres, what limit does this impose on the depth to which he can go? (Do not allow a safety margin in working out this question.)

6 A U-tube containing mercury is used as a manometer. What difference of pressure does it indicate when the difference between the two mercury levels is 100 mm? ($g = 10$ m/s²; density of mercury = 13 600 kg/m³)

7 In a hydraulic jack like that shown in Figure 8.1, the diameter of the piston which is moved by the effort is 10 mm and the diameter of the piston which moves the load is 20 mm. a) What is the velocity ratio? b) If, because of friction, the efficiency is only 50%, what is the mechanical advantage? c) If the effort moves the smaller piston by means of a lever of velocity ratio 3, as shown in Figure 8.9, what is the velocity ratio of the whole system?

Fig. 8.9

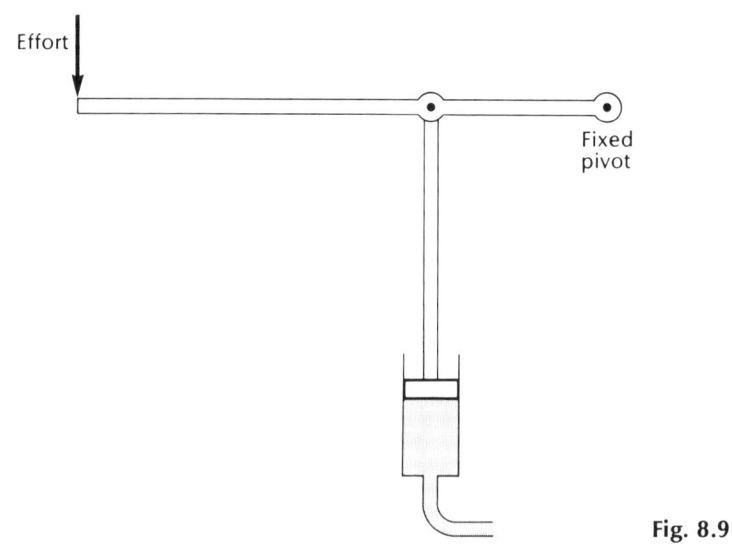

8 Figure 8.10 represents a hydraulic braking system in which the effort is applied to a pedal at the end of a lever arm, 200 mm from a pivot. On the other side of the pivot, 40 mm away, the lever connects to a piston of area 50 mm². The piston transmits pressure through oil to another piston, of area 100 mm², connected to the brake.

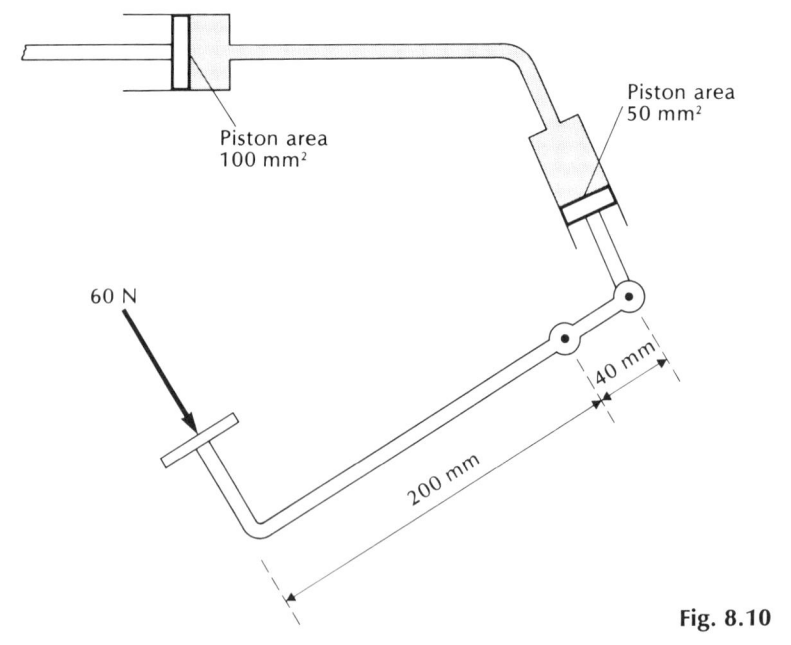

Fig. 8.10

a) When the effort applied is 60 N, what is:
   (i) the force applied to the first piston;
   (ii) the pressure on the oil?
b) What force is applied to the brake at the end of the system if frictional forces can be ignored?
c) What is the velocity ratio of this system, and what steps could be taken to increase it?
d) With a small amount of air trapped in the oil, why would the system work badly, if at all? (O)

Chapter 9

Archimedes' Principle

> If a body is immersed or partly immersed in a fluid (that is, a liquid or a gas), then an upward force acts on it and this force is equal to the weight of the fluid which is displaced.

This force is called the upthrust. In Figure 9.1(a) the spring balance indicates the weight of the stone. In Figure 9.1(b) the spring balance shows the 'apparent weight' which is less than the weight of the stone; it is labelled T in the diagram, standing for the tension in the thread. The difference between the two spring balance readings equals the upthrust. This leads to an accurate way of measuring density.

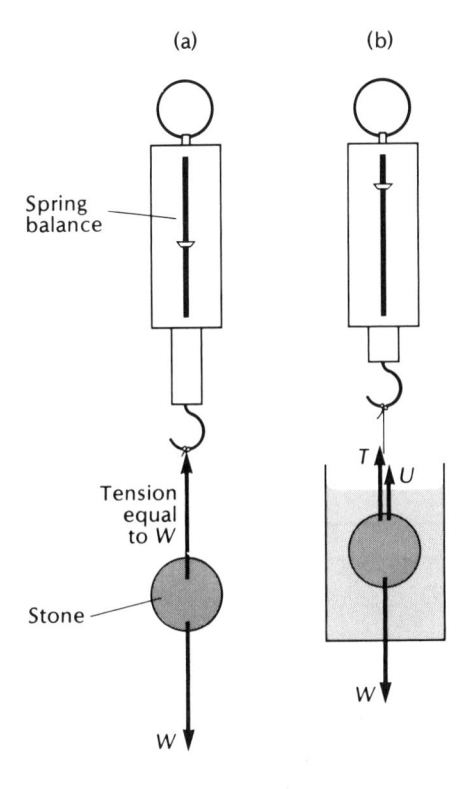

Fig. 9.1

Measurement of Density by Archimedes' Principle

The method is as follows.

Hang a solid body on a balance and record its weight. Call the weight W. Next, suspend it in water or in some other liquid as in Figure 9.1(b) and record the balance reading, calling it T.

Now $\quad W - T =$ Upthrust $=$ Weight of liquid displaced

and $\quad\quad\quad W =$ Weight of body

$$\therefore \quad \frac{W}{W-T} = \frac{\text{Weight of body}}{\text{Weight of liquid displaced}}$$

$$= \frac{\text{Mass of body}}{\text{Mass of equal volume of liquid}}$$

$$= \frac{\text{Density of body}}{\text{Density of liquid}}$$

If the liquid is water, you know its density to be 1000 kg/m^3 and you can work out the density of the solid. Alternatively, if you use a liquid of unknown density but the density of the solid is known, you can find the density of the liquid.

To compare the densities of two liquids, suspend some suitable solid body in both liquids in turn. Then if, for example, the liquids are oil and water:

$$\frac{\text{Density of oil}}{\text{Density of water}} = \frac{\text{Upthrust in oil}}{\text{Upthrust in water}} = \frac{W - T_{oil}}{W - T_{water}}$$

You can find the density of oil from this because the density of water is known.

The Principle of Flotation

The principle of flotation is the special case of Archimedes' principle for freely floating bodies like a boat, a stationary submerged submarine, or a balloon which is not rising or descending. In such cases the upthrust equals the weight, and so:

> When a body is floating freely, its weight is equal to the weight of fluid which it displaces.

Archimedes' Principle

■ A hydrometer (Figure 9.2) works on this principle to measure densities of liquids. When it floats in a liquid it always displaces the same weight of liquid — a weight equal to its own weight — and so it floats higher in denser liquids and lower in less dense ones.

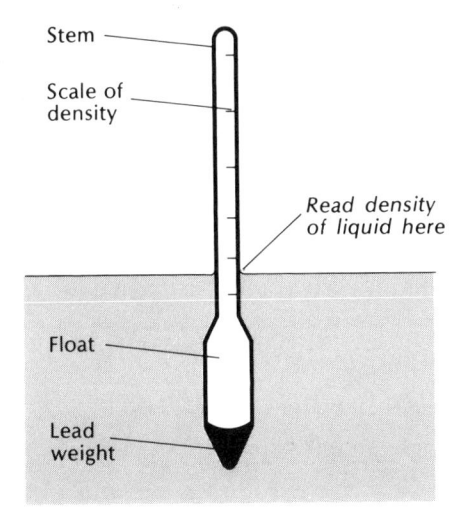

Fig. 9.2

Questions on Chapter 9

1 A concrete block with a volume of $2\,m^3$ and a density of $2500\,kg/m^3$ is lowered into water by a crane. What are:
 a) the mass of the block,
 b) the weight of the block,
 c) the tension in the crane rope when the block is in the air,
 d) the mass of water displaced,
 e) the weight of water displaced,
 f) the upthrust,
 g) the tension in the crane rope when the block is under water?
 ($g = 10\,m/s^2$; density of water $= 1000\,kg/m^3$)

2 A wooden plank has a volume of $0.05\,m^3$ and a density of $800\,kg/m^3$. Find a) its mass, b) its weight, c) the upthrust acting on it when it is completely submerged in water and d) the force needed to submerge it. ($g = 10\,m/s^2$; density of water $= 1000\,kg/m^3$)

3 As part of a laboratory experiment a one kilogram iron mass is suspended in paraffin. What is its apparent weight? The density of iron is $8000\,kg/m^3$ and that of paraffin is $800\,kg/m^3$.

4 To find the density of a stone it is weighed first in air and then while suspended in water. The results are:

weight of stone in air 7.0 N

apparent weight of stone in water 4.0 N

Find:
a) the upthrust which acts on the stone;
b) the weight of water displaced by the stone;
c) the mass of water displaced by the stone;
d) the volume of water displaced by the stone;
e) the volume of the stone;
f) the density of the stone.

5 A glass stopper is suspended from a balance and weighed, first in air and then dipping into a liquid as shown in Figure 9.1(b). The results are:

weight of stopper in air 1.00 N

apparent weight in water 0.60 N

apparent weight in salt solution 0.55 N

Find a) the density of the glass stopper and b) the density of the salt solution.

6 A hydrogen-filled balloon has a volume of 2 m^3 and the mass of its envelope is 0.3 kg. Find:
a) the total weight of the balloon including the hydrogen;
b) the upthrust;
c) the downward force which is needed to keep the balloon from rising.

Assume the density of hydrogen to be 0.1 kg/m^3, the density of air 1.3 kg/m^3 and the acceleration due to gravity 10 m/s^2.

7 An iceberg of mass 36 000 kg floats in water of density 1000 kg/m^3. The density of the ice is 900 kg/m^3. Find:
a) the volume of the ice;
b) the volume of water displaced;
c) the volume of that part of the iceberg which is above the water surface.

8 A flat-bottomed test-tube is weighted with lead shot so that it will float upright. Its area of cross-section is 4.0 cm^2. When it is floated in a salt solution it is found that adding a 10 g mass to the test-tube makes it float 2.0 cm lower in the liquid. Find the density of the solution.

Section B:
HEAT

A steam engine transforms heat energy into mechanical energy.

Chapter 10

Temperature

In studying heat we have two different things to measure. One is the amount of energy in a hot body, and we will come to that in Chapter 14. The other, the subject of this chapter, is how hot a body is, and this is called its **temperature**. Any instrument which measures temperature is called a **thermometer**. Since different kinds of thermometer do not all agree with each other, it is necessary to agree on a standard kind of thermometer, and on a standard way of calibrating it. Otherwise, one scientist's temperature measurement will not be meaningful to another scientist. The standard thermometer is the gas thermometer, which we will meet on p. 84, but the familiar mercury-in-glass thermometer agrees with the gas thermometer sufficiently accurately for most purposes, and so we can nearly always think of temperature as being the reading of a mercury thermometer.

The Fixed Points

The standard way of calibrating a thermometer uses two 'fixed points'. On the familiar Celsius scale these are numbered 0 °C and 100 °C respectively.

- The **lower fixed point** (the 'ice point') is the melting point of pure ice at standard atmospheric pressure, though pressure changes are unimportant except for very accurate work. When checking that a thermometer reads correctly at the ice point, good drainage of the melting ice is important. The arrangement shown in Figure 10.1 is suitable.

- The **upper fixed point** (the 'steam point') is the temperature of steam from pure boiling water at standard atmospheric pressure. In this case pressure changes are important as they can alter the boiling point considerably.

The rough method of checking the reading of a thermometer at the steam point, shown in Figure 10.2, has these errors:

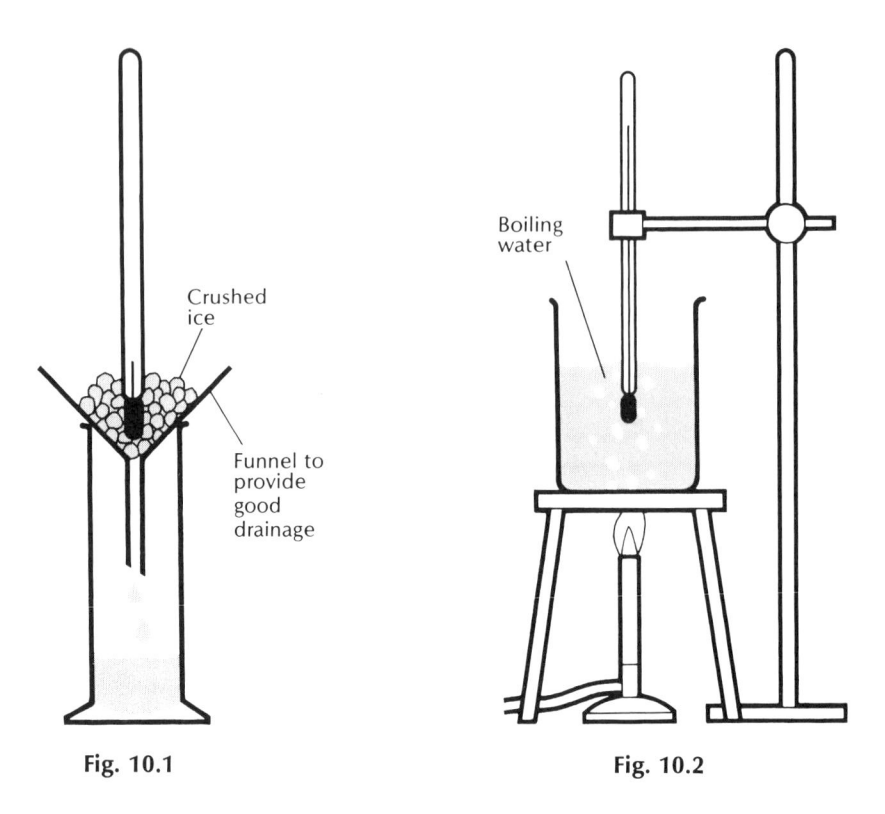

Fig. 10.1

Fig. 10.2

- *impurities* dissolved in the water raise the boiling point — this error can be avoided by using distilled water or by the method given below — and

- *irregular boiling*, or 'bumping', allows the temperature to rise a little above the boiling point between each 'bump' and the next, so that the mean temperature is too high. This error can be reduced by adding porcelain chips to the water, but to avoid it completely use the method which is described below.

Variations of the pressure of the atmosphere will also cause an error unless a correction is applied.

The accurate method of checking the upper fixed point uses a hypsometer (Figure 10.3). In this apparatus the bulb of the thermometer is not in the boiling water but in the steam. The radiation shield prevents the thermometer bulb from exchanging heat by radiation with anything which is not at steam temperature. A barometer is used to find how much the atmospheric pressure differs from 760 mmHg; by looking up this difference in the appropriate table it is possible to find what correction to apply to the temperature to allow for the effect of pressure change on the boiling point.

Temperature

Radiation shield

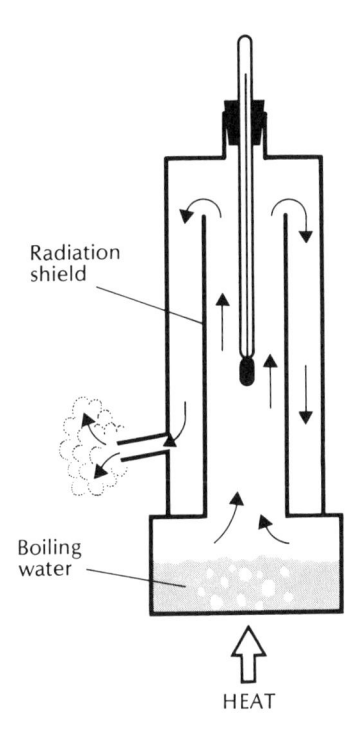

Boiling water

HEAT   Fig. 10.3

Scales of Temperature

Two temperature scales concern us.

- The **Celsius** scale (which used to be called the 'centigrade' scale) has the fixed points at 0 °C and 100 °C.
- The **Kelvin** scale has units the same size as a Celsius degree and its zero is at the absolute zero, that is, the temperature of a body which contains no internal energy.

To change:

°C to K, add 273 (accurate enough for us)

K to °C, subtract 273.

For example:

$$20°C = 293 K$$
$$100°C = 373 K$$
$$0 K = -273°C$$

Note that the kelvin is an SI unit, and '°K' is wrong.

Quick Question 20

What are a) −20 °C expressed in kelvin and b) 77 K expressed in °C?

Thermometers

- The **mercury-in-glass** thermometer is the most familiar type. Together with the less common alcohol-in-glass version it has the advantage of being portable, easy to use and comparatively cheap.

- The **clinical** thermometer (Figure 10.4) is a specialised form of the mercury-in-glass thermometer for medical use. Its special features are:
  - a constriction (narrowing) of the bore just above the bulb so that the mercury above this will not run back into the bulb until it is shaken, giving time for the reading to be taken after the thermometer is removed from the patient's mouth;
  - an extra narrow bore so that the expansion caused by a temperature rise of only ten degrees (35 °C to 45 °C) is enough to move the mercury surface right along the stem;
  - a bulge in the glass down one side of the stem to act as a magnifier so that the mercury in the extra narrow bore can be seen.

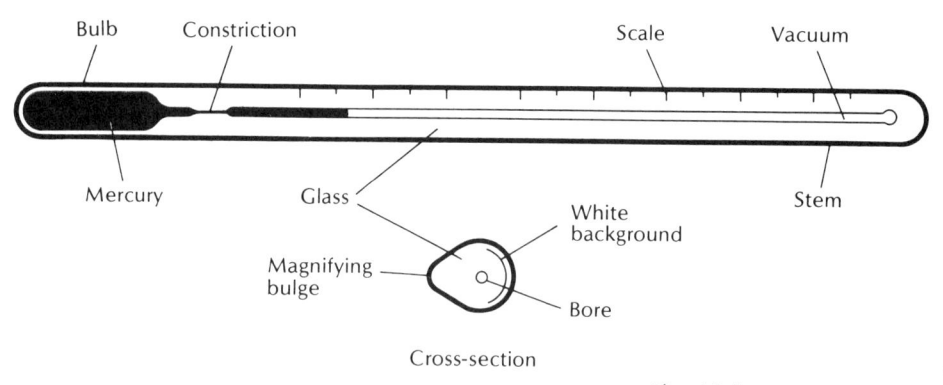

Fig. 10.4

- The **thermocouple** (or thermo-electric) thermometer is shown in Figure 10.5. It is especially useful for measuring high temperatures and quickly changing ones. It can also measure temperatures inside a closed apparatus or in an inaccessible place, because the wires leading to the hot junction can be made long and thin and flexible.

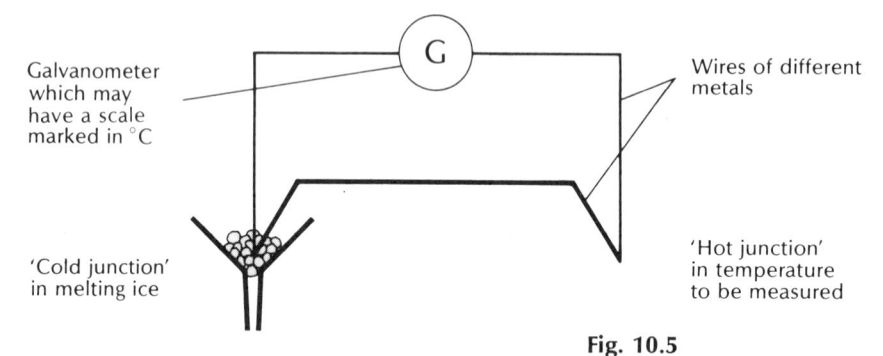

Fig. 10.5

Questions on Chapter 10

1. Change a) 27°C to kelvin and b) 500 K to °C.
2. The boiling point of liquid oxygen is 90 K. What is that in °C?
3. Aluminium melts at 660°C. What is that in kelvin?
4. A body has a temperature of 17°C. It is then heated so that its kelvin temperature is doubled. What is its new temperature, measured on the Celsius scale?

Chapter 11

Thermal Expansion

Solids expand when their temperature rises. As they expand they keep their shape (except for bodies made of two or more different materials, like a bi-metal strip). In other words the length of a body and its width and its thickness, as well as the diameter of a hole in it, all increase in the same ratio.

Liquids also, with a few exceptions, expand when their temperature rises. Water, when its temperature is between 0°C and 4°C, is one of the exceptions (see p. 107).

Gases expand more than solids and liquids do if their pressure is kept constant. They can be prevented from expanding by being kept in a strong container and in this case the pressure increases when the temperature rises.

Expansivity

When a solid body expands (or contracts), the increase (or decrease) of its length is given by:

$$x = l\alpha\theta$$

where x is the expansion, or increase in length, in any unit

l is the original length, in the same unit

θ (the Greek letter 'theta') is the change of temperature in °C or in K

α (the Greek letter 'alpha') is the expansivity of the material; it may be called 'linear expansivity' to distinguish it from the quantity which measures volume change in a liquid.

The unit of expansivity is 'per degree Celsius' or 'per kelvin', /°C or /K.

Thermal Expansion

Since the other dimensions of the body increase in the same ratio as the length does, the same equation can be used to calculate (for example) the increase in the diameter of a hole in the body. If l means any dimension of the body, x means the increase of that dimension.

To measure α, fit a rod or tube of the material in question so that it rests against a fixed stop at one end and against a micrometer screw gauge at the other. Figure 11.1 shows an apparatus which may be used for this. Pass cold water first, and then steam, through a jacket round the rod or through the tube, and read the micrometer each time, remembering to screw the micrometer back out of the way while the expansion is taking place to avoid straining the apparatus. x is found by subtracting one micrometer reading from the other.

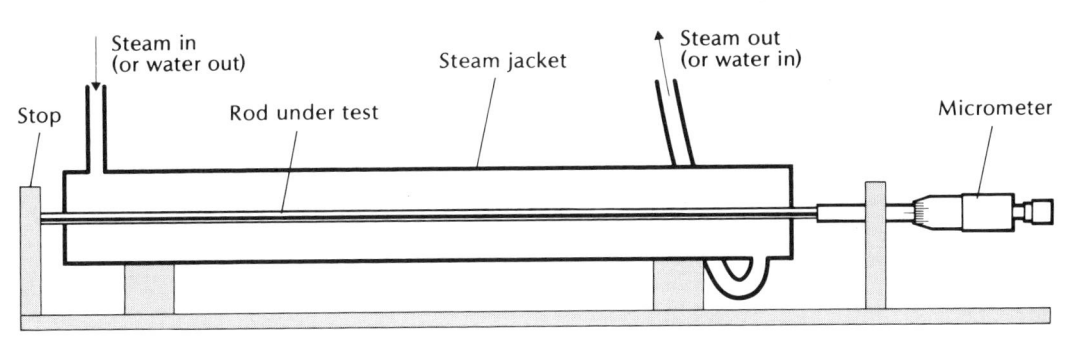

Fig. 11.1

Example 11.1 To what temperature must a copper rod one metre long at 20°C be heated for its length to increase by 5 mm? (The expansivity of copper is 0.000 02 /K.)

Solution

$$x = l\alpha\theta$$

$$\therefore \quad \theta = \frac{x}{l\alpha} = \frac{5}{1000 \times 0.000\,02}$$

$$= 250 \text{ K}$$

Adding this change of temperature to the original 20°C, the answer is 270°C.

Quick Question 21 What rise of temperature will make a copper rod increase in length by 1%?

Allowances for Expansion

In some cases expansion is a nuisance and allowance must be made for it. Bridges provide an example of this — some types of bridge are fixed at one end only, while the other end rests on steel rollers.

For an example of an allowance for expansion of a liquid, consider the radiator of a car. Space is left at the top of the header tank to allow room for the water to expand. Sometimes an overflow pipe is provided as well.

Uses of Expansion

■ Here are some examples of uses (or 'applications') of expansion of a **solid**:

- Steel tyres for wooden cart-wheels are made too tight a fit to be put on when cold. They are fitted to the wheels when hot and then cooled quickly so as to contract and hold the wheel together very firmly.
- Cog wheels are fitted to their shafts by cooling the shafts in liquid nitrogen to contract them, since heating the wheels would soften the teeth.
- **Bi-metal strips** are used to operate switches in thermostats and to move the pointers of dial-type thermometers. The strip bends when it is heated (Figure 11.2) because one metal has a higher expansivity than the other and therefore expands more. Bi-metal strips are often made in the form of a spiral so that they curl up or uncurl as the temperature changes.

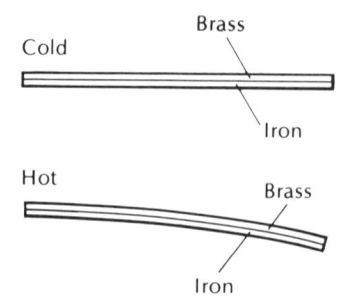

Fig. 11.2

Quick Question 22

The expansivity of iron is 0.000 011 /K. What can you say about the expansivity of brass, after looking at Figure 11.2?

Thermal Expansion

■ The most important use of **liquid** expansion is the liquid-in-glass thermometer, either the mercury or the alcohol type.

Questions on Chapter 11

Assume that $\alpha = 1.1 \times 10^{-5}$ /K for steel.

1 A steel-built ship is 150 m long. How much longer does it become when the temperature of its hull rises by 10°C?

2 A steel rule has a scale of millimetres which is correct when the rule is at 0°C. To what temperature must the rule be heated for its scale to be wrong by 1%?

3 In an experiment to measure the expansivity of lead, a lead bar half a metre long increases its length by 1.20 mm when its temperature rises from 20°C to 100°C. What is its expansivity?

Chapter 12

Gases

The Gas Laws

Boyle's law states:

> The pressure and the volume of a constant mass of gas are inversely proportional to each other, if the temperature does not change.

Charles' law states:

> The volume of a constant mass of gas is proportional to the kelvin temperature, if the volume does not change.

The **law of pressures** states:

> The pressure of a constant mass of gas is proportional to the kelvin temperature, if the volume does not change.

The last two laws can also be stated in the form:

> The volume (or pressure) of a fixed mass of gas increases by $\frac{1}{273}$ of its value at $0°C$ for each $1°C$ rise of temperature, if the pressure (or volume) does not change.

The table summarises the three laws in mathematical form.

Boyle's law	If T is constant,	$p \propto \dfrac{1}{V}$ $V \propto \dfrac{1}{p}$ $p \times V$ is constant
Charles' law	If p is constant,	$V \propto T_{kelvin}$
Law of pressures	If V is constant,	$p \propto T_{kelvin}$

Gases

> **Quick Question 23**
> A gas cylinder is at a temperature of 0 °C. It would burst if the pressure of the gas inside it was doubled. If this cylinder is heated by a fire, at what temperature would you expect it to burst?
>
> $p \propto T$

■ The combined form of the three laws is called the **ideal gas equation**, an ideal gas being one that always obeys the laws exactly and so cannot liquefy. (Real gases turn liquid if cooled sufficiently and do not exactly obey the laws.) Two forms of the ideal gas equation are:

$$\frac{pV}{T} = \text{constant}$$

and

$$\frac{p_1 V_1}{T_1} = \frac{p_2 V_2}{T_2}$$

where the temperatures are in kelvin and the subscripts, 1 and 2, mean before and after some change — but not a chemical change, and not one which alters the mass.

Example 12.1 Twenty gas cylinders, each having a volume of 10 dm³, contain helium gas at 27 °C and at a pressure of 100 atmospheres. When this gas is used to fill a balloon at a pressure of one atmosphere, its temperature falls to 7 °C. What is the volume of the gas in the balloon?

Solution

$V_1 = 20 \times 10 \text{ dm}^3 = 200 \text{ dm}^3 = 0.20 \text{ m}^3$

$T_1 = 27 + 273 \text{ K} = 300 \text{ K}$

$T_2 = 7 + 273 \text{ K} = 280 \text{ K}$

$$\frac{p_1 V_1}{T_1} = \frac{p_2 V_2}{T_2}$$

$$\frac{100 \times 0.20}{300} = \frac{1 \times V_2}{280}$$

$$V_2 = \frac{100 \times 0.20 \times 280}{300}$$

$$= 18.7 \text{ m}^3$$

Of this, 0.2 m³ remains in the cylinders and so the volume of the gas in the balloon is 18.5 m³.

Gas Law Graphs

The graph in Figure 12.1 illustrates Boyle's law.

The graph in Figure 12.2 illustrates:
- Charles' law, if V is plotted vertically and p is constant;
- the law of pressures, if p is plotted vertically and V is constant;
- the general case, if $p \times V$ is plotted vertically.

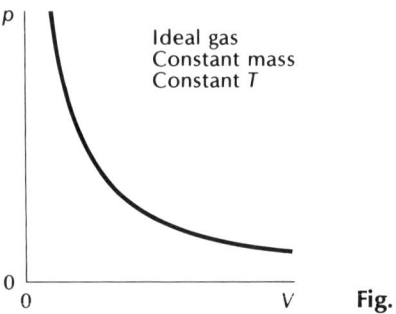

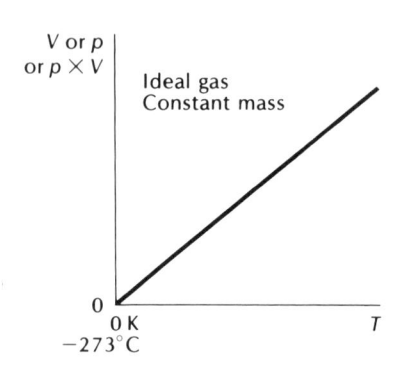

Fig. 12.1 (Ideal gas, Constant mass, Constant T): p vs V curve.

Fig. 12.2 (Ideal gas, Constant mass): V or p or $p \times V$ vs T, straight line through 0 K / $-273°C$.

An Experimental Test of Boyle's Law

The apparatus in Figure 12.3 can be used to test Boyle's law. The method is as follows.

Read the length of the air column, l, and the pressure, p. Record them in a table like this:

l	p	$l \times p$

Pump more air into the reservoir. Wait a minute to ensure that the air under test is again at room temperature, and take another pair of readings. Do this several more times. The figures in the third column should be the same every time, within experimental error.

This method is not accurate but has the merit of simplicity.

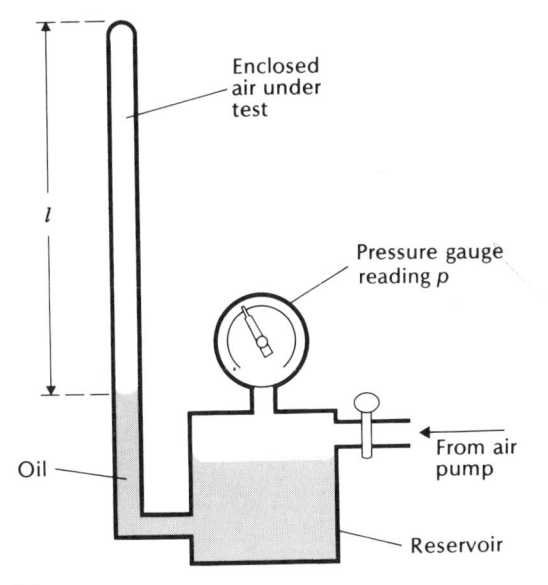

Fig. 12.3

Notes

- Readings of the length, l, can be used as a measure of the volume of the enclosed air because l is proportional to the volume.
- It has been assumed that the pressure gauge indicates total pressure. If, instead, it indicates pressure difference from atmospheric pressure, it is necessary to read a barometer and add atmospheric pressure to the gauge reading.
- The difference of pressure between the air under test and the air in the reservoir, due to the difference of the oil levels, will be too small to matter in an experiment of this sort.

An Experimental Test of Charles' Law

The apparatus in Figure 12.4 can be used to test Charles' law as follows.

The length, l, of the enclosed air column and the temperature, θ, of the water bath are measured and recorded. The process is repeated at various temperatures from the ice point up to the boiling point of water. l is plotted against θ (Figure 12.5). The best straight line is drawn, to pass as nearly as possible through all the points. If the experiment was sufficiently accurate this would be found to cut the temperature axis at $-273\,°C$.

Fig. 12.4

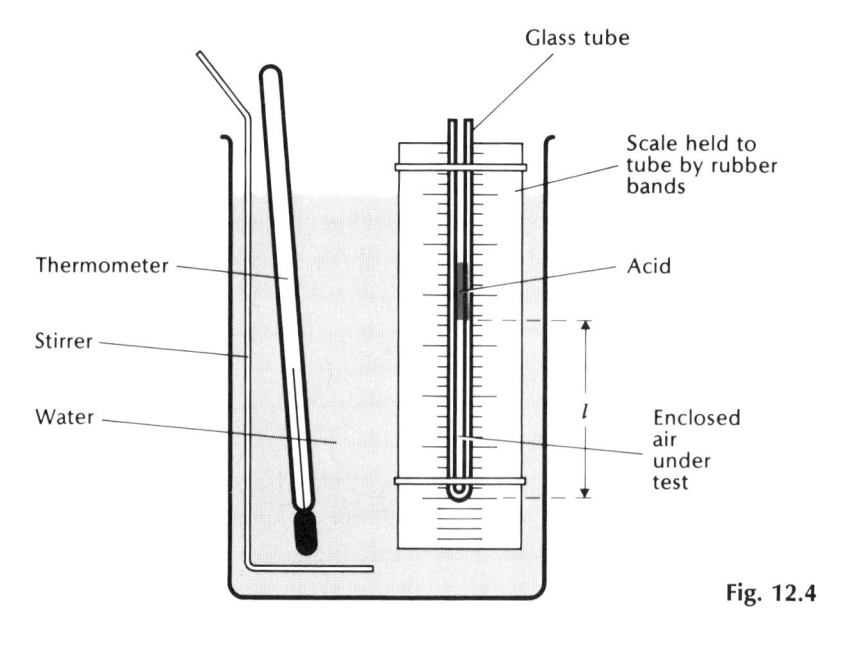

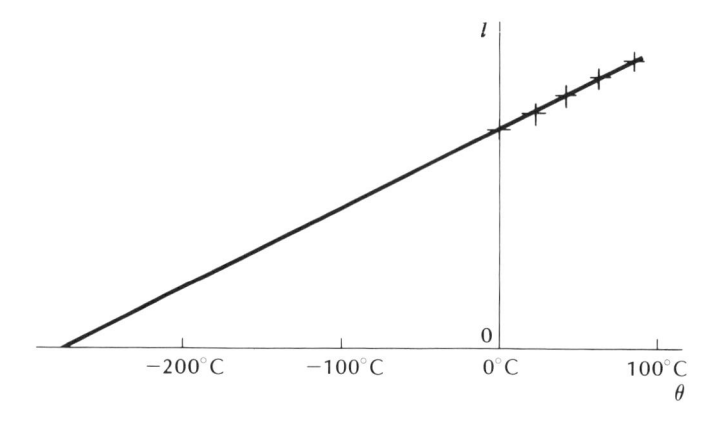

Fig. 12.5

Notes

- The pressure of the enclosed air is constant because it is equal to atmospheric, apart from a very slight extra pressure due to the weight of the acid.
- Concentrated sulphuric acid is used to enclose the air sample because it absorbs water vapour and so dries the enclosed air. If this was not done, slight condensation and evaporation would cause the mass of enclosed gas to vary.

An Experimental Test of the Law of Pressures

This can be done with the apparatus of Figure 12.6. This apparatus is a simple form of gas thermometer, and it can also be used for measuring temperatures. The total pressure of the enclosed air is found by adding the atmospheric pressure to the pressure difference shown on the manometer. This total pressure can be plotted against temperature to give a graph similar to Figure 12.5.

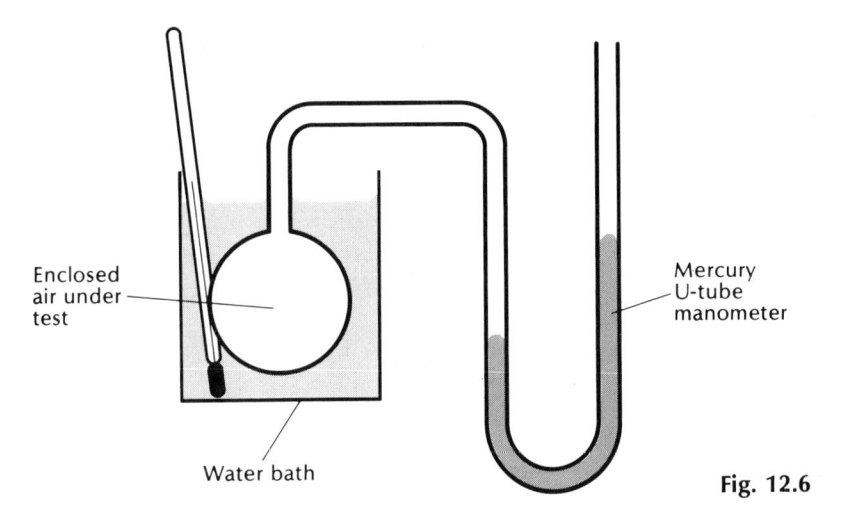

Fig. 12.6

Measurement of the Absolute Zero of Temperature

The absolute zero has been measured on the Celsius scale by both the last two experiments, but these methods depend on the accuracy of a mercury thermometer. A more satisfactory way is described next.

Use either apparatus, Figure 12.4 or 12.6. Pack crushed ice around the tube or the bulb, and take a reading. Surround the tube (or bulb) with boiling water — or, for greater accuracy, with steam in a properly designed steam jacket — and take a second reading. Measure atmospheric pressure to see how much it differs from 760 mmHg and apply a correction for the effect of pressure on the boiling point. Plot a graph like Figure 12.5 but with just two points on it, one at 0°C and the other at 100°C. Draw a line through these two points and read where it cuts the temperature axis.

Quick Question 24

In a rather inaccurate version of the experiment to find the absolute zero of temperature, the pressure of the gas sample is kept constant and these readings are taken:

volume of the gas at the ice point   6 cm^3
volume of the gas at the steam point   8 cm^3

What value does this give for the absolute zero?

Questions on Chapter 12

1. An air compressor delivers 100 litres of air every minute at a pressure of 4 atmospheres. What volume of air (in litres) does it take in at atmospheric pressure in each minute? Assume that there is no change of temperature.

2. A balloon contains 10.0 m³ of hydrogen at a temperature of 27°C. What volume will this hydrogen occupy if it cools to 12°C, assuming that its pressure does not change?

3. A diver's air cylinder contains air at a pressure of 20 atmospheres when its temperature is 7°C. What is the pressure of the air after the cylinder has been warmed by the sun to 35°C?

4. Air which is initially at atmospheric pressure is compressed into one quarter of its previous volume. Compressing the air causes its temperature to rise from 7°C to 77°C. What is the new pressure of the air?

5. In a chemical experiment, 48.5 cm³ of gas is collected at a temperature of 20°C and a pressure of 740 mmHg. What would the volume of the gas be at STP? (STP stands for standard temperature and pressure, which is 0°C and 760 mmHg.)

6. The density of oxygen at 1 atmosphere pressure and 288 K is 1.3 kg/m³. What is the mass of oxygen contained in a cylinder of volume 0.004 m³ at 50 atmospheres pressure at this temperature?
(O)

7. Early in the morning the pressure in a car tyre was 2.00×10^5 Pa when the temperature was 7°C. What would you expect the pressure in the tyre to be when the temperature has risen to 27°C in the afternoon? (Assume that the volume of the tyre does not change.)
(L)

8. In Figure 12.7, dry air is trapped in the closed end of a horizontal glass tube by mercury which occupies a 250 mm length of the tube. The other end of the tube is open to the atmosphere, the atmospheric pressure being 750 mmHg. The temperature is 290 K.

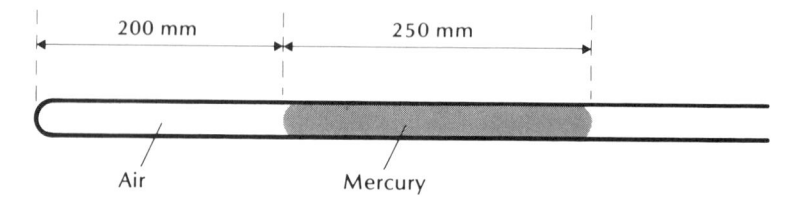

Fig. 12.7

a) The open end is now raised until the tube is vertical.
   (i) What is now the pressure on the trapped air?
   (ii) What length of the tube does the trapped air now occupy?
b) With the tube still vertical, the temperature is raised to 348 K. What length of the tube does the trapped air now occupy?
c) With the tube returned to the horizontal position at 348 K, what length of the tube does the trapped air now occupy?   (O)

9   A closed vessel has a volume of 0.50 m³ and contains gas at a pressure of 2000 mmHg and a temperature of 300 K.
Calculate the pressure exerted by the same mass of gas if the volume of the vessel is increased to 0.80 m³ and the temperature is raised to 450 K.   (C)

Chapter 13

The Kinetic Theory

The kinetic (movement) theory states that matter is made up of small particles in continual motion.

In a **solid** these particles are the atoms, and they vibrate about fixed positions. These fixed positions — the centres of vibration of the various atoms — form a regular pattern if the solid is a crystal.

In a **liquid** it is the molecules that move. Each molecule is made up (in most cases) of several atoms bonded together, and it moves as a whole, both vibrating and moving about through the body of the liquid.

In a **gas** each molecule moves in a straight line (except for the slight effect of gravity) until it collides with another molecule and bounces off it.

Molecules vary greatly in size but one nanometre (see p. 248) is a typical diameter. The next experiment gives some evidence for this order of magnitude.

The Oil Film Method of Estimating the Size of a Molecule

Use an oil which will spread on a water surface to form a layer one molecule thick. Drop a very small drop of the oil on to the surface of some clean water in a wide tray. Measure the resulting patch of oil when it has spread fully. Then:

Volume of oil = Area of patch × Thickness of patch

But the thickness of the oil patch is the length of one molecule, and so the length of an oil molecule equals:

Volume of oil ÷ Area of patch

If the layer was actually not one but two molecules thick, or more than that, then the length of a molecule would be half, or a smaller fraction, of the thickness of the oil patch. This experiment therefore gives an upper limit to the length of a molecule.

Notes

- To make the estimation of the volume of the oil easier, the oil may be dissolved in a solvent. A comparatively large drop of the solution can then be used, and after it has been put on the water surface the unwanted solvent evaporates away.

- A powder may be sprinkled on the water surface before adding the oil, to make the spreading of the oil more visible.

Kinetic Theory Explanations

- **Pressure** in a gas is explained as the effect of the impacts of the molecules when they hit the wall of the container or some other surface. The number of molecules which hit each bit of the surface in each second is so large that the total effect seems to be steady.

- **Temperature** is explained as being a measure of how fast the molecules move. The higher the temperature the faster the molecules are moving.

- **Boyle's law** is explained because halving the volume of a gas doubles the number of molecules in each cubic metre, and so doubles the number of impacts on each square metre of the wall in each second. This assumes that each single impact is just as hard as it was before the volume was halved, and this is true if the temperature does not change.

- The **increase of pressure on heating** can be explained like this. When the temperature rises, the gas molecules start to move faster, and so they hit the container wall both harder and more often, causing a greater pressure.

- The explanation of **evaporation** is illustrated in Figure 13.1. Molecule A, at the surface of the liquid, is in equilibrium. If the motions of the molecules next to it knock it out to B, further from its neighbours, it will immediately return because of the

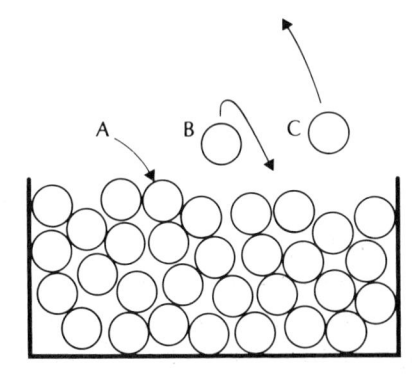

Fig. 13.1

attractive forces between molecules. Since molecules do not all have equal energy, a few of them at any one moment will happen to have considerably greater energy than the average. If C is one of these, it may be moving fast enough to escape against the attractive forces and become part of the gas.

- **Cooling by evaporation** occurs because it is the fastest moving molecules which are able to escape. Those left behind have, on average, less energy after the escape of the most energetic ones, and so the temperature of the remaining liquid is lowered.

- **Saturated vapour pressure** (see p. 102) is explained in terms of a balance between evaporation and condensation. At this vapour pressure, the number of molecules hitting the surface and therefore entering the liquid in each second is equal to the number escaping. If the temperature rises, more molecules have enough energy to escape and the gas pressure starts to increase, until balance is restored at a higher pressure.

- **Diffusion** is readily understood if the molecules are continually moving. Diffusion of a *liquid* is shown in Figure 13.2(a). The blue colour of the copper sulphate slowly spreads right to the top of the beaker although the solution is denser than the water which lies on top of it. Figure 13.2(b) shows how diffusion of a *gas* may be demonstrated. Bromine is used because its brown colour makes the effect of the diffusion visible. First the rubber tube is squeezed to break the capsule and release the bromine into the side tube. Then the tap is opened to allow the bromine to enter the main tube. If there is a vacuum in the main tube the brown colour

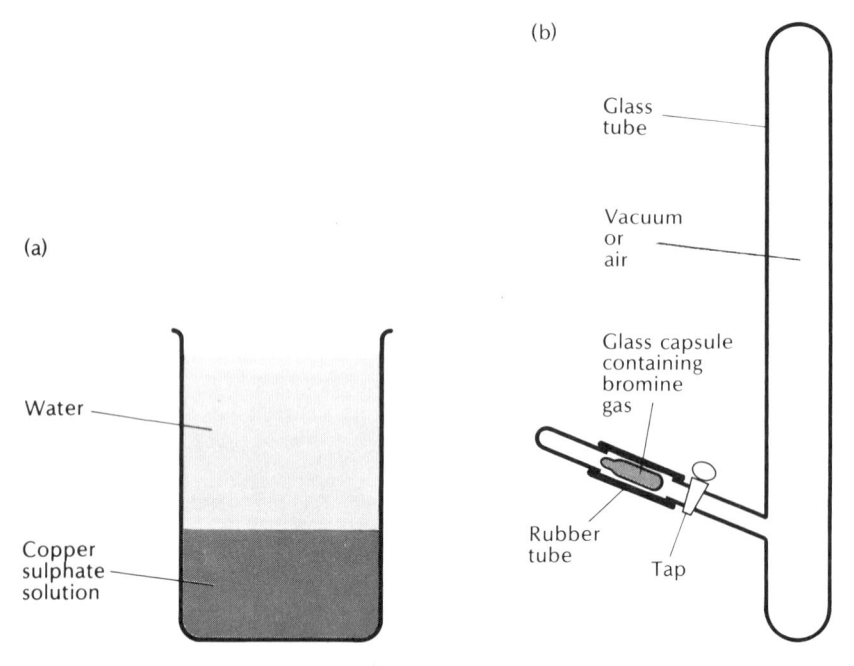

Fig. 13.2

appears to reach the top of the apparatus instantaneously; diffusion of a gas into a vacuum is very fast, showing that gas molecules move very fast at ordinary temperatures. If the main tube contains air at atmospheric pressure, the bromine goes to the bottom of the main tube when the tap is opened, because it is denser than air. It takes several minutes for the brown colour to spread throughout the tube, showing that the presence of the air has caused the diffusion to take place much more slowly.

Brownian Motion

Brownian motion gives clear evidence for the truth of the kinetic theory.

Very small smoke particles in air, or pollen grains in water, are seen to dance about continually. Because of the minute size of the particles it is necessary to use a microscope to see the motion, with a dark background and strong illumination from the side.

The cause of the motion is that, although the impacts of the surrounding molecules on opposite sides of the small particle balance each other on average, they do not balance exactly at any one time owing to the random nature of the impacts.

Chapter 14

Heat Capacity

To raise the temperature of a body, energy is needed. The amount of energy required depends both on the body and on the number of degrees through which the temperature is to be increased.

- The **heat capacity** of a body is the quantity of energy needed to raise its temperature by one kelvin — or by one Celsius degree, which means the same thing. So the energy put in (or taken out) when the temperature rises (or falls) is:

$$E = C\theta$$

where E is the energy put in (or taken out)   (in J)
       C is the heat capacity   (in J/K)
       θ is the rise (or fall) of temperature (in K)

The heat capacity of a body depends both on its mass and on the substance of which it is composed. The constant which is characteristic of the substance alone is called the 'specific heat capacity'.

- The **specific heat capacity** of a substance is the quantity of energy needed to raise the temperature of one kilogram of it by one kelvin. Note that the word 'specific' means 'for one unit of mass'. So another, more useful expression for the amount of energy gained or lost when the temperature changes is:

$$E = mc\theta$$

where m is the mass of the body   (in kg)
       c is its specific heat capacity (in J/kg K)

This assumes that the body does not change state — for example, that it does not change from the solid state to the liquid state by melting. We will consider changes of state in the next chapter.

Quick Question 25

How much energy is needed to heat up half a kilogram of ice-cold water to its boiling point? The specific heat capacity of water is 4200 J/kg K.

Measurement of Specific Heat Capacity

■ **For a liquid** the following method can be used, with the apparatus shown in Figure 14.1.

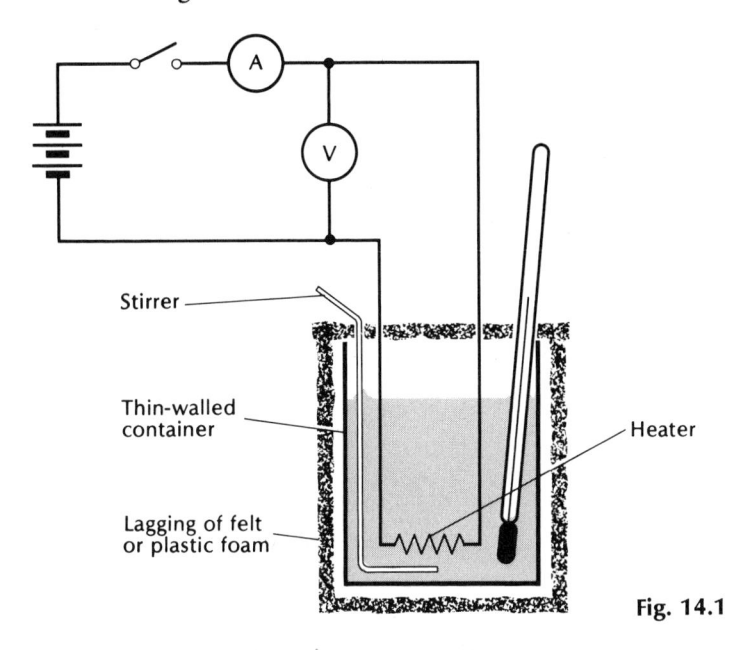

Fig. 14.1

Weigh the container both empty and with the liquid in it. Subtract to find the mass of liquid, m. Read the initial temperature. Switch on the current for long enough for the temperature to rise by 20° or so. Record the current, I, the potential difference, V, and the time, t (in seconds), during which the current flowed.

After switching off, stir the liquid and read the highest temperature which the thermometer reaches; this is the final temperature. Subtract to find the change of temperature, θ.

Then:

$$mc\theta = VIt$$

$$\therefore \quad c = \frac{VIt}{m\theta}$$

(For the expression VIt, see p. 201.)

■ **For a solid** the same method can be used (apart from details such as stirring) with the apparatus shown in Figure 14.2.

The solid is in the form of a block with two holes in it, one being the right size for an immersion heater and the other for a thermometer. A very small amount of a suitable liquid may be put in each hole to aid the transfer of heat from the heater to the block and from the block to the thermometer.

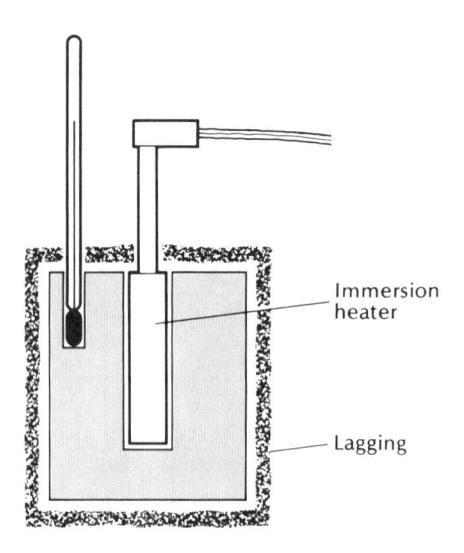

Fig. 14.2

Quick Question 26

If 0.1 kg of copper is heated through 10 K by an electric current of 1 A flowing for 40 s at a voltage of 10 V, what is the specific heat capacity of copper?

Two *errors* in these experiments will cause the values obtained for the specific heat capacity to be too high. They are:
- heat lost to the surroundings, and
- heat gained by the container, thermometer and heater.

In more advanced work these errors are corrected.

Two other methods of measuring specific heat capacity are given in the next two examples.

Example 14.1 A half kilogram iron mass is heated in boiling water and then put into a plastic beaker of negligible heat capacity which contains 400 g of water at 20 °C. The water is stirred, and its temperature rises to 30 °C. What value does this give for the specific heat capacity of iron? (The specific heat capacity of water is 4200 J/kg K.)

Solution The water temperature rises from 20 °C to 30 °C, and so:

$$\theta_{water} = 10 \text{ K}$$

The iron temperature falls from 100 °C to 30 °C, and so:

$$\theta_{iron} = 70 \text{ K}$$

(There is no need to call it -70 K.)

$$\text{Heat lost by iron} = \text{Heat gained by water}$$
$$(mc\theta)_{\text{iron}} = (mc\theta)_{\text{water}}$$
$$0.5 \times c_{\text{iron}} \times 70 = 0.4 \times 4200 \times 10$$
$$\therefore \quad c_{\text{iron}} = \frac{0.4 \times 4200 \times 10}{0.5 \times 70} = 480 \text{ J/kg K}$$

(This method of comparing one specific heat capacity with another is called the **method of mixtures**.)

Example 14.2 A liquid flows at a steady rate past two thermometers and an electric heater as shown in Figure 14.3. The thermometer readings are: left, 16°C; right 26°C. 120 g of the liquid is collected in the beaker in one minute. The power of the heater, measured by an ammeter and a voltmeter, is 40 W. Calculate the specific heat capacity of the liquid.

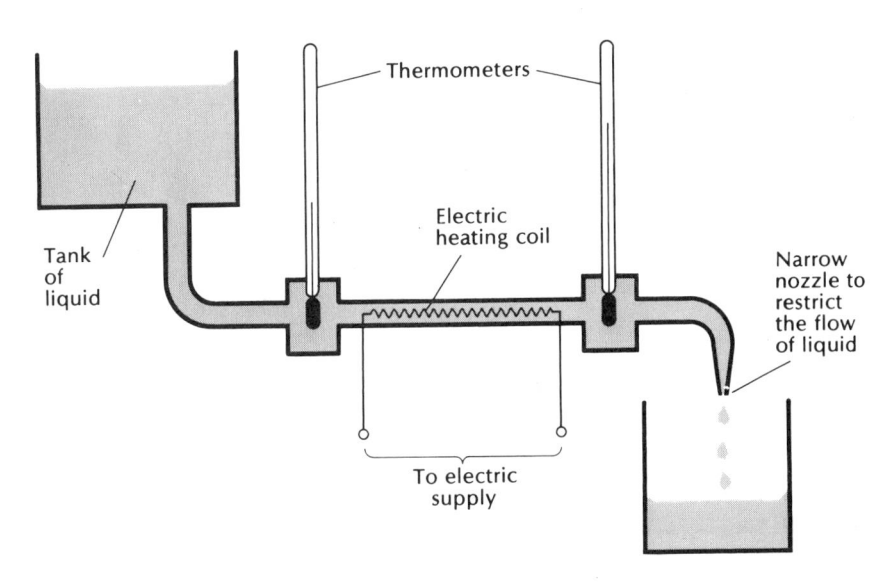

Fig. 14.3

Solution Energy put into liquid in 60 s is:
$$mc\theta = \text{Power of heater} \times \text{Time}$$
$$0.120 \times c \times 10 = 40 \times 60$$
$$\therefore \quad c = \frac{40 \times 60}{0.12 \times 10} = 2000 \text{ J/kg K}$$

(This is called a **constant-flow method**.)

Questions on Chapter 14

Use these values of specific heat capacity:
- water $c = 4200$ J/kg K
- aluminium $c = 900$ J/kg K
- iron $c = 475$ J/kg K
- copper $c = 400$ J/kg K

1 How much heat is needed to heat up:
a) 2 kg of water from 20°C to 30°C,
b) 100 g of copper from 20°C to 100°C,
c) 4 kg of iron from 300 K to 1300 K,
d) 1 g of aluminium from 0°C to 100°C?

2 An aluminium saucepan of mass 0.5 kg contains 1.0 kg of water. How much heat is needed to heat up the whole thing from 20°C to 100°C, if no heat is wasted?

3 Water at 10°C is to be heated to 60°C by an immersion heater. How much energy is needed to heat 25 kg of water? What power of immersion heater is needed to do this in half an hour?

4 125 g of water is put into a container which has a heat capacity of 75 J/K. The container is lagged to reduce heat losses. Find:
a) the total heat capacity of the container and the water together;
b) the amount of heat needed to raise their temperature by 50 K;
c) the length of time that this will take if the heating is done by a 50 W heater and heat losses are negligible.

5 In an experiment to measure the specific heat capacity of one kind of oil, a lump of copper of mass 100 g is heated in boiling water and then quickly transferred into a plastic beaker of negligible heat capacity which contains 200 g of the oil at 12°C. The resulting temperature, after stirring, is 20°C. Calculate the specific heat capacity of the oil.

6 To measure the specific heat capacity of paraffin, some paraffin is passed at a steady rate through a tube so that 40 g of it goes through in each minute. The tube contains a heater with a power of 28 watts and this causes the paraffin to rise in temperature by 20°C. Ignoring heat losses, calculate the specific heat capacity of paraffin.

7 In a simple experiment to determine the specific heat capacity of aluminium a 50 W immersion heater is inserted in a 2 kg block of aluminium, which also holds a thermometer, as shown in Figure 14.4.

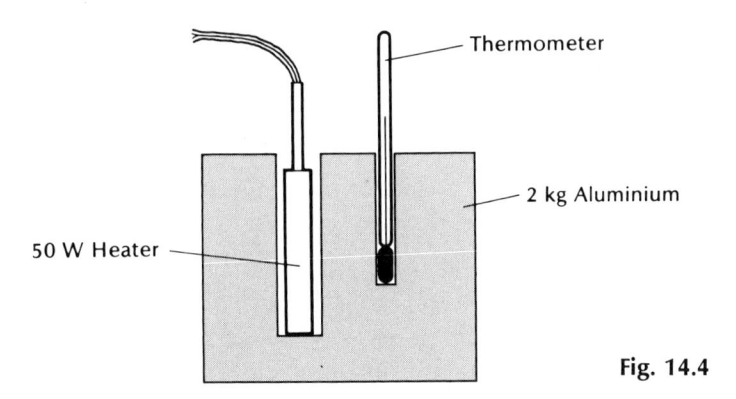

Fig. 14.4

a) How much heat is supplied by the heater every second?
b) How much heat is supplied by the heater in 5 minutes?
c) It is found that the temperature of the block rises 8 K in 5 minutes. Neglecting heat losses, calculate from this the value of the specific heat capacity of aluminium. (O*)

8 The heat capacity of an empty storage tank is 32 000 J/K. 200 kg of water are added to this tank.

(Take the specific heat capacity of water to be 4200 J/kg K.)

a) How much energy must be supplied to raise the temperature of the water alone from 18°C to 68°C?
b) How much energy must be supplied to raise the temperature of the tank alone from 18°C to 68°C?
c) How long will it take to raise the temperature of the tank and water together from 18°C to 68°C if the energy is supplied by a 3 kW immersion heater, and there are no heat losses to the surroundings?
d) How much longer will it take if the average rate of loss of heat to the surroundings is 250 W? (O)

Chapter 15

Change of State

Consider what would happen to the temperature of some ice taken straight out of the freezer at $-10\,°C$ if heat is put into it at a steady rate. In practice the surface layers are likely to melt before any of the heat has reached the middle of the lump of ice, but if the heat is given to all of the ice evenly this will happen:

  (i) first the temperature of the ice will rise to $0\,°C$, the melting point;
 (ii) the temperature will then stay at $0\,°C$ until the ice has melted;
(iii) when the melting is complete, the water so formed will again show a rise of temperature.

Again, consider the temperature changes when water is brought to the boil and then boiled away:

  (i) the temperature rises to the boiling point;
 (ii) the temperature then stays at the boiling point while the water boils away;
(iii) if it was possible to collect the steam and to go on heating it, its temperature would rise again once there was no liquid left.

So, while a change of state is taking place, either from solid to liquid or from liquid to gas, heat is being put in but the temperature does not rise. This heat is called latent heat.

■ The **latent heat** of a body is the quantity of energy needed to change its state without changing its temperature.

■ The **specific latent heat** of a substance is the quantity of energy needed to change the state of one kilogram of it without changing its temperature. The specific latent heat of *fusion* (melting) applies to the change from solid to liquid or from liquid to solid, and the specific latent heat of *vaporisation* applies to the change between the liquid and gas (or vapour) states. These two latent heats are not equal. So the energy put in or taken out when a body changes its state without change of temperature is:

$$E = ml$$

where E is the quantity of energy   (in J)
       m is the mass   (in kg)
       l is the specific latent heat (in J/kg)

Change of State

Quick Question 27

How much heat is needed to boil away half a kilogram of water which has already been heated to its boiling point? The specific latent heat of vaporisation of water is 2.25 MJ/kg.

Calculations often involve both a change of temperature and a change of state. Both expressions, $mc\theta$ and ml, must then be used one after the other and the results added.

Example 15.1 How much heat is needed to turn 0.50 kg of ice-cold water into steam at 100°C? How long would it take to do this using a 5 kW electric heater, if no heat is wasted? The specific heat capacity of water is 4200 J/kg K and its specific latent heat of vaporisation is 2.25 MJ/kg.

Solution First, the water is heated to 100°C. The amount of energy needed for this is:

$$E_1 = mc\theta = 0.5 \times 4200 \times 100 = 210\,000 \text{ J}$$

Then it is vaporised with no further change of temperature. The additional energy needed for this is:

$$E_2 = ml = 0.5 \times 2\,250\,000 = 1\,125\,000 \text{ J}$$

Therefore the total energy needed is:

$$E = E_1 + E_2 = 1\,335\,000 \text{ J}$$
$$= 1.34 \text{ MJ}$$

$$5 \text{ kW} = 5000 \text{ W} = 5000 \text{ joule per second}$$

and so the time taken is:

$$t = \frac{1\,340\,000}{5000} \text{ s} = 268 \text{ s} = 4\tfrac{1}{2} \text{ minutes, very nearly}$$

Measurement of the Specific Latent Heat of Vaporisation of Water

An approximate way of doing this is shown in Figure 15.1. Water is boiled away by means of an immersion heater and the mass, m, which has vaporised is found by weighing the beaker beforehand and again afterwards. Then, if V and I are the voltmeter and ammeter readings and t is the time in seconds during which the current was flowing:

$$ml = VIt$$
$$\therefore l = \frac{VIt}{m}$$

(For the expression VIt, see p. 201.)

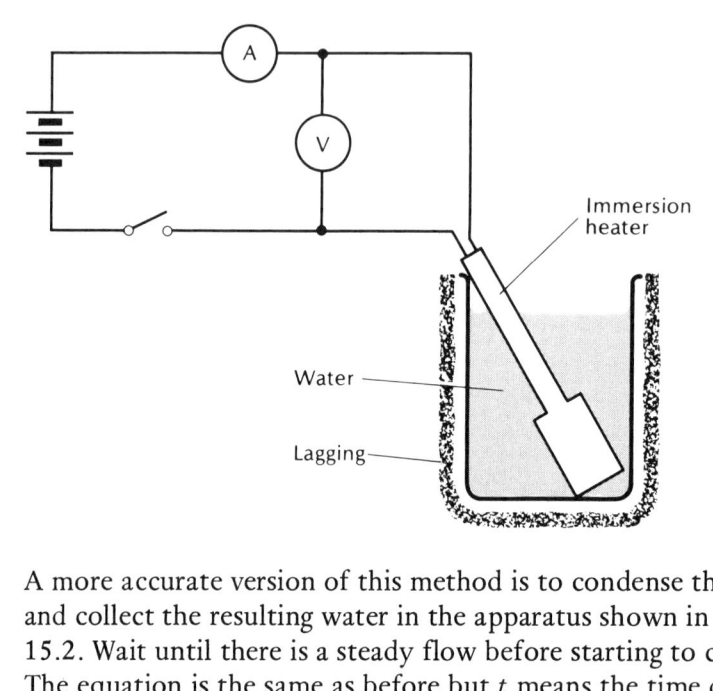

Fig. 15.1

A more accurate version of this method is to condense the steam and collect the resulting water in the apparatus shown in Figure 15.2. Wait until there is a steady flow before starting to collect it. The equation is the same as before but t means the time during which the water was being collected and m the mass collected during that time.

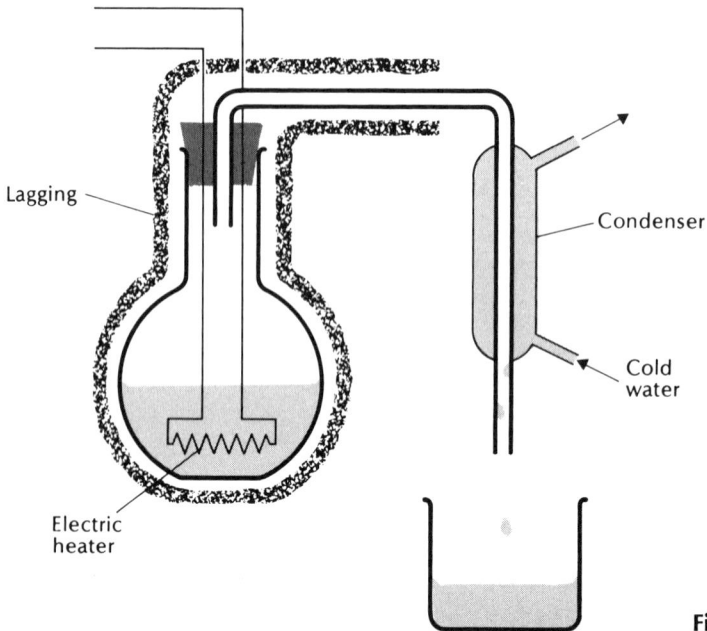

Fig. 15.2

Change of State

Quick Question 28

If an electric current of 1 A flowing for 100 s at a voltage of 10 V is enough to boil away 5 g of liquid nitrogen, what is the specific latent heat of vaporisation of nitrogen?

Some Definitions

- **Melting** is the change from the solid state to the liquid state. It takes place at the **melting point** (melting temperature).

- **Freezing** (or 'solidification') is the change from the liquid state to the solid state. It takes place at the melting point.

- **Evaporation** is the change from the liquid to the gas (or vapour) state when the change happens at the surface of the liquid. It takes place at all temperatures up to the boiling point.

- **Boiling** is the change from liquid to gas when the change happens in the body of the liquid or wherever heat is put in. It takes place at the **boiling point**.

- **Vaporisation** is a word that covers both evaporation and boiling.

- **Condensation** is the change from gas (or vapour) to liquid. It is the opposite of evaporation and can take place at any temperature below the boiling point if the vapour is saturated. (For saturated vapours, see p. 102.)

- **Sublimation** is the change from solid to gas (or vapour) without passing through the liquid state. An example is the slow disappearance of snow without melting if the weather is cold and dry. The opposite change — gas to solid — has no accepted name; an example of it is the formation of hoar frost.

Variations of Melting Point and Boiling Point

The melting point (freezing point) and boiling point of any substance depend on the pressure and also on whether the substance is pure. For water:

$$\text{m.p.} = 0\,°C$$
$$\text{b.p.} = 100\,°C$$

if the water is pure and if the pressure is one standard atmosphere. These two temperatures are the 'fixed points' of the temperature scale (see p. 71).

Increasing the pressure, and dissolving salt or some other substance in water, both have the same effect, and that is to move the melting point and the boiling point further apart. For example, sea-water freezes at a lower temperature and boils at a higher temperature than pure water; water boils at a higher temperature than 100 °C at the bottom of a deep mine where the pressure is higher, and conversely it boils at a lower temperature at the top of a mountain where the pressure is lower; ice melts at a lower temperature than 0 °C where the blade of a skate exerts a very big pressure on it.

Vapours

A gas is called a 'vapour' if it is a substance which is familiar to us as a liquid. For example, water or petrol which have turned into gases by evaporation are referred to as vapours, but hydrogen would not be called a vapour, although it can be turned into a liquid by cooling it. When water is in its gaseous state it is usually called 'water vapour' at temperatures below 100 °C and 'steam' at temperatures of 100 °C and above. Steam is an invisible gas; the white clouds that can be seen when a kettle boils are not steam, but drops of water formed when some of the steam condenses.

■ A **saturated vapour** is one that is in equilibrium with its liquid. In the right-hand part of Figure 15.3, evaporation and condensation are taking place at equal rates so that the net rate of evaporation is zero. If air is present in the flask as well as water and water vapour, then it takes a considerable time for equilibrium to be reached. The vapour is only saturated if it has been left to stand for long enough since the flask was sealed.

■ The **saturated vapour pressure** of a liquid — that is, the pressure of a saturated vapour over its surface — depends only on the nature of the liquid and on the temperature. The SVP of pure water at 100 °C is one standard atmosphere.

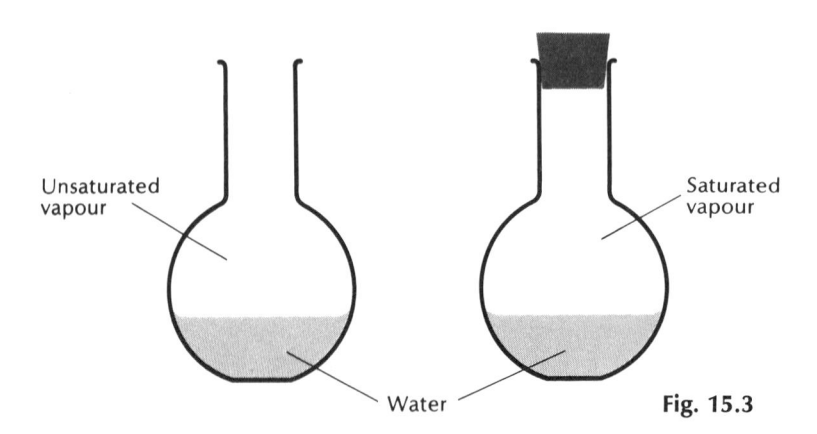

Unsaturated vapour

Saturated vapour

Water

Fig. 15.3

Change of State

If a saturated vapour is compressed, some of it immediately condenses and the pressure does not increase unless the temperature rises. This gives us an alternative definition of a saturated vapour: a saturated vapour is a vapour which is exerting the greatest pressure that it can exert at that temperature.

■ An **unsaturated vapour** is one whose pressure is less than the SVP at that temperature. An example of an unsaturated vapour is the water vapour mixed with the air — unless fog or dew is just on the point of forming, or fog has already formed, for in these cases the water vapour in the air is saturated.

dew point

Factors Affecting Rate of Evaporation

Evaporation takes place from a water surface as long as the vapour in contact with it is unsaturated. To increase the rate of evaporation:

- *increase the temperature*, or
- *increase the draught* (wind speed) over the surface, or
- spread the water out to *increase the surface area*, or
- in cases where it is practicable, *reduce the pressure* over the surface by using a vacuum pump.

Questions on Chapter 15

Assume that:
- latent heat of fusion of ice = 330×10^3 J/kg
- latent heat of vaporisation of water = 2.25×10^6 J/kg
- specific heat capacity of ice = 2100 J/kg K
- specific heat capacity of water = 4200 J/kg K

1 How much heat is needed to turn:
  a) 2 kg of ice at 0°C into water at 0°C,
  b) 100 g of water at 100°C into steam?

2 How much heat is needed to turn:
  a) 2 kg of water at 0°C into water at 100°C,
  b) 2 kg of water at 100°C into steam,
  c) 2 kg of water at 0°C into steam?

3 How much heat must be removed from 10 kg of water at 20°C to turn it into ice at −10°C?

4 A heater supplying energy at a constant rate of 500 W is completely immersed in a large block of ice at 0°C. In 1320 s, 2.0 kg of water at 0°C are produced. Calculate a value for the specific latent heat of fusion of ice. (C)

5 A lump of copper has a mass of 250 g and a specific heat capacity of 400 J/kg K. It is heated in boiling water until it reaches a temperature of 100°C and then quickly moved on to a block of ice which is at 0°C. As a result the copper cools to 0°C and some of the ice melts. Find a) the amount of heat lost by the copper and b) the mass of ice which melts, assuming that all of the heat lost by the copper goes into the ice.

6 A plastic beaker of negligible heat capacity contains 100 g of dried ice at 0°C. 150 g of water at 50°C is poured in. After thorough stirring it is found that all the ice has melted and the water in the beaker is at 0°C. Find:
a) the amount of heat lost by the 150 g of water in cooling to 0°C;
b) the value of the specific latent heat of fusion of ice that can be calculated from these results.

7 2 kg of water at 298 K are cooled until the water becomes a block of ice at the Freezing Point. How much energy has been extracted from the water? (Specific heat capacity of water = 4 200 J kg^{-1} K^{-1}; specific latent heat of ice = 330 000 J kg^{-1}.) (SUJB)

8 A refrigerator cools 0.2 kg of water from 20°C to its freezing point in 20 minutes. If the specific heat capacity of water is 4 200 J/kg °C and the specific latent heat of fusion of ice is 340 000 J/kg, calculate:
(i) the heat energy removed **per minute** from the water, and
(ii) the further time taken for the water to be changed into ice. (W)

9 A small quantity, 0.010 kg, of water at 17°C is added to a larger mass of ice at 0°C contained in a vacuum flask. Calculate the greatest mass of ice which can be melted.
(Take the specific heat capacity of water as 4200 J/kg°C and the specific latent heat of fusion of ice as 340 × 10^3 J/kg.) (O & C)

10 A beaker contains 200 g of water at 15°C. 25 g of ice at 0°C is added to the water which is stirred until the ice is completely melted.
a) How much heat is needed to melt all the ice?
b) What is the mass of water produced by melting all the ice?
c) Calculate the lowest temperature of the mixture, assuming that all the heat to melt the ice is taken from the water and that no heat enters or leaves the system.
(Assume Specific heat capacity of water = 4200 J/kg K.
Specific latent heat of fusion of ice = 336 000 J/kg.)
(JMB)

Chapter 16

Heat Transfer

Conduction

- Conduction is the transfer of internal energy (heat) through a body from a hotter to a colder part. It happens in solids, liquids and gases but it is usually only noticeable in solids; the reason for this is that liquids and gases are mostly poor conductors of heat, and also they can carry heat by convection.

- The mechanism of conduction is as follows:
  - *In metals*, heat is carried by electrons (see p. 178) which are also responsible for the conduction of electricity. This is why good conductors of electricity are generally speaking good conductors of heat.

  - *In non-metals*, each atom passes on vibrational energy to neighbouring atoms by means of the forces between them. This also happens in metals, but it is much less effective than the conduction of heat by electrons.

Figure 16.1 shows a way of demonstrating that copper conducts heat better than iron does.

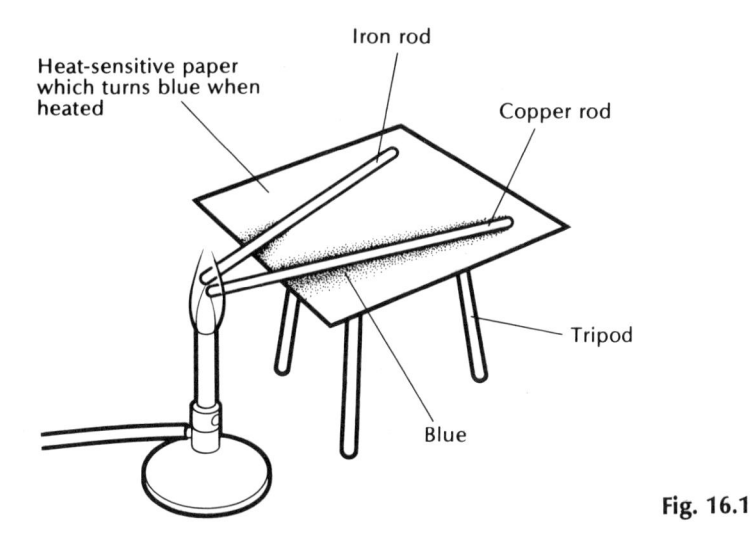

Fig. 16.1

Uses of good and bad conductors — here are some examples:
- The bit of a soldering iron is made of a good conductor (usually copper) so that heat flows easily to the tip.
- In clothing, the trapped air is a bad conductor, and there is little room for convection.
- A saucepan has a good conductor for the bottom, to let heat through and to spread it evenly. The handle is a bad conductor (plastic or wood) so that little heat is conducted to the cook's hand.

Convection

■ Convection is the transfer of heat by a body moving and carrying heat with it. It happens in liquids and gases. Figure 16.2 shows how it may be demonstrated using water. The currents may be made visible by means of ink or a dye.

CONVECTION IN A LIQUID

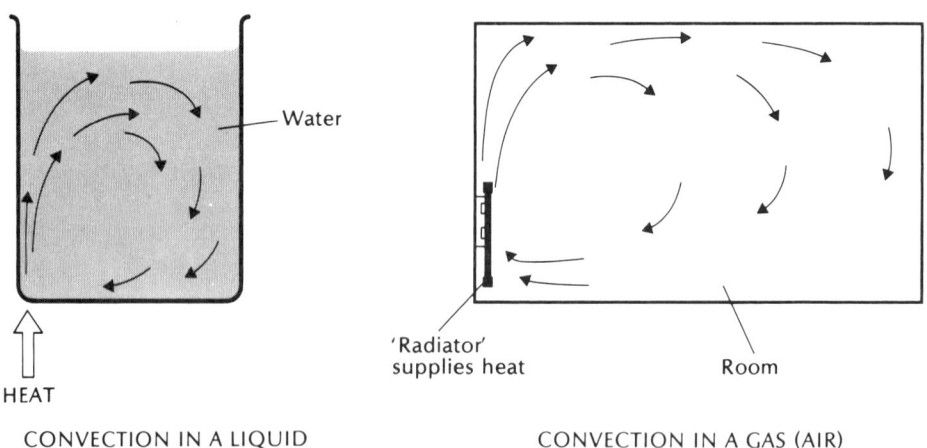

Fig. 16.2

CONVECTION IN A GAS (AIR)

Fig. 16.3

■ The mechanism of convection is:
  (i) one part of the liquid or gas increases in temperature;
  (ii) it therefore expands;
  (iii) its density therefore decreases;
  (iv) its density is then less than that of the surrounding fluid and so it rises.

Convection can also be caused by a fan or a pump and that is called 'forced convection', as opposed to 'natural convection' which is caused, as described above, by a change of density.

Heat Transfer

Uses of convection — here are two examples:
- The water in the pipes of a central heating system (Figure 16.4) is heated in the boiler. A convection current carries this heat to the 'radiators'.
- Convection of the air in each room distributes the heat throughout the house (Figure 16.3).

Note that it is conduction which transfers the heat through the thickness of the radiator, from the water to the air. Radiation plays little part here, and so a 'radiator' is badly named.

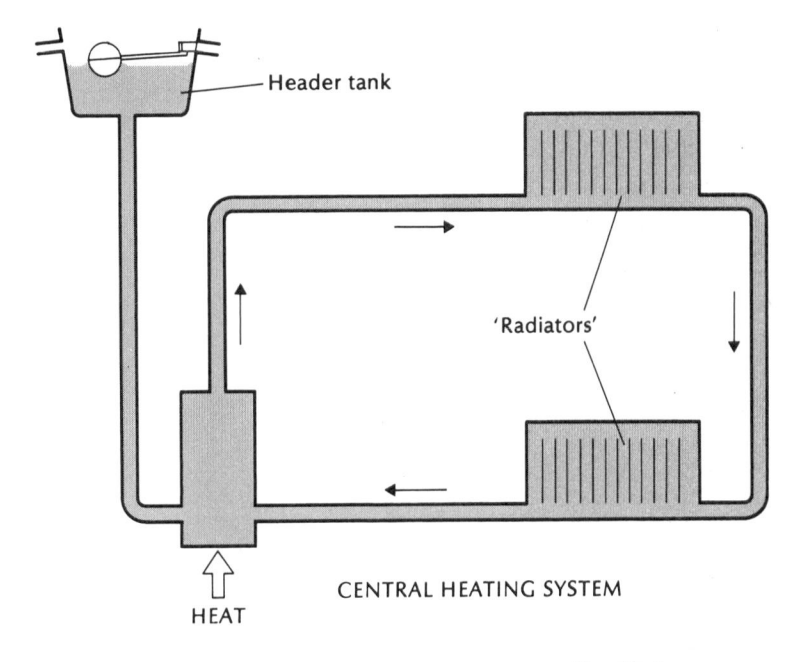

Fig. 16.4 CENTRAL HEATING SYSTEM

Peculiarities of Water

Above a temperature of 4°C water behaves like other liquids in that it expands when it is heated. If the surface of a pond is cooled by a cold wind, convection takes place: cooling causes contraction, so the density increases and the cooled water sinks down from the surface. But below 4°C water expands when it is cooled (and contracts if it is heated). Therefore the cooled water becomes less dense and stays at the surface, where it may then freeze. The bottom of the pond remains at 4°C and fish can survive there below the ice.

Water expands when it freezes, and so ice is less dense than water and therefore floats. Most liquids do the opposite of this.

Radiation

- Thermal radiation is the transfer of heat in the form of infra-red rays, which travel at the speed of light. It can pass through a vacuum or a gas, and to some extent through glass and certain other solids and liquids.

- The **mechanism of radiation** is that all bodies emit infra-red rays but hot bodies emit very much more than cool ones do. So a hot body loses much more heat by radiation than it gains from the cooler bodies around it.

The **nature of the surface** affects the amount of radiation emitted: matt black surfaces emit the most at a given temperature, mirror-like surfaces emit least, and in general:

> Good absorbers are good emitters.

To test this, fill two cans with hot water, one can being shiny and the other blackened on the outside, and compare their rates of cooling. Since the cans also cool by convection of the surrounding air they must be equally shielded from draughts. A better way is shown in Figure 16.5. This uses a single can, and the radiation given out by each surface in turn is measured with an infra-red detector, which may be a thermopile or a phototransistor.

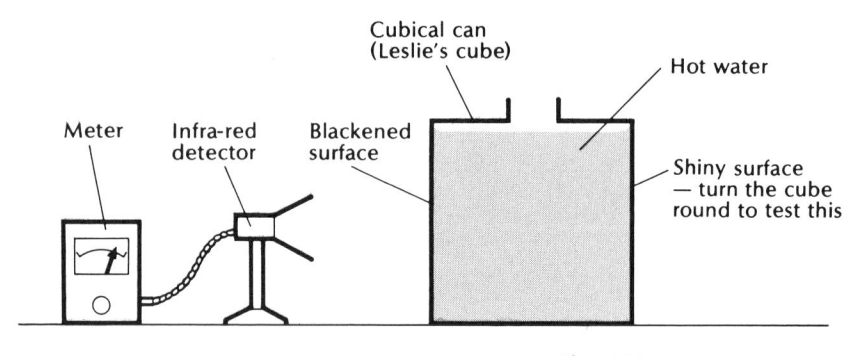

Fig. 16.5

The Greenhouse Effect

The Sun, because it is so hot, gives out most of its heat radiation in the form of 'near infra-red' rays, that is, rays with wavelengths near to those of visible light; these can mostly pass through glass (Figure 16.6). The plants and shelves inside a greenhouse, being only warm, give out their heat radiation as 'far infra-red' — that is, with wavelengths much greater than the wavelengths of visible light. These cannot pass through glass. So the greenhouse traps the energy of the Sun's rays and becomes considerably warmer than its surroundings.

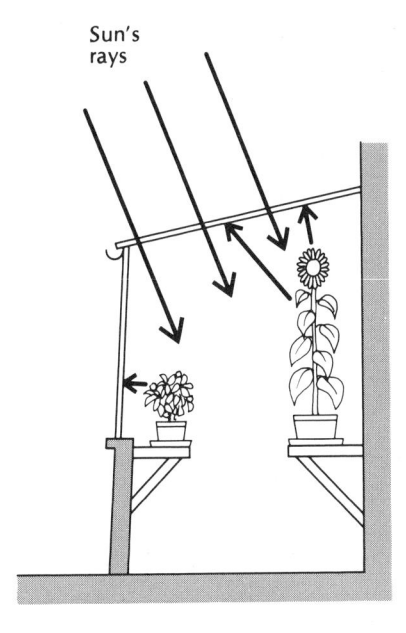

Fig. 16.6

The Vacuum Flask (Dewar Vessel)

A vacuum flask may be used to keep hot things from losing heat, or to keep cold things from gaining heat. Figure 16.7 shows how the heat loss is minimised if the flask contains a hot liquid.

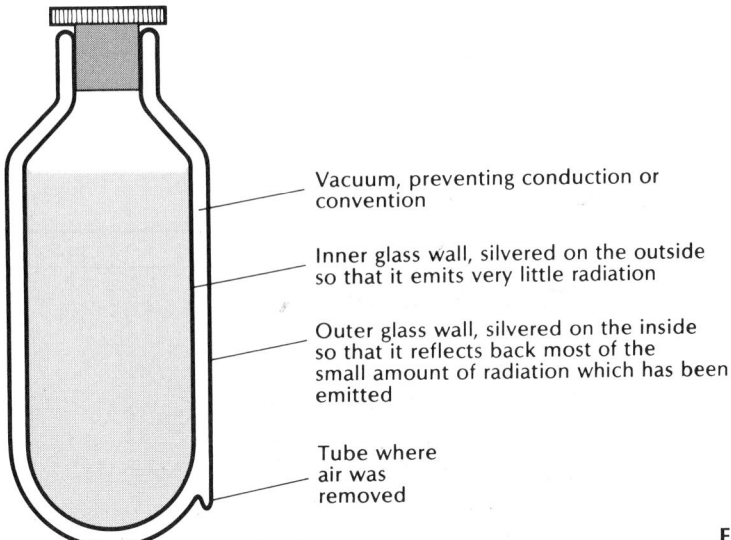

Vacuum, preventing conduction or convention

Inner glass wall, silvered on the outside so that it emits very little radiation

Outer glass wall, silvered on the inside so that it reflects back most of the small amount of radiation which has been emitted

Tube where air was removed

Fig. 16.7

A cork, or else a hollow plastic stopper, helps to reduce heat loss through the neck of the flask, as it is a bad conductor of heat.

Vacuum flasks are better at keeping cold things cold — for example, ice, or liquid nitrogen — than they are at keeping hot things hot. This is because, when the contents of the flask are cold, the air in the neck of the flask is cooled at the bottom and so there is no convection there. The stopper may then not be needed.

Section C:
LIGHT

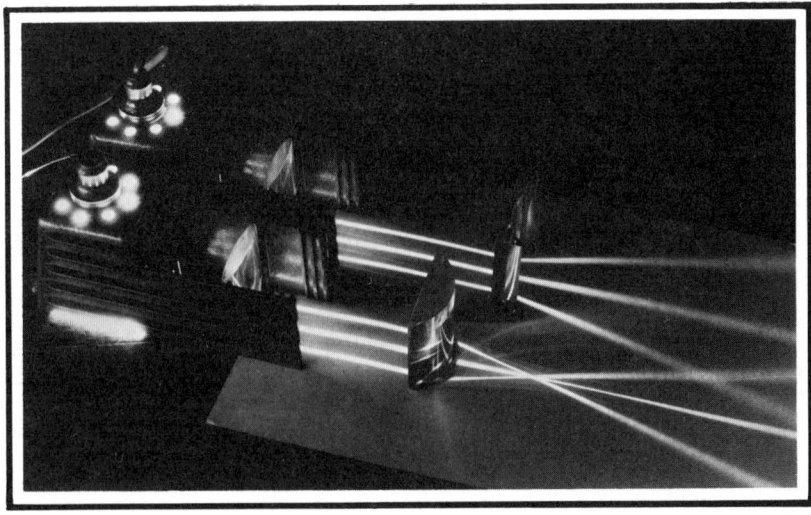

The effects of different lenses on parallel beams of light is shown by using two ray-boxes.

Chapter 17

Properties of Light

It is easier to start by studying the *properties* of light (what it *does*) than by investigating the *nature* of light (what it *is*). We will see later that light is a wave, but just what sort of a wave it is will be easier to find out after studying other kinds of wave. So we will return to the question of the nature of light on p. 168. For the present, the questions for us to answer are:

- How is light produced?

- How does light travel?

- How does light behave when it meets a mirror, or when it enters or leaves a transparent substance?

Production of Light

The chief methods by which light is produced are:

- **Hot-body radiation** such as the production of light by the Sun or by the filament of an electric light bulb. As we saw on p. 108, infra-red rays are given out by hot bodies. If they are hot enough they emit light as well. The red-hot bar of an electric fire is not nearly as hot as the Sun or the light bulb filament, and for this reason it only gives out a little red light; most of its radiation is in the form of infra-red.

- **Molecular collisions** when an electric current flows through an ionised gas. This happens in a lightning flash and also in the gas inside an advertising sign.

- **Fluorescence** — for example, the emission of light by the fluorescent coating on the inside of the front of a television tube when electrons hit it. Fluorescence can be caused by ultra-violet rays as well as by electrons; we will return to this on p. 169.

Propagation of Light

'Propagation of light' means 'how light travels'. The propagation of light is 'rectilinear' — that is, in straight lines — except when it is being reflected or refracted.* Shadows and the pinhole camera can both be used to check that the propagation of light is rectilinear.

Shadows

A compact light source, such as an electric lamp which has a small filament inside a clear glass bulb, throws a sharp shadow.

(a) COMPACT LIGHT SOURCE — Compact filament, Clear bulb, Sharp shadow

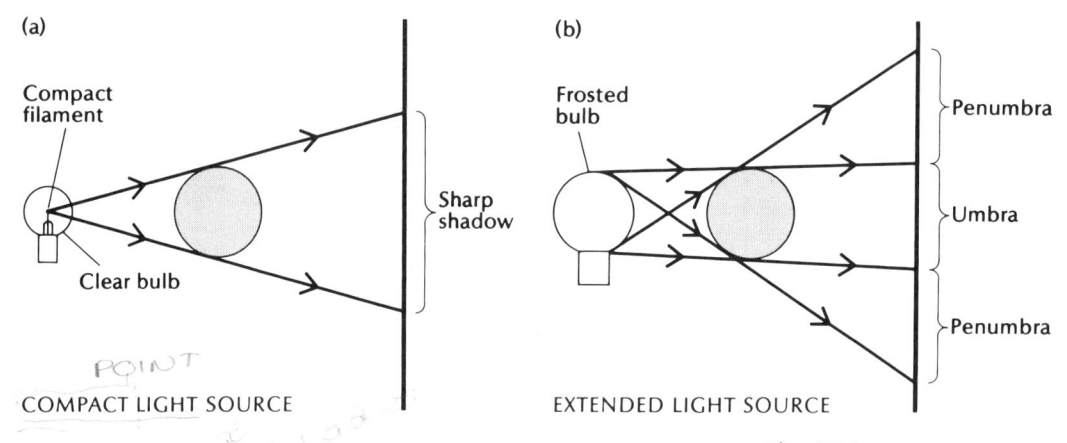

(b) EXTENDED LIGHT SOURCE — Frosted bulb, Penumbra, Umbra, Penumbra

Fig. 17.1

An extended light source is one which emits its light from a considerable area. An example is a frosted light bulb. In this case the shadow consists of a dark part called the 'umbra', which receives no direct light from any part of the source, and a hazy 'penumbra' around it; each point in the penumbra receives light from part of the source.

Quick Question 29

a) A frosted light bulb 80 mm in diameter is placed near a white wall in a darkened room. A tennis ball, 60 mm in diameter, is hung on a thin thread half-way between the bulb and the wall. How big is the umbra?

b) If the tennis ball is now removed and a table tennis ball, diameter 38 mm, is put in its place, what difference will this make to the shadow?

*We will meet a slight exception to this on p. 164.

The Pinhole Camera

There are two versions of this. One has a frosted screen at the back, perhaps with a hood around it to exclude stray light, and this is used for observing the image. The other has an opaque back, and a piece of photographic film can be fixed inside it so as to take a photograph, but the exposure will need to last several minutes even in a good light. The exposure can be shorter if the pinhole is made large, but then the image will be more blurred.

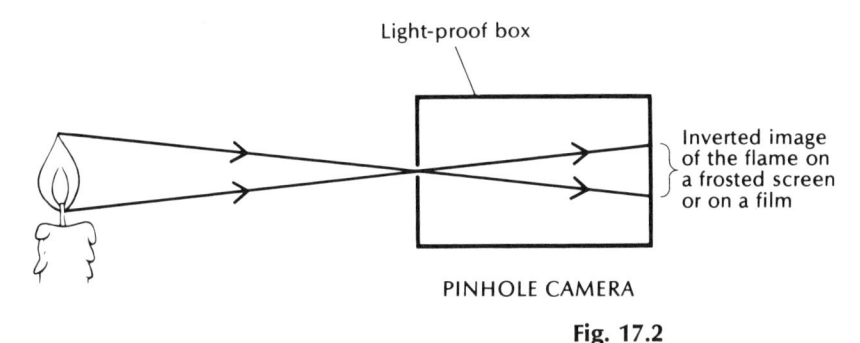

PINHOLE CAMERA

Fig. 17.2

Quick Question 30

What will be the effect of doubling the length of a pinhole camera?

The Speed of Light

Light travels so fast that for many purposes we can assume that it takes no time at all to travel. The speed is almost exactly 3×10^8 m/s in a vacuum or in air, but we will see later that it is slower than this in other media such as glass.

Quick Question 31

If you flash a signalling lamp from one hill-top so that the light is reflected back to you from a mirror on another hill-top 15 km away, how long will the light take for the double journey?

To an astronomer, light travel is by no means instantaneous. Light takes about 8 minutes to reach us from the Sun, a number of years from the stars, and millions of years from other galaxies.

Questions on Chapter 17

1. A man 1.75 m tall stands at a distance of 7.0 m from the pinhole of a pinhole camera. The distance of the film from the pinhole is 0.20 m. Find the length of the image of the man which is formed on the film. (C*)

2. A radio signal is sent to the Moon which reflects it back to the radio telescope which sent it. Given that the distance to the Moon is 390 000 km and that radio signals travel at the same speed as light, find how long the signal takes to make the double journey.

3. A radio transmitter directs pulses of waves towards a satellite from which reflections are received 10 milliseconds after transmission. If the speed of radio waves is 3×10^8 m s^{-1}, how far away is the satellite? (SUJB)

Chapter 18

Reflection and Refraction

When white paper reflects light, the reflected light goes in all directions. This is called 'diffuse' reflection. When a mirror reflects light, each ray of the incident light (the light falling on the mirror) is reflected in one definite direction, and this direction is described by the **laws of reflection**:

1. The reflected ray is in the same plane as the incident ray and the normal.
2. The angle of reflection is equal to the angle of incidence.

The **normal** is the line at right angles to the surface. The two angles are shown in Figure 18.1.

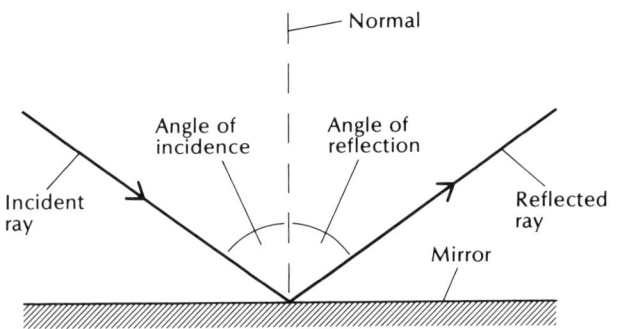

Fig. 18.1

The Image in a Plane Mirror

A 'plane' mirror means a flat one — one which forms part of a geometrical plane. The image formed by a plane mirror does not appear to be on the surface of the mirror, like a painting, but behind it, like a scene viewed through a window. Figure 18.2 shows how one point of the image is formed.

The image is:
- as far behind the mirror as the object is in front of it,
- on the same normal as the object,
- the same size as the object (magnification = 1),

- laterally inverted (object F gives image ꟻ),
- virtual, that is, light does not go to the image but appears to come from it.

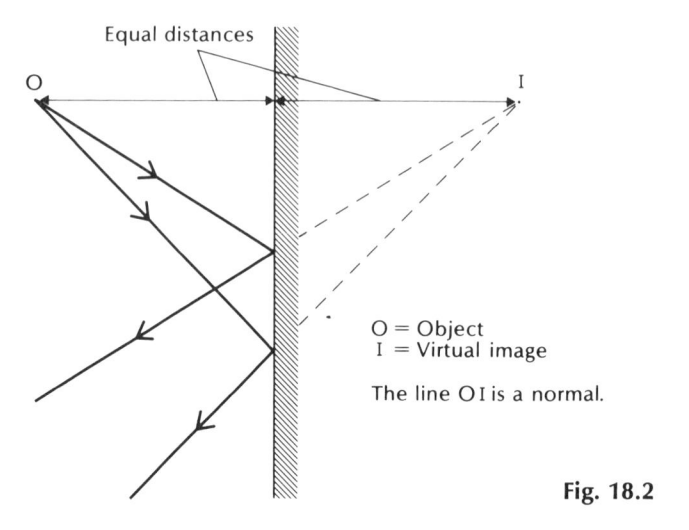

Equal distances

O = Object
I = Virtual image

The line OI is a normal.

Fig. 18.2

Quick Question 32

> Two mirrors are stood up on edge at right angles to each other with a piece of chalk in front of them. Figure 18.3 shows the arrangement in plan view. How many images are formed, and how are these images arranged?
>
> Chalk
>
> **Fig. 18.3**

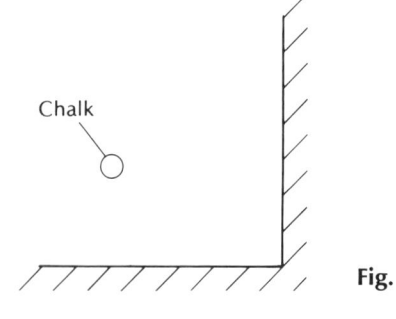

The symbol for a mirror used in Quick Question 32 is a generally accepted one. Being easier to draw than the symbol used in other figures, it is the one you should use in hand-drawn diagrams.

Spherical Mirrors

Some mirrors form part of a sphere instead of part of a plane. They are either concave (caving in) or convex (bulging out). When beams of light fall on spherical mirrors:

Reflection and Refraction

Concave mirrors tend to make light **converge**.

Convex mirrors tend to make light **diverge**.

We will see in the next chapter that lenses do the opposite of this: a convex lens is a converging one.

Concave mirrors are used by dentists and sometimes for shaving as they can give magnified images (see Figure 19.13 on p. 134). Convex mirrors are used as wing mirrors on cars to give a large field of view.

F is the focal point
f = Focal length

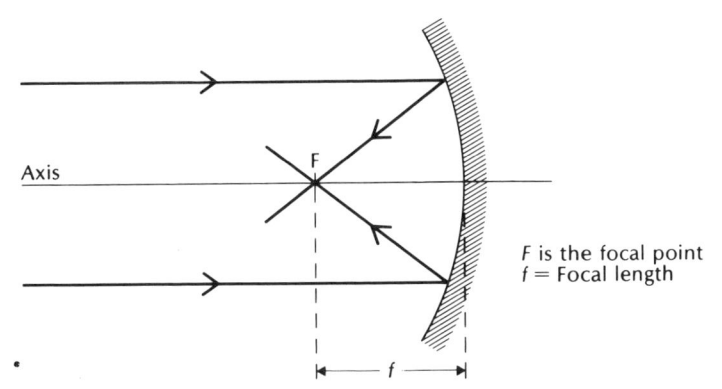

Fig. 18.4

If the incident rays are all parallel to the axis of a concave mirror, the point where the reflected rays meet is the **focal point** (or 'principal focus') — see Figure 18.4. The distance from the focal point to the pole (centre of the mirror) is the **focal length**. The focal length is equal to half of the radius of curvature:

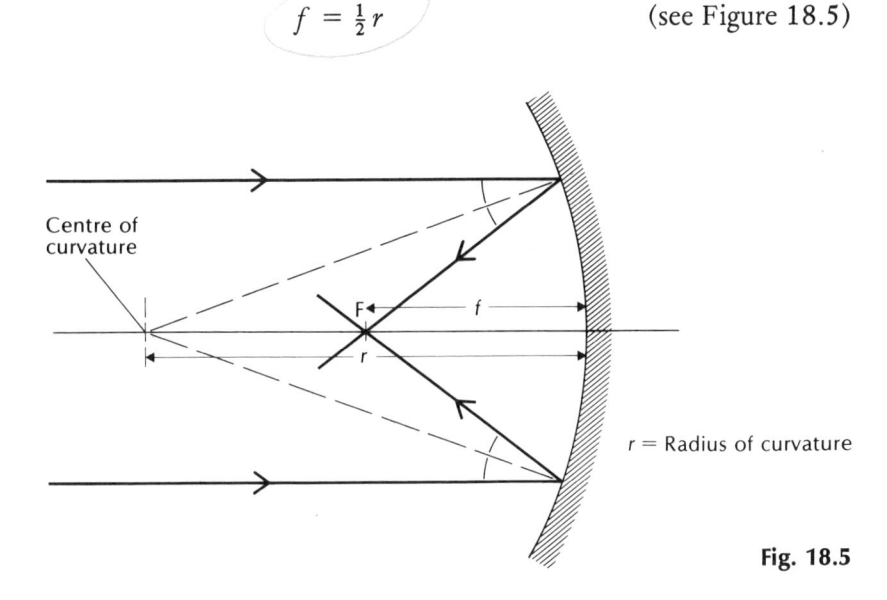

$$f = \tfrac{1}{2} r \qquad \text{(see Figure 18.5)}$$

r = Radius of curvature

Fig. 18.5

Methods of measuring the focal length of a concave mirror, and the way that it forms an image, are left until Chapter 19.

Refraction

Refraction of light is the bending of rays when they pass from one medium to another — for example, from air into the glass of a lens, or from the vacuum of space into the air of the Earth's atmosphere.

The laws of refraction are:

1. The refracted ray is in the same plane as the incident ray and the normal.

2. The ratio of the sine of the angle of incidence to the sine of the angle of refraction is always the same for a given pair of media and for a given colour of light. This is called **Snell's law**, and it can be written as an equation like this:

$$\frac{\sin i}{\sin r} = n$$

where n is the 'refractive index'* of that pair of media for one particular colour of light.

Light is refracted towards the normal when it enters a denser medium and away from the normal as it emerges (Figure 18.6). To observe these two things happening, a rectangular block of glass or plastic is convenient (Figure 18.7). There is a practical point to notice: unless the lower surface of the block is painted white or else roughened, the ray A will not be visible (for a reason that we will discover on p. 124).

(a) From air to a denser medium

(b) From a denser medium to air

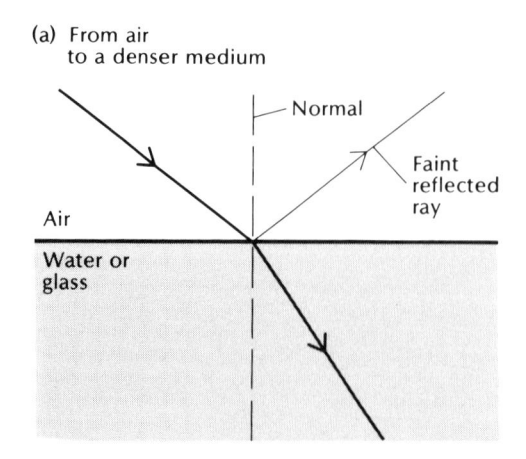

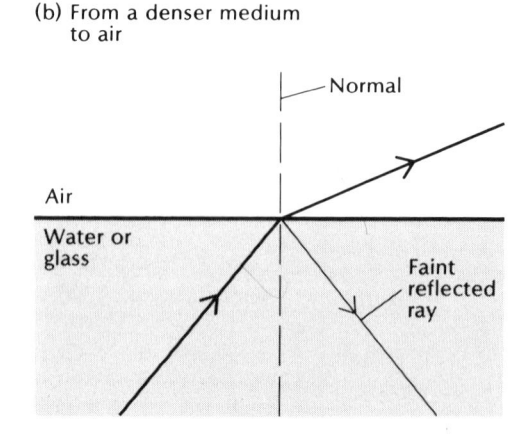

Fig. 18.6

*Some examination boards use the older symbol μ (the Greek letter 'mu') for refractive index.

Reflection and Refraction

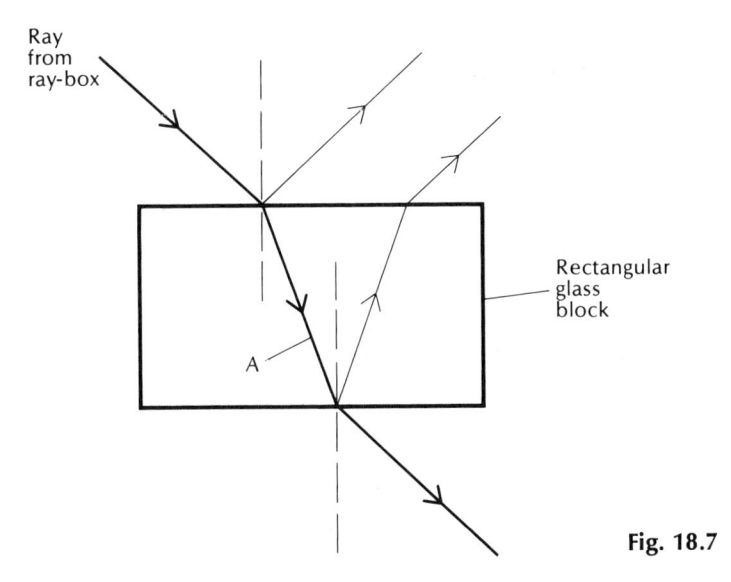

Fig. 18.7

Example 18.1 Light travelling downwards at 45° to the vertical meets a smooth water surface. Through what angle is the refracted light deviated? The refractive index of water is $1\frac{1}{3}$. (*Note*. Refractive indices are usually given for light travelling from air — or a vacuum — to the material in question. Colour makes little difference and only needs to be stated in accurate work.)

Solution

$$\frac{\sin i}{\sin r} = n$$

$$\therefore \quad \sin r = \frac{\sin i}{n} = \frac{\sin 45°}{\frac{4}{3}}$$

$$= \frac{3}{4} \times 0.707 = 0.530$$

$$\therefore \quad r = 32°$$

The deviation, as shown in Figure 18.8, is 13°.

Deviation = 45° − 32° = 13°

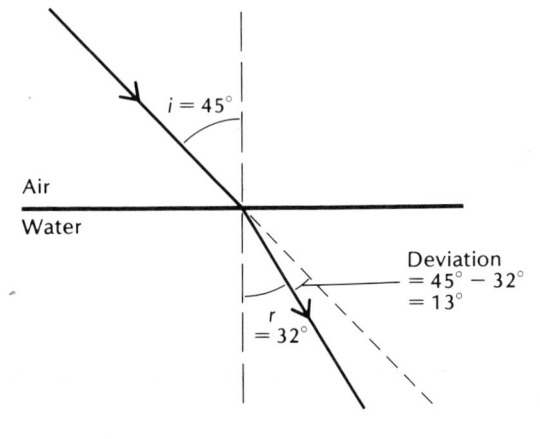

Fig. 18.8

Example 18.2 Light travelling upwards through water at 30° to the vertical meets the water surface and emerges into air. What is the angle of refraction? ($n = 1\frac{1}{3}$ for water)

Solution You can *either* say that since $n = \frac{4}{3}$ from air to water, therefore $n = \frac{3}{4}$ from water to air (Figure 18.9(a)) *or* you can say that for a ray entering the water along the same path (Figure 18.9(b)) you would multiply by $\frac{4}{3}$ if you wanted to find $\sin i$ from $\sin r$. In either case, the sine of the required angle is equal to

$$\frac{4}{3} \times \sin 30° = \frac{4}{3} \times 0.500 = 0.667$$

∴ Angle of refraction = 42°

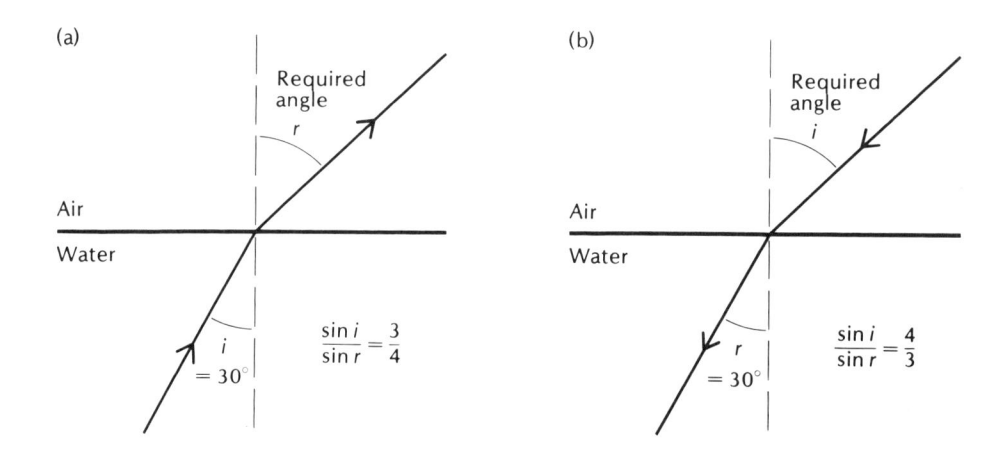

Fig. 18.9

Real and Apparent Depth

If you look vertically downwards into the calm water of a pond the bottom seems nearer to you than it really is. Looking into a glass block along a normal, the far end again seems nearer to you. In both cases (see Figure 18.10):

$$\frac{\text{Real depth}}{\text{Apparent depth}} = \frac{d}{a} = \text{Refractive index}$$

If you look at an angle to the normal, as in Figure 18.11, the equation is no longer true and the pond looks shallower still.

Reflection and Refraction

Fig. 18.10

d = Real depth
a = Apparent depth

Fig. 18.11

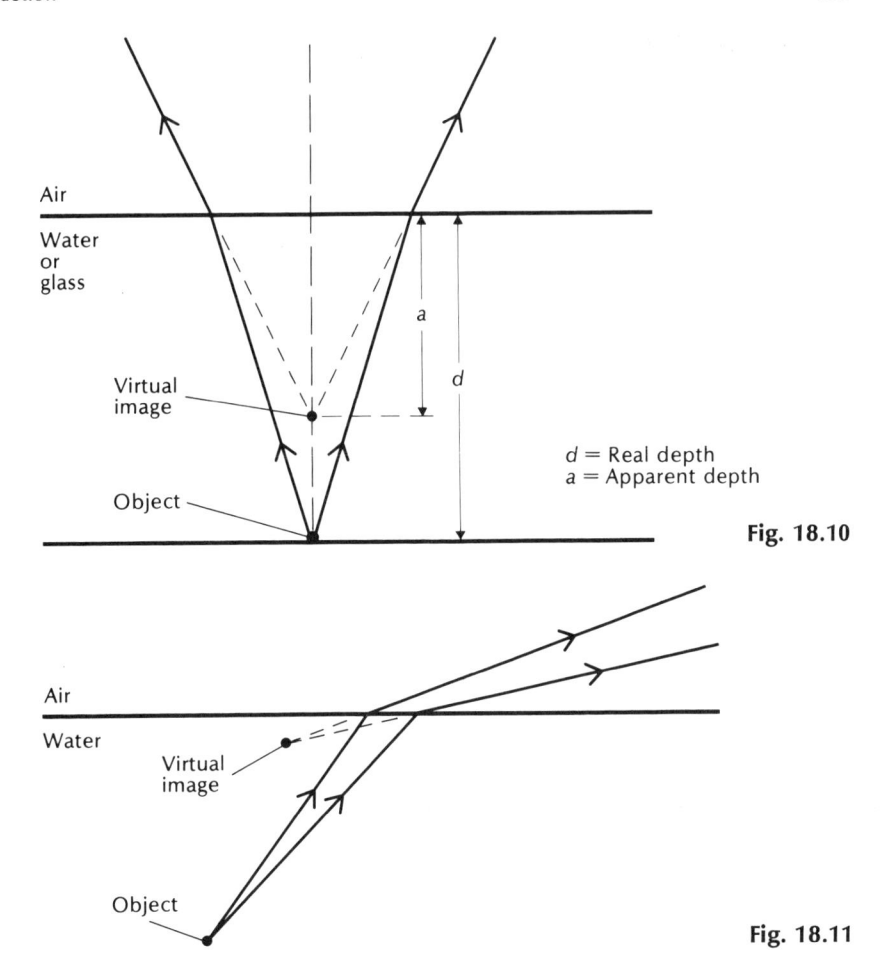

Total Internal Reflection

Light cannot emerge from an optically denser medium if the angle of incidence is too big; instead, it is totally internally reflected, as shown in Figure 18.12(b). 'Optically denser' means 'with higher refractive index'.

C = Critical angle

(a) $i < C$: PARTIAL REFRACTION AND PARTIAL REFLECTION

(b) $i \geq C$: TOTAL INTERNAL REFLECTION

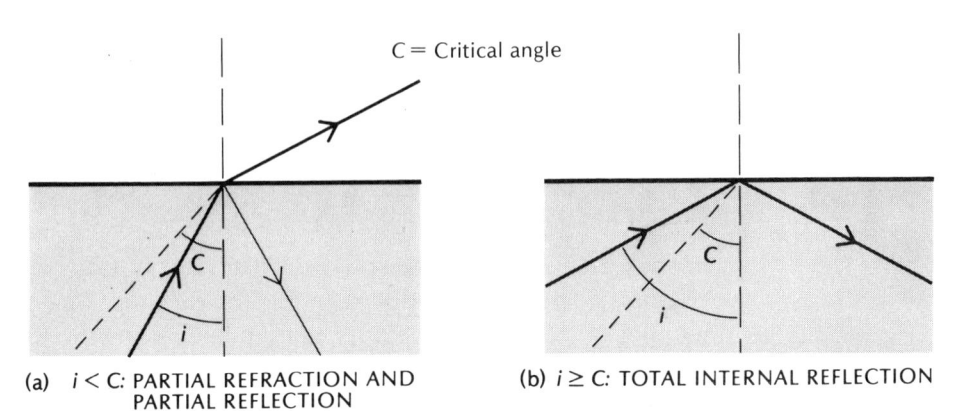

Fig. 18.12

- **Total internal reflection** takes place when the angle of incidence is bigger than the **critical angle**, C, which is related to the refractive index by:

$$\sin C = \frac{1}{n}$$

Quick Question 33

> In Example 18.2 on p. 122, if the ray had been travelling through the water at $60°$ to the vertical, instead of $30°$, it would have been totally internally reflected. How does the method of calculation of that example show that there is no refracted ray?

We are now in a position to see why the glass block of Figure 18.7 on p. 121 had to have its lower surface either painted or roughened if ray A in that diagram was to be visible. The light from the ray-box slants downwards at about $10°$ from the horizontal, and this makes the angle of incidence of the light striking the lower surface about $80°$ (Figure 18.13). This is greater than the critical angle and so all the light is reflected and none of it emerges from the bottom of the glass block to illuminate the paper.

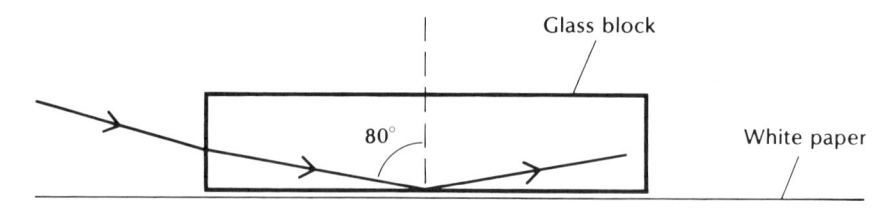

Fig. 18.13

Prisms

Since the critical angle of glass is less than $45°$, prisms can be used to turn light through $90°$ or $180°$ by total internal reflection as shown in Figure 18.14. This principle is used in periscopes, range-finders and prism binoculars.

Prisms can also be used to split up white light into its component colours. A spectrum produced by the arrangement of Figure 18.15 will not be pure, as the colours overlap because of the width of the original beam of white light. To produce a pure spectrum a narrow slit is needed; Figure 18.16 shows how it can be done. Notice that red is bent the least and violet the most.

Reflection and Refraction

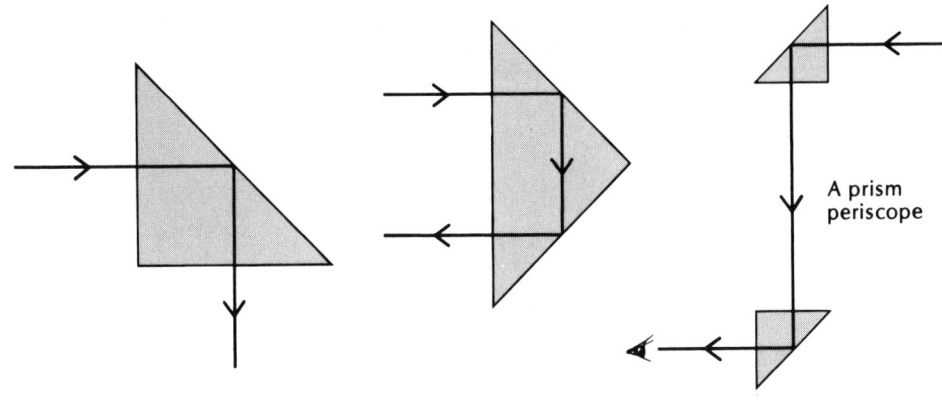

Fig. 18.14

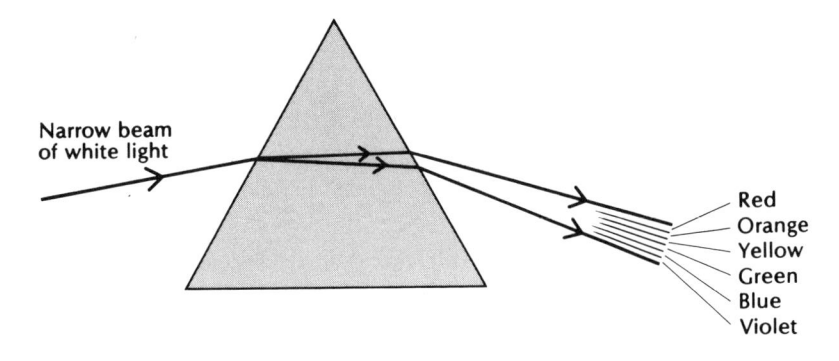

Fig. 18.15

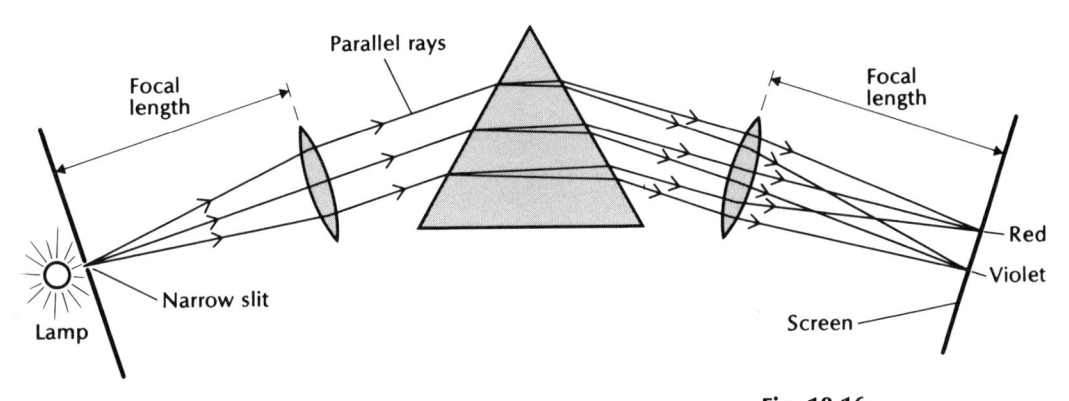

Fig. 18.16

Questions on Chapter 18

1 A man 1.8 m high stands in front of a mirror which is fixed to a wall. How tall must the mirror be if the man is to be able to see the whole of himself without moving? Illustrate your answer with a ray diagram.

2 An object is placed on the principal axis of a concave mirror of radius of curvature 20 cm. State whether the image is real/virtual and magnified/diminished when the object distance from the mirror is a) 50 cm, b) 15 cm, c) 5 cm. What is significant about the reflected rays if a suitable object is at a distance of 10 cm from the mirror? (Ray diagrams are **not** expected for these answers.)   (SUJB)

3 A searchlight directs its beam on a calm water surface so that the light is travelling at 20° from the horizontal. Taking the refractive index of water to be 1.33, find a) the angle of incidence, b) the angle of refraction and c) the angle through which the light turns as it enters the water.

4 A diver working at night shines his waterproof torch upwards at an angle of 40° from the vertical. At what angle from the vertical is the refracted beam? Use $n = 1.33$ and assume that the water surface is perfectly calm.

5 A triangular glass prism ABC of refractive index 1.50 has a right angle at A. Angle B is 30° and angle C is 60°. A beam of light enters the face AB, travelling along the normal, and passes through the prism to strike face BC from inside the prism. Find:
a) the angle of incidence on face BC;
b) the angle of refraction as the light emerges from face BC;
c) the angle through which the beam has been turned.

6 Figure 18.17 shows a parallel beam of light entering a glass block ABCD of refractive index 1.6, the angle of incidence being 45°. Half of the light strikes face BC after refraction at face AB, and the other half of the light strikes face CD, as shown in the diagram.
a) What is the angle of refraction at AB?
b) What happens to the light which meets BC?
c) What happens to the light which meets CD?
d) What is the angle between the two beams of light which emerge from the block?
e) Illustrate your answer with a ray diagram.

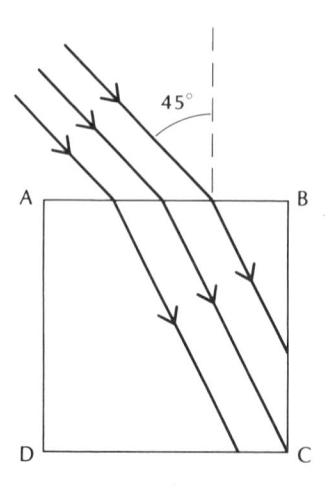

Fig. 18.17

7 a) The deep end of a swimming bath is 4.0 m deep. How deep does it appear to be when looked at vertically?
   b) The apparent depth at another place in the bath is 1.5 m. What is the true depth at this position?
   ($n = 1\frac{1}{3}$ for water)

8 A diver wearing a face mask sees a fish that is apparently 0.9 m from his face. How far away is the fish really? ($n = 1\frac{1}{3}$)

9 What is the critical angle of a) water of refractive index 1.33 and b) diamond of refractive index 2.4?

10 The critical angles of two types of glass are measured and found to be a) 40° and b) 37°. What are their refractive indices?

Chapter 19

Lenses

The action of a lens can be explained by comparing it with prisms, as shown in Figure 19.1. Like prisms, lenses produce colour effects, and this must be allowed for in designing cameras and other optical instuments.

Convex (bulging out) lenses tend to make light **converge**.
Concave (caving in) lenses tend to make light **diverge**.

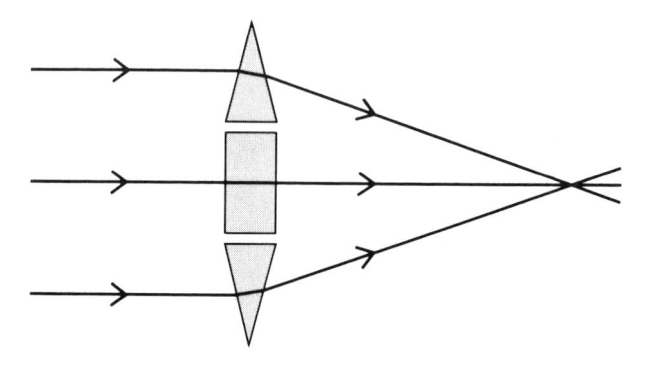

Fig. 19.1

■ The **focal point** (or 'principal focus') of a lens is the point of intersection of rays which were parallel to the axis before they entered the lens (Figure 19.2). There are two focal points, one on each side of the lens. In the case of a diverging lens the rays do not meet (see Figure 19.3) and to find the point of intersection the rays must be extended backwards as we do for a virtual image.

F is the focal point
f = Focal length

CONVERGING (CONVEX) LENS

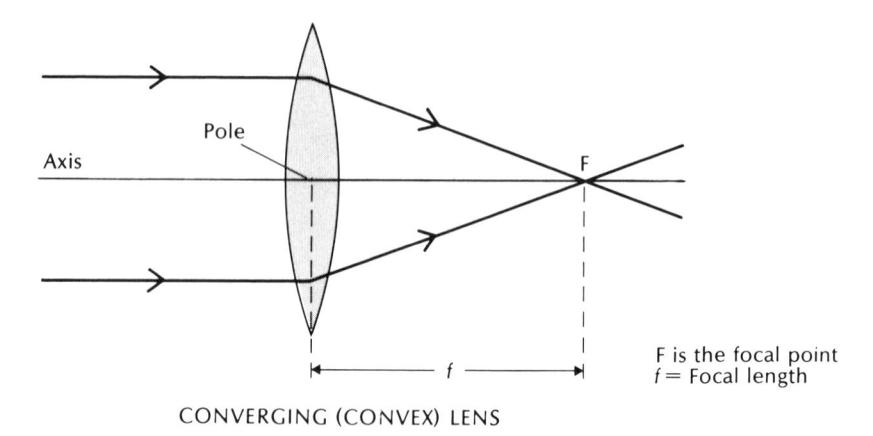

Fig. 19.2

DIVERGING (CONCAVE) LENS

F is the focal point
f = Focal length

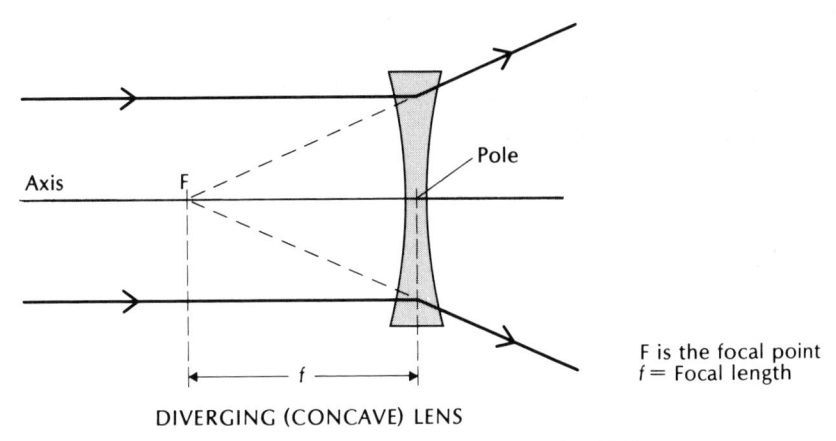

Fig. 19.3

■ The **focal length** is the distance from the lens to the focal point.

■ The **power** of a lens is measured in dioptres (D) and it is the reciprocal of its focal length in metres:

$$\text{Power} = \frac{1}{f}$$

For example:

if focal length = 2 m,   power = 0.5 D
if focal length = 1 m,   power = 1 D
if focal length = 20 cm, power = 5 D

Measurement of the Focal Length of a Converging Lens

■ The **distant object method** (Figure 19.4) is quick but not accurate.

Choose a distant object, such as a chimney seen through the laboratory window. Focus its image on a screen or on the wall. Measure from the lens to the screen.

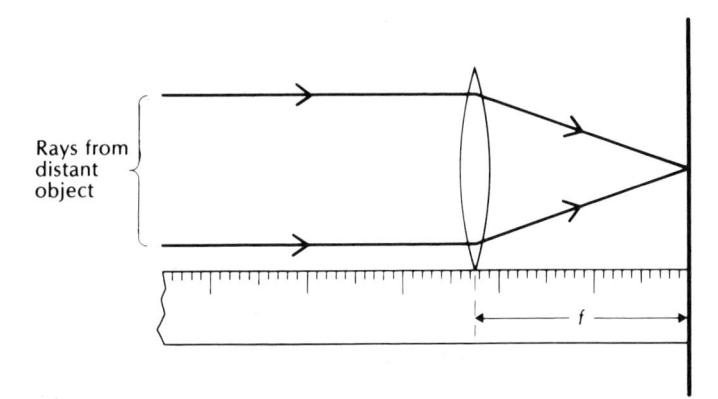

Fig. 19.4

■ The **plane mirror method** is accurate but not so quick.

Arrange the apparatus as shown in Figure 19.5. The object is a hole in the screen, covered with tracing paper and lit up by a lamp behind it. Move the lens and the mirror until a clear image of the object is formed on the screen beside the hole. Measure from the lens to the screen. The distance from the lens to the mirror does not matter, though it should not be too big.

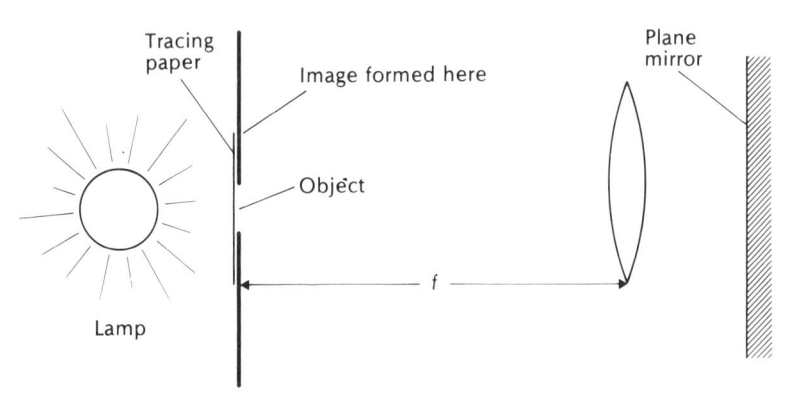

Fig. 19.5

If the focal length of the lens is quite long — half a metre or more — then it is not necessary to use a special object; the filament of a lamp can be used as the object, as shown in Figure 19.6.

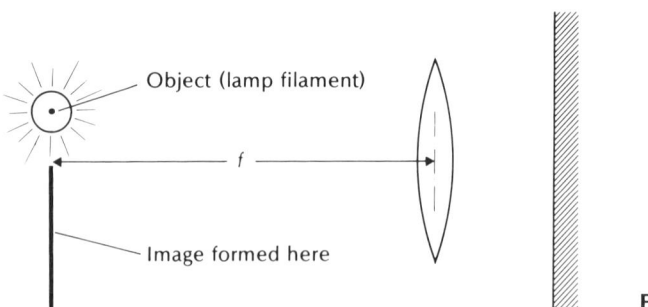

Fig. 19.6

Measurement of the Focal Length of a Converging Mirror

There are two methods, and they are similar to those for a converging lens. The distant object method is shown in Figure 19.7. The more accurate method (Figure 19.8) is similar to the plane mirror method for a converging lens but it does not use a plane mirror. The measurement from the concave mirror to the screen is not the focal length but the radius of curvature; it must be halved to find the focal length (see p. 119).

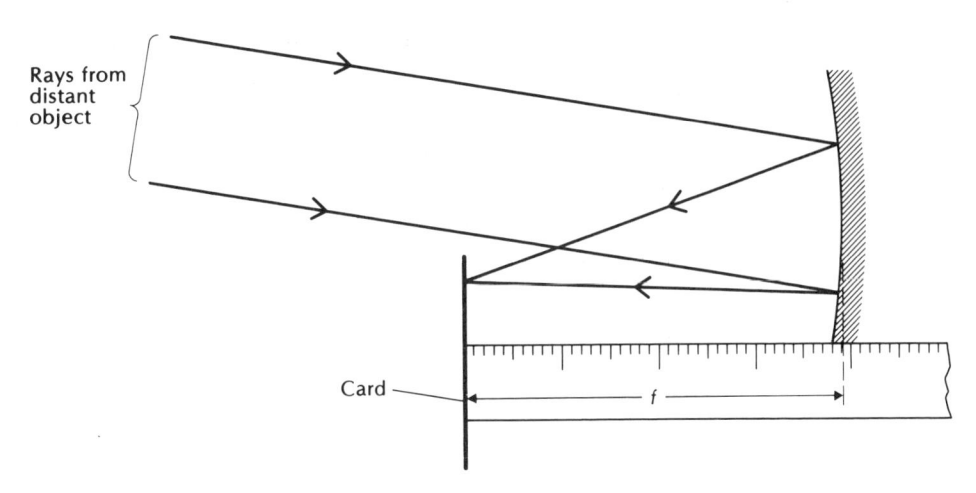

Fig. 19.7

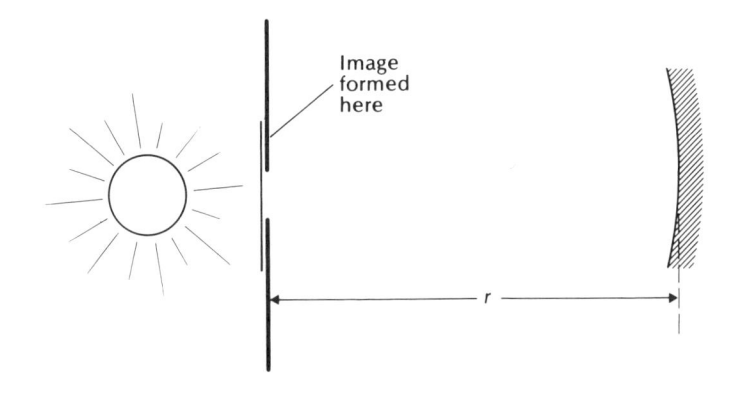

Fig. 19.8

Images Formed by Converging Lenses

In the following diagrams the thickness of the lens is ignored and the lens is represented by a straight line. The ray changes direction as it crosses this line. The curved 'lens' shape is just a form of labelling; you may prefer to omit the curves and to label the line 'convex lens' or 'concave lens'. (Refraction actually takes place at both surfaces of the lens as shown in Figure 19.11.) The same principle applies to curved mirrors. These, too, are represented by a line in Figures 19.13 and 19.14, and the curves added to the ends of the line are only a form of labelling.

To find the position and size of an image by a diagram, two rays are needed but three are better. In Figure 19.9:

ray (a) runs parallel to the axis and then through the far focal point, F_2,

ray (b) goes to the pole (centre of the lens) and straight on,

ray (c) passes through the near focal point, F_1, and runs parallel to the axis on the far side of the lens.

If the object is close to the lens — between the lens and the near focal point, F_1 — these three rays will still be diverging when they emerge from the lens (Figure 19.10). The image is virtual and its position can be found by extending the rays backwards.

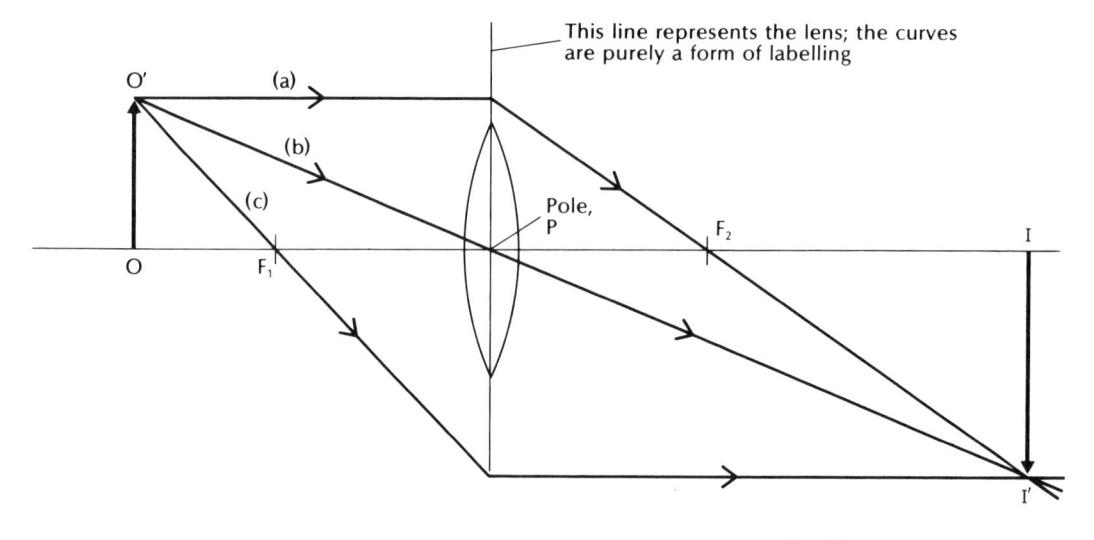

Fig. 19.9

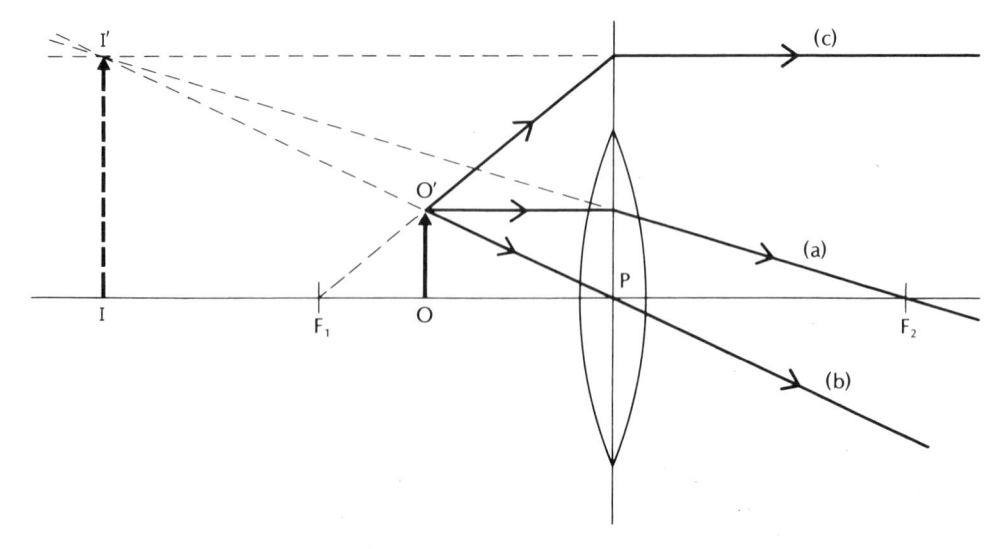

Fig. 19.10

Fig. 19.11

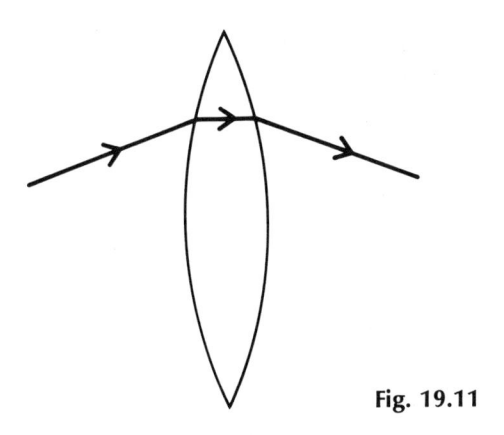

Solving Lens Problems by Scale Drawing*

When drawing ray diagrams to scale, remember these points.
(i) Use a *sharp pencil*.
(ii) Choose a *horizontal scale* and write it down. If the object, O, is nearer to the lens than it is to the focal point, then the image will be farther from the lens than the object is; you must be careful to choose your scale so as to leave enough room for it.
(iii) Choose a *vertical scale*, usually larger than the horizontal scale, and write it down too. Aim to make the steepest rays in the drawing slope at 45° or so.
(iv) If the three rays don't meet in a point but form a small *triangle*, take the centre of the triangle as the image point.
(v) If the *magnification* is asked for, find it by dividing II' by OO'. You can still do this even if the size of the object is not given in the question.

Images Formed by Diverging Lenses

Compare this case (Figure 19.12) with the convex lens: each ray which passed through a focal point in the convex lens case now travels so that the line of its path, if extended through to the other side of the lens, passes through the other focal point.

The image in this case is always virtual, erect and diminished.

*Not required by all examination boards.

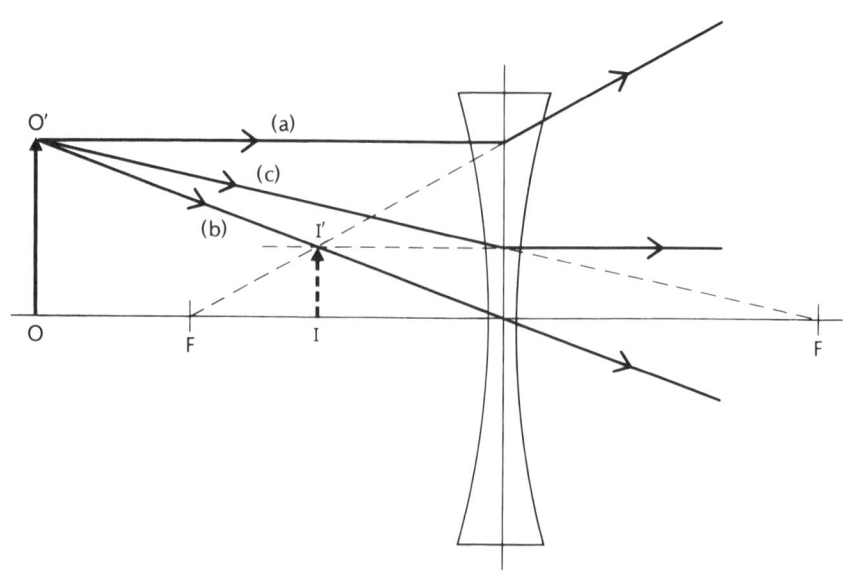

Fig. 19.12

Images Formed by Converging Mirrors

Note that Figure 19.13 is just like Figure 19.9 with the right-hand half folded over on to the left-hand half. In the virtual image case, Figure 19.14 is like Figure 19.10 except that the reflected rays and the image have undergone a left–right reversal.

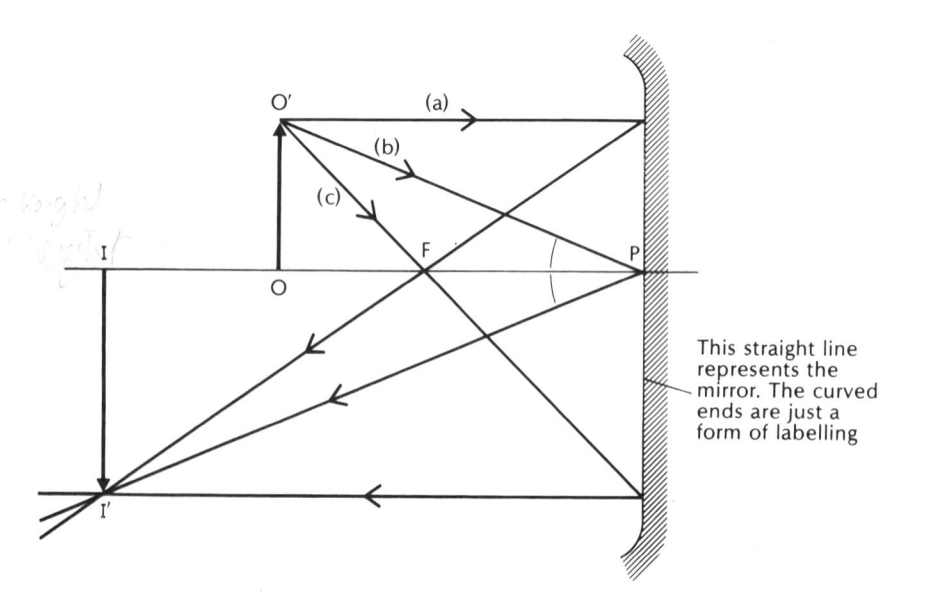

This straight line represents the mirror. The curved ends are just a form of labelling

Fig. 19.13

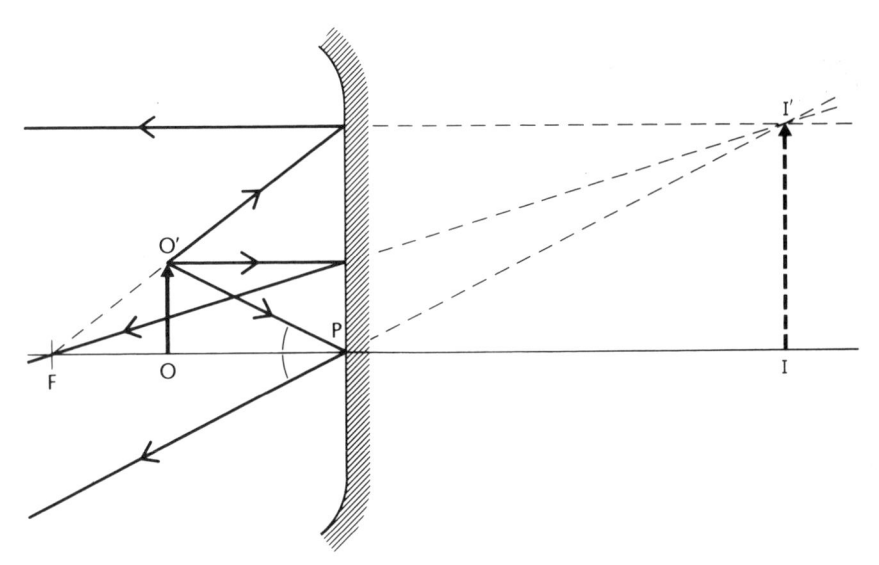

Fig. 19.14

Questions on Chapter 19

1. A camera has a lens of focal length 100 mm. It is placed so that the lens is 220 mm from an object 60 mm high in order to take a close-up photograph of the object. Find a) how far from the lens the film must be and b) the size of the image.

2. A convex lens of focal length 100 mm is used as a magnifying glass. It is placed 60 mm from a small object. Find a) the distance from the lens to the image and b) the magnification. Also state c) whether the image is real or virtual, upright or inverted, and magnified or diminished.

3. A lamp with a filament 8 mm long is placed 250 mm from a converging lens of focal length 150 mm so that the length of the lamp filament is at right angles to the axis of the lens. Find the position, size and nature of the image formed by the lens.

4. An illuminated object 10 mm high and a white screen are placed parallel to each other and 250 mm apart. A convex lens placed in between forms a clear image of the object, 15 mm high, on the screen. Find the focal length of the lens and its distance from the object.

5. A diverging lens of focal length 60 mm forms an image of an object placed on its axis and 120 mm from it. Find a) the distance of the image from the lens and b) the magnification.

Chapter 20

Optical Instruments

The Camera

The essentials of a camera are:
(i) a light-proof box,
(ii) a converging lens (unless a pinhole is used instead),
(iii) a light-sensitive film or plate,
(iv) a shutter (or a lens-cap may be used instead).

The following adjustments are found on many cameras.

- **Focusing** by moving the lens — the focal point of the lens is on the film when the camera is adjusted for an object at infinity (for distant views) and the lens is moved farther from the film for photographing nearer objects. Figure 20.1 illustrates this.

- **Variable aperture** to let in less light by reducing the size of the hole on bright days or to obtain greater depth of focus.

- **Variable exposure time** so that the shutter can be opened for a shorter interval on bright days or to photograph fast-moving objects.

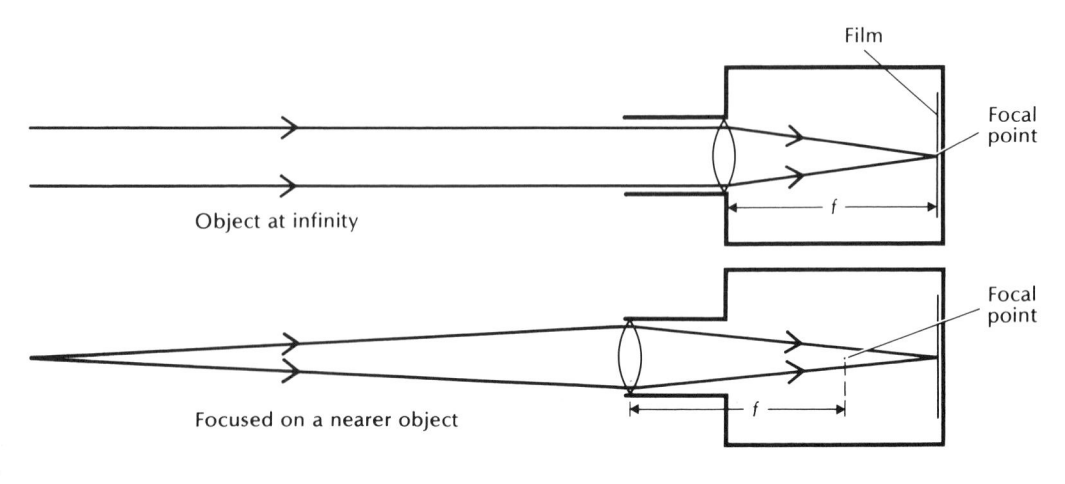

Fig. 20.1

The Eye

Figure 20.2 shows the parts of the eye which are important for a physics course. The light is refracted both by the liquid-filled cornea and by the lens.

The eye has the following adjustments.

- **Focusing** by changing the shape of the lens — it becomes fatter for looking at nearer objects.

- **Variable aperture** — in bright light, the iris (the coloured part) expands inwards to reduce the size of the pupil (the hole).

- **Variable sensitivity** of the retina, especially in adapting for night vision or 'getting used to the dark'.

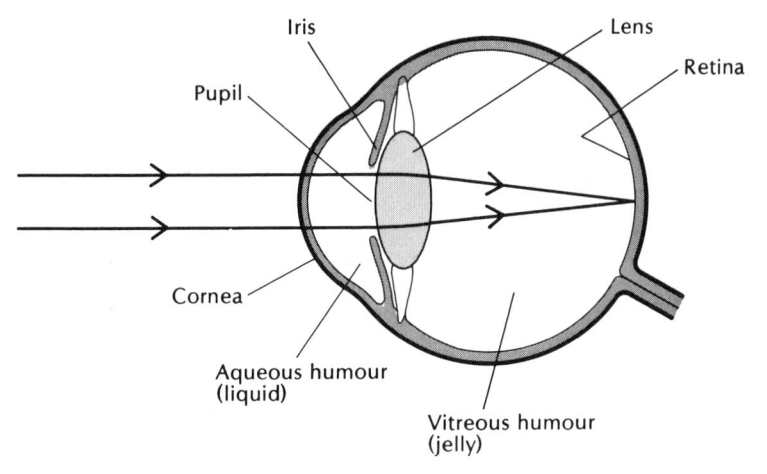

Fig. 20.2

The Projector

Where a camera has its object (usually) many focal lengths away from the lens and its image at the focal point or just outside it, the projector (Figure 20.3) is the opposite: its object is just outside the focal point and its image is many focal lengths away.

The concave mirror brings into use light which would otherwise be wasted. The condensing lens ensures that the light reaching the object is going in the right direction to go through the projecting lens. The diagram does not show the casing which stops stray light from escaping, nor the cooling fan.

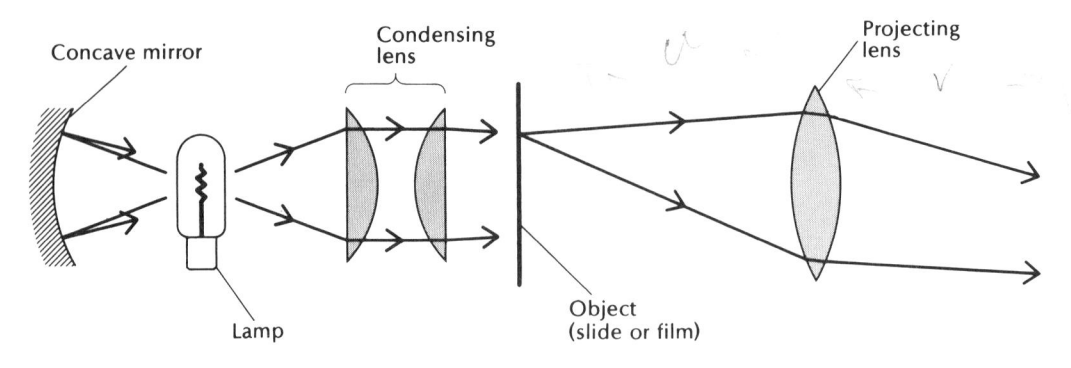

Fig. 20.3

The Magnifying Glass

This is a single convex lens. It is also called a 'simple microscope'. Figure 20.4 shows the position of the image, which is virtual, erect and magnified. For another ray diagram — one that shows why it magnifies — see Figure 19.10.

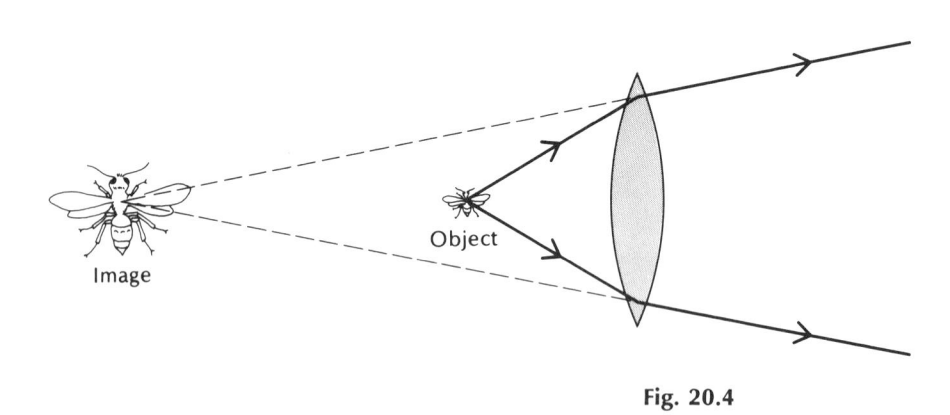

Fig. 20.4

Telescopes*

Three types of telescope are shown in Figures 20.5 to 20.7. The reflecting telescope (Figure 20.6) is not so good as a refracting one (Figure 20.5) of the same size because the plane mirror stops some of the incident light. Reflecting telescopes can be made in larger sizes than refractors can. Both types produce inverted images, but this is no disadvantage for astronomical work.

*Only required by one examination board.

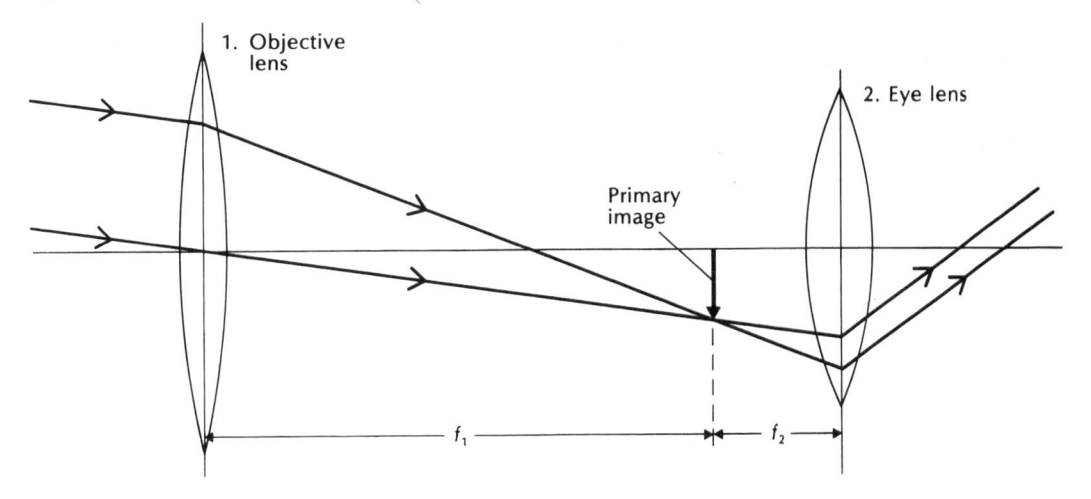

Optical Instruments   139

ASTRONOMICAL REFRACTING TELESCOPE

Fig. 20.5

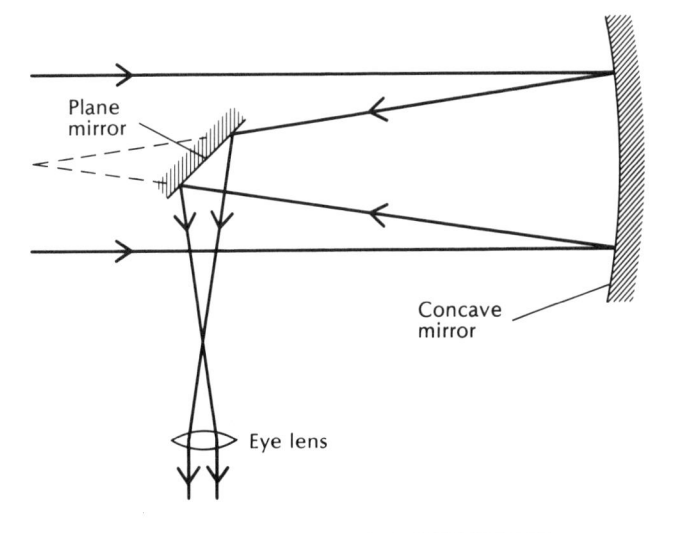

NEWTONIAN REFLECTING TELESCOPE   **Fig. 20.6**

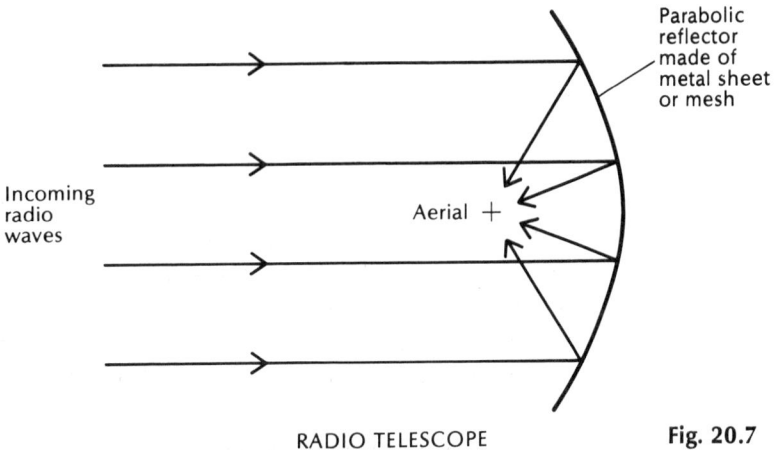

RADIO TELESCOPE   **Fig. 20.7**

The Compound Microscope*

The two-lens microscope is usually called a 'compound' microscope (Figure 20.8). The objective lens forms a magnified real image and the eye lens acts as a simple microscope to look at this image.

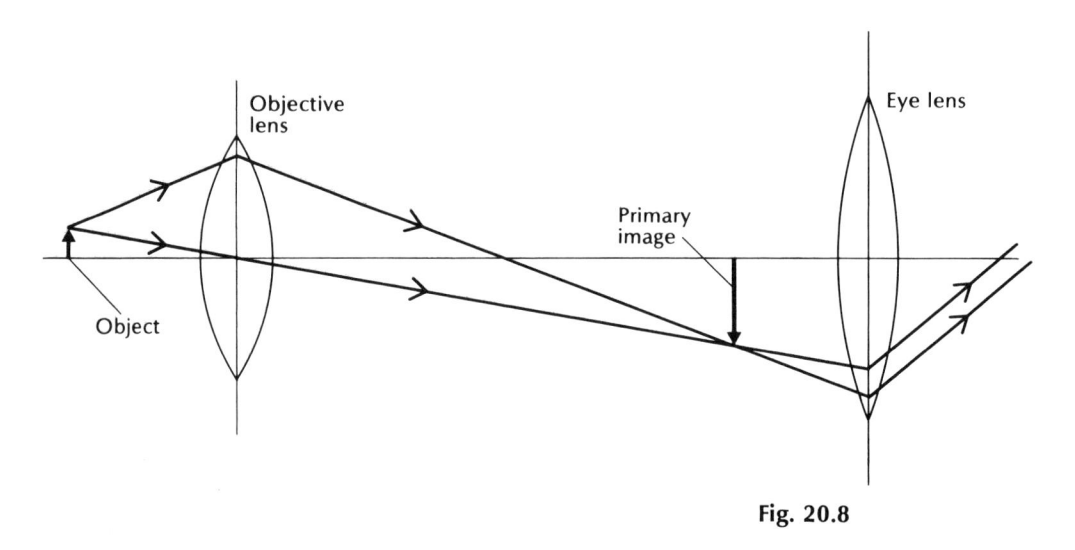

Fig. 20.8

---

*One examination board includes this in its syllabus.

Section D:
WAVES

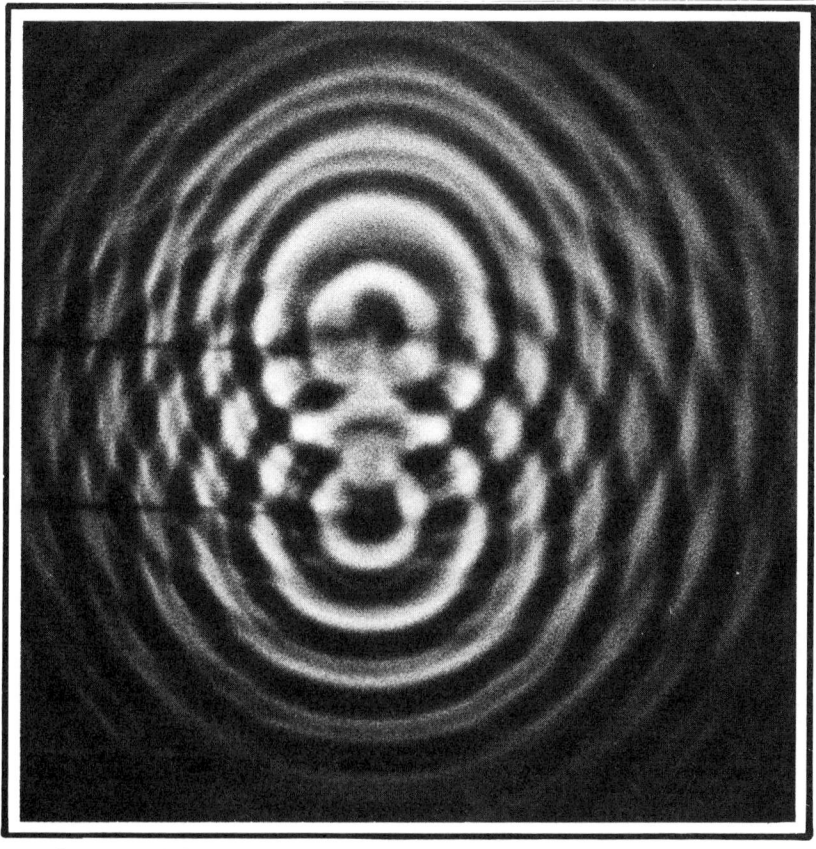

Interference of ripples
Compare this photograph with Fig. 24.4

Chapter 21

Oscillations and Waves

An **oscillation** is a movement or change which keeps on repeating regularly. A familiar example is the motion of a pendulum. However, a pendulum moves along a curve, and in some ways it is better to consider a movement which is not along a curve but along a straight line. An example of an oscillation along a straight line is provided by the mass on a spring shown in Figure 21.1

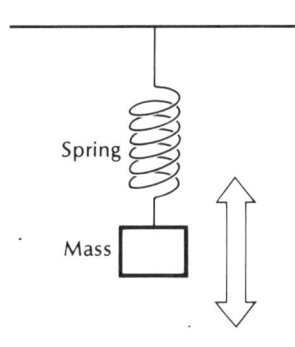

Fig. 21.1

Since a **wave** is made up of oscillations, the definitions which follow apply to waves as well as to oscillations. Figure 21.2 illustrates some of these definitions. In this figure, the vertical scale may represent the vertical displacement of the mass shown in Figure 21.1, but it may equally well represent many other things, such as the height of one point on the water surface in a water wave, or the pressure at one point in the air as a sound wave is passing.

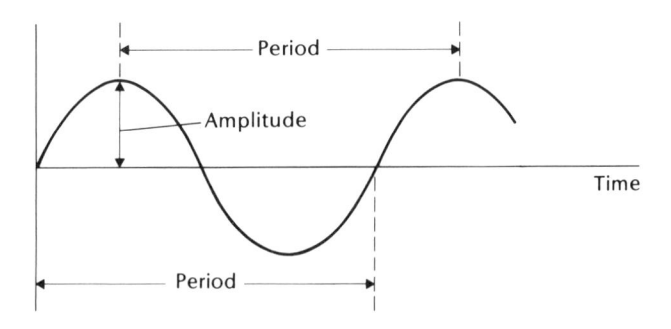

Fig. 21.2

- The **amplitude** of an oscillation is the distance from the centre to one extreme.

- The **period** is the time taken for one complete swing — for example, from one extreme to the other and back again.

- The **frequency** is the number of complete swings that take place in one second. The SI unit of frequency is the hertz (Hz); one hertz equals one complete swing per second.

- The **wave-form** of an oscillation is the shape of the graph that represents it. For simple oscillations this may be a sine curve.

- The **phase** of an oscillation is the timing of it in comparison with another oscillation. In Figure 21.3, the oscillations represented by curves A and B are *in phase* with each other but have different amplitudes, while C is opposite in phase to A and B. D and E are slightly *out of phase* with each other.

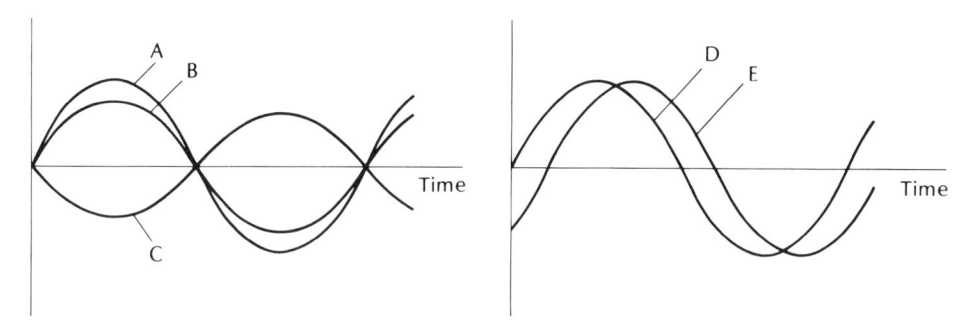

Fig. 21.3

Stroboscopes

A stroboscope is a device for seeing an oscillating body, or a rotating one, at certain moments only, so that it seems to be stationary or only slowly moving. It can be used to observe the motion or to measure the frequency.

The **flashing-light stroboscope** is best used in a darkened room; it emits a brief flash of light at regular intervals, the period being adjustable in a typical instrument from 1 s down to $\frac{1}{250}$ s. The **rotating-wheel stroboscope** has a wheel with one or more radial slits in it and it is driven round by hand or by an electric motor. Looking through it, you have a glimpse of the oscillating or rotating body every time a slit passes in front of your eye.

Imagine that the wheel shown in Figure 21.4, which has a white arrow painted on it, rotates once every $\frac{1}{50}$ s. If you observe it once every $\frac{1}{50}$ s with a stroboscope, it will have turned 360° between each glimpse and the next, and so it will seem to be still. Now if the stroboscope frequency is increased very slightly, the wheel will only have time to turn perhaps 359° instead of 360°. It will look as if it has turned 1° in the other direction, and you will seem to see a slow, backward rotation. Similarly, decreasing the stroboscope frequency will make the wheel seem to turn slowly forwards.

Fig. 21.4

Quick Question 34

What will be the appearance of the wheel of Figure 21.4, which is rotating at a frequency of 50 Hz, if it is observed with a stroboscope which has a frequency of a) 100 Hz, b) 25 Hz?

Free and Forced Vibrations

- When a bell is struck or a guitar string is plucked, it vibrates at its own natural frequency. This kind of vibration is called a **free vibration** (or a free oscillation).

- A **damped** oscillation is one which is losing energy. Figure 21.5 shows a free oscillation which is heavily damped so that its amplitude decreases quickly.

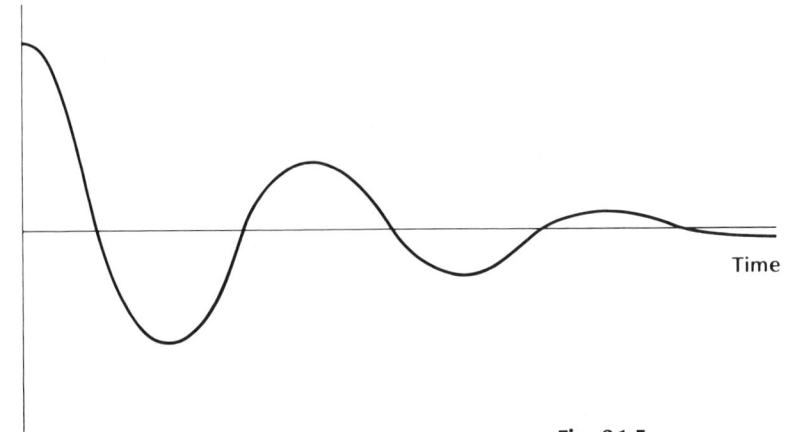

Fig. 21.5

- A **forced vibration** is one which takes place at a frequency imposed on it by some outside cause, like the vibration of the cone of a loudspeaker in response to the oscillating electric current which is being sent through its coil. If the frequency imposed from outside is equal to the natural frequency of the vibrating body, then the amplitude becomes much bigger; this is called **resonance**. One way to demonstrate resonance is to strike a tuning fork and hold it over the open end of a resonance tube while water is running slowly out of the tube. (Figure 21.6 — compare this with Figure 23.4.) The tuning fork makes the column of air inside the tube vibrate. As the water level drops and so the air column becomes longer, its natural frequency changes. When the length is just right for the natural frequency of the air column to be equal to the frequency of the tuning fork, the air column resonates and produces a loud enough note to be heard.

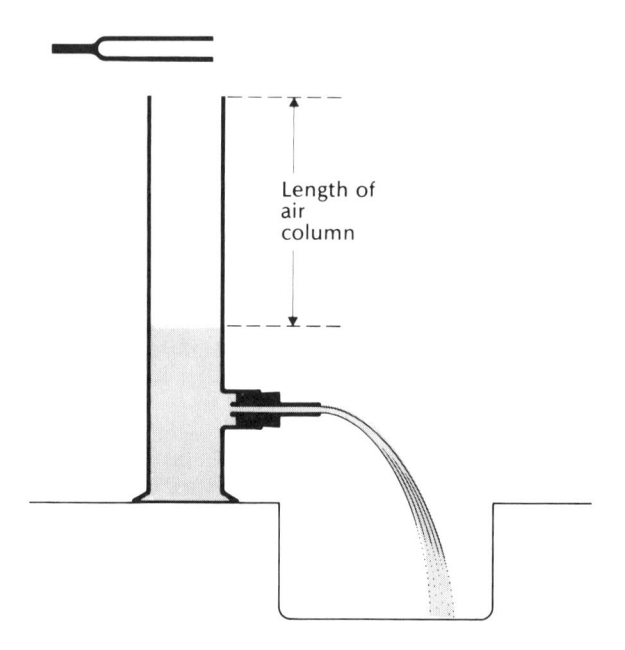

Fig. 21.6

Progressive Waves

A progressive (or 'travelling') wave is composed of oscillations which are not all in phase with each other. Figure 21.7 is an instantaneous view of a travelling wave. As the wave moves, the oscillations of points A and B are slightly out of phase with each other because they reach their maxima at slightly different times as the wave passes them. Points A and C are in opposite phase. A and D are in phase with each other, and they are one wavelength apart.

■ The **wavelength** is the distance between two points on consecutive waves which are oscillating in phase with each other. In the case of a water wave it is simply the distance from one wave-crest to the next. It is written as λ (the Greek letter 'lambda').

Oscillations and Waves

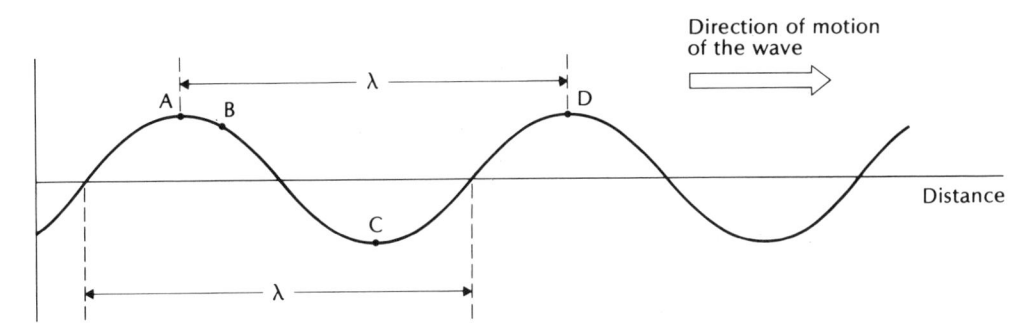

Fig. 21.7

Equations

$$f = \frac{1}{T} \quad \text{and} \quad T = \frac{1}{f}$$

where f is the frequency   (in Hz)
        T is the period   (in s)

$$v = f\lambda$$

where v is the speed of the wave   (in m/s)
        λ is the wavelength   (in m)

Example 21.1 The period of a sound wave, measured with an oscilloscope, is found to be 2.5 milliseconds. The wavelength, measured with a resonance tube, is found to be 0.80 m. What is the speed of sound?

Solution

$$T = 2.5 \text{ ms} = 0.0025 \text{ s}$$

$$f = \frac{1}{T} = \frac{1}{0.0025} \text{ Hz} = 400 \text{ Hz}$$

$$v = f\lambda = 400 \times 0.8 = 320 \text{ m/s}$$

Example 21.2 Radio 4 has a frequency of 200 kHz. What is its wavelength? (The speed of light — and therefore also of radio waves — is 3×10^8 m/s.)

Solution

$$v = f\lambda$$

$$\therefore \quad \lambda = \frac{v}{f} = \frac{3 \times 10^8}{200\,000} = 1500 \text{ m} = 1.5 \text{ km}$$

Types of Wave

Waves may be divided into two types, longitudinal and transverse. Both kinds may be made to travel along a spiral spring by jerking one end in the appropriate direction.

- In a **transverse** wave the movement of each particle is at right angles to (across) the path of the wave. It may be called a 'shake' wave. Transverse waves may be sent along a rope by shaking one end; other examples are water waves or ripples, and electromagnetic waves such as light and radio waves.

- In a **longitudinal** wave the movement of each particle is parallel to (along) the path of the wave. It may be called a 'push' wave. Sound waves are longitudinal.

Questions on Chapter 21

1. Waves on the sea are observed to have their crests 10 m apart and to travel at a speed of 4 m/s. What are *a*) their frequency and *b*) their period?

2. A VHF transmitter works on a frequency of 100 MHz. What is the wavelength of the waves that it sends out? (For the speed of radio waves, see Example 21.2 on p. 147.)

3. A perfectly symmetrical three-spoked wheel rotates 40 times in every second. It is illuminated by a flashing-light stroboscope. What will the appearance of the wheel be if the stroboscope frequency is *a*) 20 Hz, *b*) 40 Hz, *c*) 80 Hz, *d*) 41 Hz?

Chapter 22

Sound

A sound wave can be thought of in two ways: as longitudinal displacements of the air or of some other medium, and as alternate compressions (pressure above atmospheric) and rarefactions (pressure below atmospheric). Figure 22.1 illustrates this.

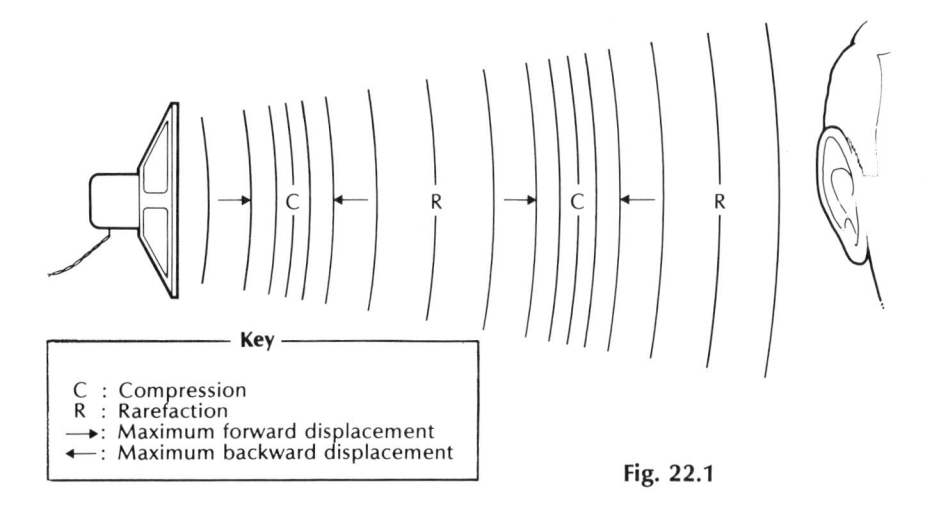

Key
C : Compression
R : Rarefaction
→ : Maximum forward displacement
← : Maximum backward displacement

Fig. 22.1

Sound can travel through solids, liquids and gases. To show that it cannot travel through a vacuum, hang up an electric bell under a bell jar connected to a vacuum pump. When all the air has been removed from around the bell, it can be seen to ring normally but no sound escapes.

Characteristics of a Musical Note

- The **pitch** of a note means how high or low it is on the musical scale. It corresponds to **frequency**. Two notes which differ in pitch by one octave have their frequencies in a ratio of 2.

- The **loudness** corresponds to the **amplitude** of the sound wave.

■ The **quality** (or timbre) enables us to distinguish, for example, between a flute and a violin. It corresponds to the **wave-form** of the sound, which may be shown on the screen of an oscilloscope connected to a microphone as illustrated in Figure 22.2. Figure 22.3 shows a wave-form which might be produced by a clarinet. Compare it with the wave-form of the tuning fork.

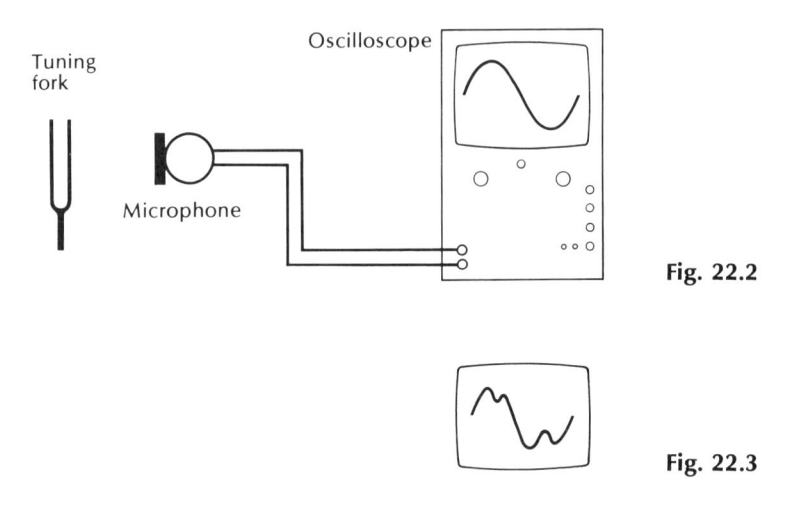

Fig. 22.2

Fig. 22.3

The Speed of Sound

The speed of sound in a gas depends on the composition of the gas and also on the temperature. In air at ordinary temperatures it is about $\frac{1}{3}$ km/s. It can be measured by:

- timing the interval between seeing the flash of a distant gun firing and hearing the sound of the explosion, since the time taken for the light of the flash to reach the observer is negligible;
- timing an echo;
- the method described on p. 156.

Quick Question 35

If thunder is heard 6 s after the lightning flash is seen, how far away is the storm?

Sound

Example 22.1 Two ships are 6 km apart and each is 4 km from a long, straight cliff, as shown in Figure 22.4. One ship sounds its fog-horn. What length of time elapses between the beginning of the fog-horn blast and the beginning of its echo from the cliff, as heard from the other ship? (Speed of sound in air = 333 m/s)

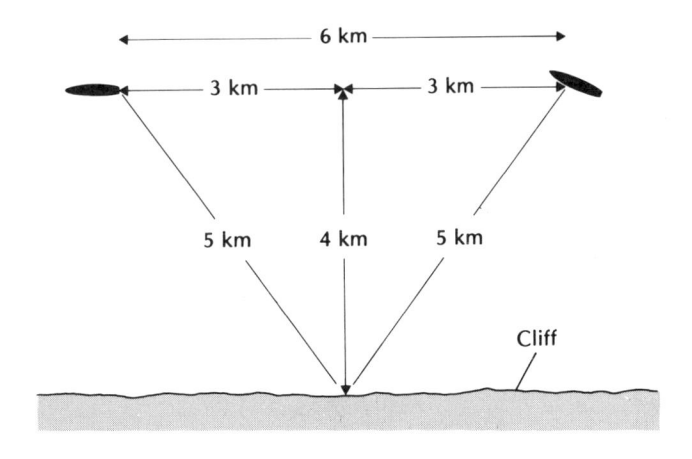

Fig. 22.4

Solution The equation for this type of problem is $v = \dfrac{s}{t}$ (p. 12). For the direct sound:

$$t_1 = \frac{s}{v} = \frac{6000}{333} = 18 \text{ s}$$

For the echo, the total distance is 10 km (by Pythagoras — see Figure 22.4)

$$\therefore \quad t_2 = \frac{s}{v} = \frac{10\,000}{333} = 30 \text{ s}$$

Therefore the interval between the arrivals of the two sounds is:

$$t = t_2 - t_1 = 30 - 18 = 12 \text{ s}$$

Example 22.2 An echo sounder in a ship transmits sound waves through the water and receives the echo from the bottom of the sea after a short delay. What length of delay corresponds to a depth of 100 m? (Speed of sound in sea water = 1500 m/s)

Solution When depth = 100 m, the sound must travel 200 m.

Therefore
$$t = \frac{s}{v} = \frac{200}{1500} = 0.133 \text{ s}$$

Questions on Chapter 22

1 *a)* A siren consists of a disc in which there are 16 equally spaced holes, all the same distance from the axle, as illustrated in Figure 22.5. When a jet of air is directed at the holes and the disc is rotated at a particular constant rate, the frequency of the note produced is 320 Hz. What is the frequency of the note produced using a disc containing 24 holes which is rotated at the same rate?

b) How does the sound of this note compare with the sound of the original note? (C)

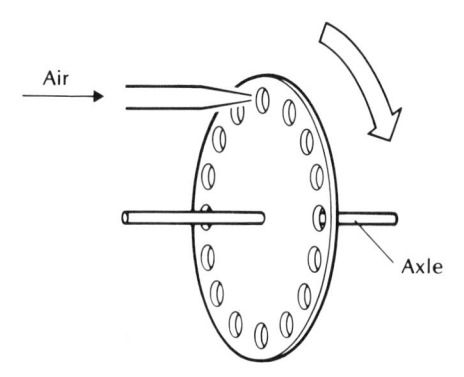

Fig. 22.5

2 To measure the speed of sound in air, two microphones are connected to a recorder and placed as shown in Figure 22.6. When the detonator is exploded, the recorder measures the interval between the times of arrival of the sound at the two microphones; it is 1.50 s. What value does this give for the speed of sound?

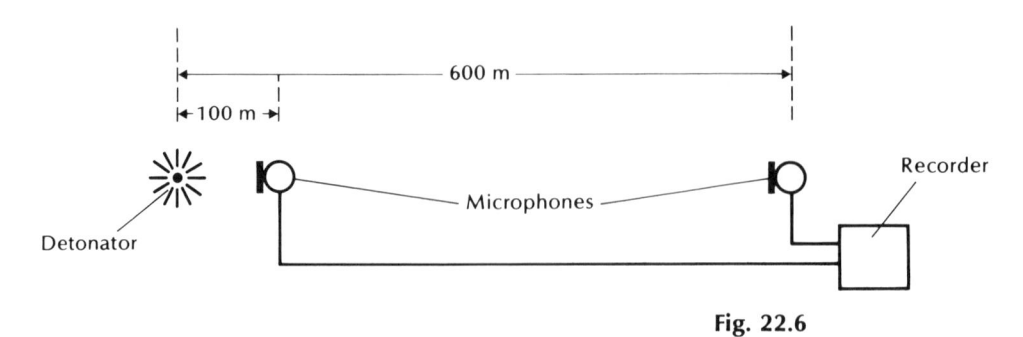

Fig. 22.6

3 A mechanical hammer at H (Figure 22.7) produces bangs at a fixed rate of 3.0 per second. An observer at O hears the bangs and their echoes from the vertical wall AB. When the perpendicular distance, OX, of the observer from the wall is 28.0 m the echoes are heard exactly in the middle of the interval between hearing the bangs. Calculate a value for the speed of sound in air. (O & C)

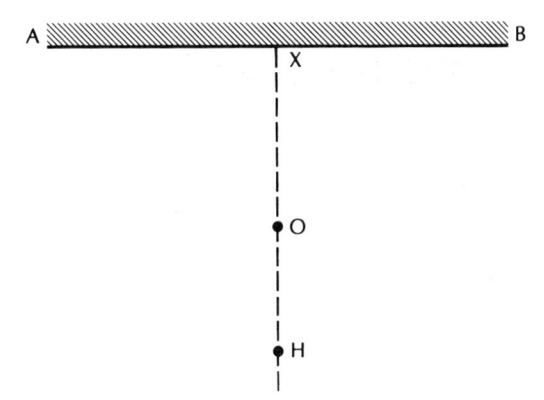

Fig. 22.7

4 A ship surveying the sea bed sends out every 0.4 s short pulses of sound at a frequency of 50 000 Hz. A special microphone on the ship receives the echoes from the sea bed.

  (i) Using the fact that the speed of sound in water is 1500 m/s and that the time interval between sending the impulse and receiving the echo is 0.1 s, calculate the depth of the sea.
  (ii) On entering a region where the sea bed slopes gradually away, the ship goes over a spot known to be 300 m deep. Calculate the time interval between the impulse and the echo, and comment on your result.
  (iii) What is significant about the timing of the transmitted and received pulses when the depth of the sea is 150 m? (AEB)

Chapter 23

Stationary Waves

Stationary Waves in a Rope

If one end of a clothes line is firmly fixed and you shake the other end transversely, trying different frequencies until you find a suitable one, the rope will form a pattern of stationary waves, also called standing waves. Some points do not move; these are called **nodes**, marked N in Figure 23.1. The points where the amplitude is greatest are called **antinodes**, marked A in the diagram. The space between two consecutive nodes is a **loop**. By comparing Figure 23.1 with Figure 21.6 you can see that the distance apart of consecutive nodes is half a wavelength.

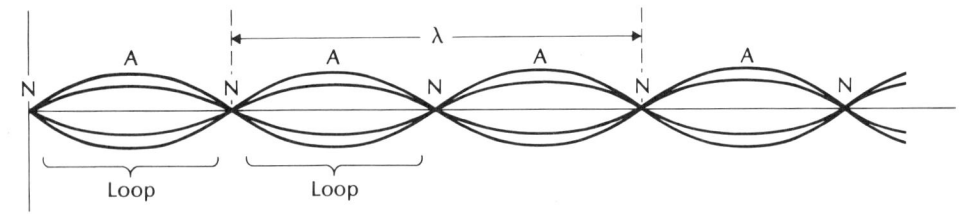

Fig. 23.1

Stretched Strings

The string of a guitar or a violin vibrates in just the same way as the rope that we have been considering, except that it is lighter and tighter and therefore vibrates at a higher frequency. Also, in ordinary playing it vibrates with only one loop.

Figure 23.2 shows a laboratory version of a stretched string. It is shown: *a)* vibrating with a node at each end and only one loop — this is called the 'fundamental' or the 'first harmonic'; and *b)* vibrating with two loops — that is, sounding its second harmonic. The frequency of the second harmonic is twice that of the fundamental.

The factors affecting the frequency of the fundamental of a stretched string are:

(i) *length* — doubling the length halves the frequency,
(ii) *tension* — a tighter string has a higher frequency,
(iii) *mass* — a thicker string has a lower frequency.

The formula for the natural frequency, f, of a stretched string sounding its fundamental is:

$$f = \frac{1}{2l}\sqrt{\frac{T}{m}}$$

where l is its length,
        T is its tension,
        m is its mass per unit length.

To find the frequency of a higher harmonic, multiply this by the number of loops.

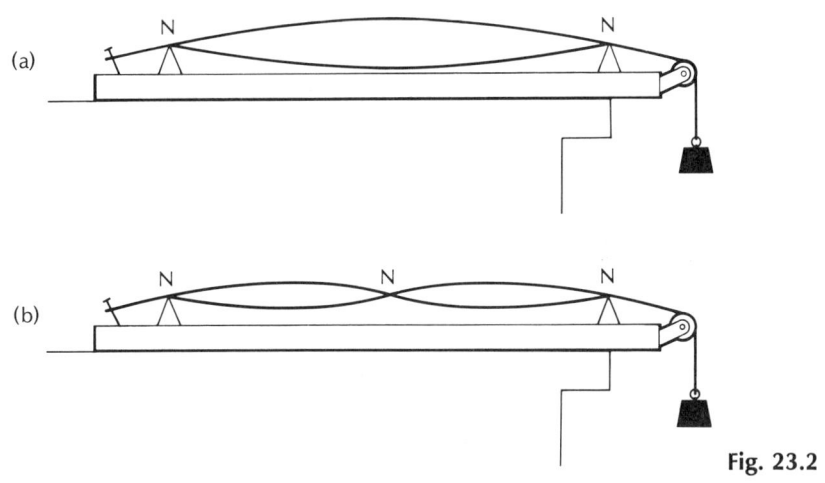

Fig. 23.2

Air Columns

The air column inside a flute or a clarinet or an organ pipe provides another example of stationary waves. Figure 23.3(a) shows the vibration of the air column inside a closed organ pipe (that is, closed at one end). The closed end is a node and the open end is an antinode if we are considering the air movements, but the pressure changes are the opposite: at the open end there is no variation of pressure and so this is a node as far as pressure changes are concerned.

Figure 23.3(b) shows a closed tube about three times as long, sounding its third harmonic; its frequency is the same as that of the pipe in Figure 23.3(a). A closed pipe can only produce odd-numbered harmonics. An open pipe (that is, open at both ends) such as a flute has a pressure node at each end and can sound all harmonics, both odd and even.

(a) FUNDAMENTAL NOTE (FIRST HARMONIC)

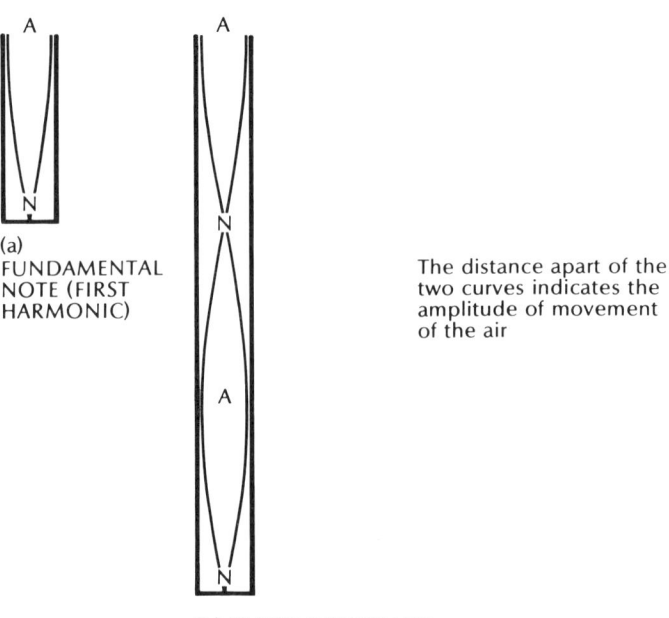

The distance apart of the two curves indicates the amplitude of movement of the air

(b) THIRD HARMONIC

A: Movement (or displacement) antinodes which are pressure nodes
N: Movement (or displacement) nodes which are pressure antinodes

Fig. 23.3

The factors affecting the frequency of the fundamental of an air column are:

(i) *length* — doubling the length halves the frequency;
(ii) the *speed of sound* in the gas — raising the temperature, or filling the tube with a less dense gas such as helium, increases the speed of sound in the gas and therefore increases the natural frequency of the air column.

Resonance Tubes

A resonance tube may be used to measure the wavelength of a sound. If the frequency of the sound is known, the speed can then be calculated. The length of the tube needs to be adjustable and one way of doing this is shown in Figure 23.4. The method for finding the speed of sound in air is described next.

Strike a tuning fork which has its frequency marked on it and hold it over the end of the tube. Raise or lower the reservoir so as to alter the length, l, of the air column in the tube; do this until you

Fig. 23.4

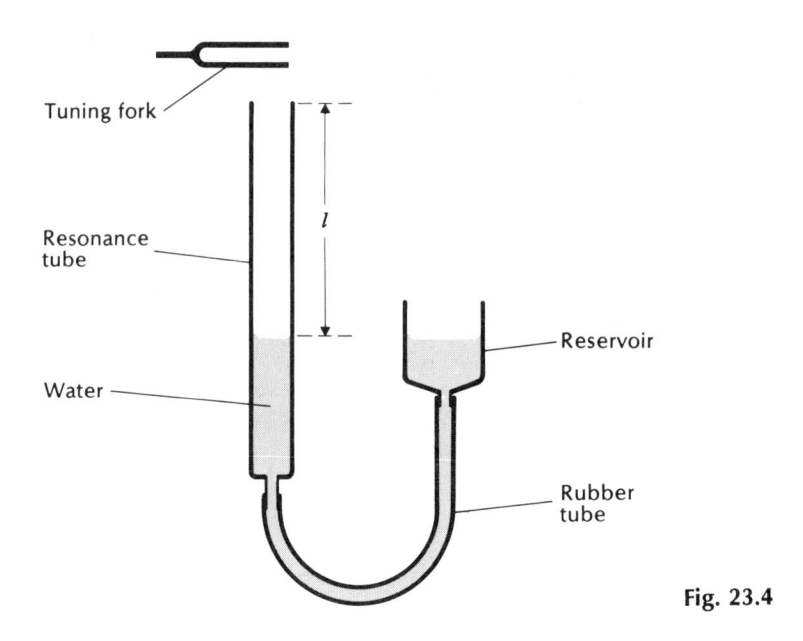

hear an extra loud sound. The air is then resonating as in Figure 23.3(a). Either measure l or mark the water level on the outside of the tube with a felt-tip pen.

Next, lower the reservoir until l is about three times as long as before and again find a resonance setting. The air is now resonating as in Figure 23.3(b). Measure l, or mark the tube, as before.

By subtracting one length from the other, or by measuring the distance apart of the two marks, find the distance between the two water levels. This is half a wavelength; double it to find the wavelength and then use $v = f\lambda$ to find the speed of sound.

Notes

To see why the difference of levels is half a wavelength, look at Figure 23.3. The difference in level equals the distance apart of consecutive nodes and the wavelength is twice this.

If the pressure node was exactly at the end of the tube, the first value of l would be one-quarter of the wavelength and the second part of the experiment would be unnecessary. Actually, the pressure node is just outside the end of the tube. The distance between the end of the tube and the pressure node is called the **end correction**.

A loudspeaker may be used instead of a tuning fork if it is driven by an oscillator whose frequency calibration is known to be accurate.

Questions on Chapter 23

1. A tuning fork of frequency 256 Hz is struck and then held over the open end of a resonance tube like the one in Figure 23.4. The loudest sound is heard when the length of the air column is 0.33 m and the air column is then sounding its fundamental note. Ignoring end correction, calculate the speed of sound.

2. A resonance tube as shown in Figure 23.4 is made to resonate by a tuning fork of frequency 440 Hz. Resonance occurs when the length of the tube above the water surface is 175 mm and again when it is 550 mm. Using both these length readings to eliminate the end correction, calculate the speed of sound.

3. A closed organ pipe 0.50 m long produces a frequency of 160 Hz. What are:
   a) the wavelength of the sound produced,
   b) the wavelength of the sound which would be produced by an open organ pipe of the same length,
   c) the frequency which would be produced by a closed pipe twice as long, that is, 1.0 m long?

   Ignore end correction in this question.

Chapter 24

Wave Patterns

A **ripple tank** is a shallow tank with a transparent bottom so that light can shine upwards or downwards through it. The sides slope to form beaches; the purpose of these is to absorb the energy of the ripples instead of reflecting them back across the tank. Ripples are made by a vibrator which drives a paddle dipping into the water, either a small paddle for circular ripples or else a long one for straight ripples. The ripples are seen by watching their shadows on a screen, using a rotating disc stroboscope.

■ **Reflection** can be shown by standing a barrier, either straight or curved, in the tank. Figure 24.1 shows the patterns which are formed. Compare Figure 24.1(b) with Figure 18.2 on p. 118, and compare Figure 24.1(c) with Figure 18.4.

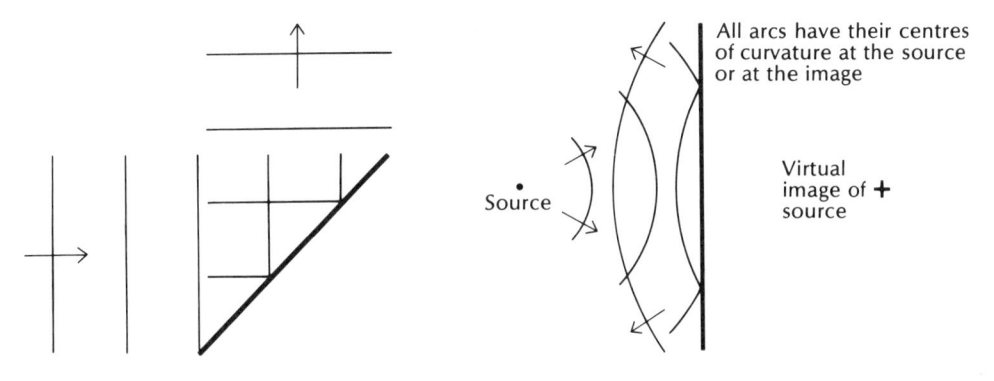

(a) STRAIGHT WAVES, STRAIGHT REFLECTOR

(b) CIRCULAR WAVES, STRAIGHT REFLECTOR

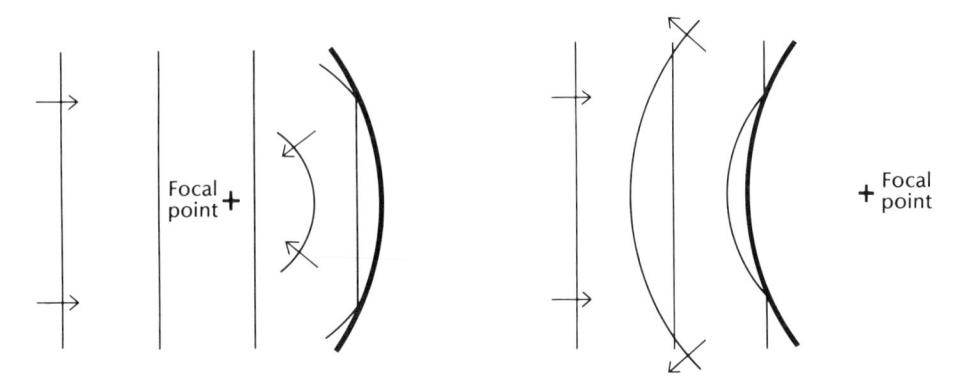

All arcs have their centres of curvature at the source or at the image

Virtual image of + source

(c) STRAIGHT WAVES, CONCAVE REFLECTOR

(d) STRAIGHT WAVES, CONVEX REFLECTOR

Fig. 24.1

■ **Refraction** can be shown by using different depths of water (Figure 24.2). As ripples enter a shallower patch of water they slow down. This causes the wavelength to decrease, but the frequency does not change.

(a) STRAIGHT WAVES, ANGLE OF INCIDENCE = 0

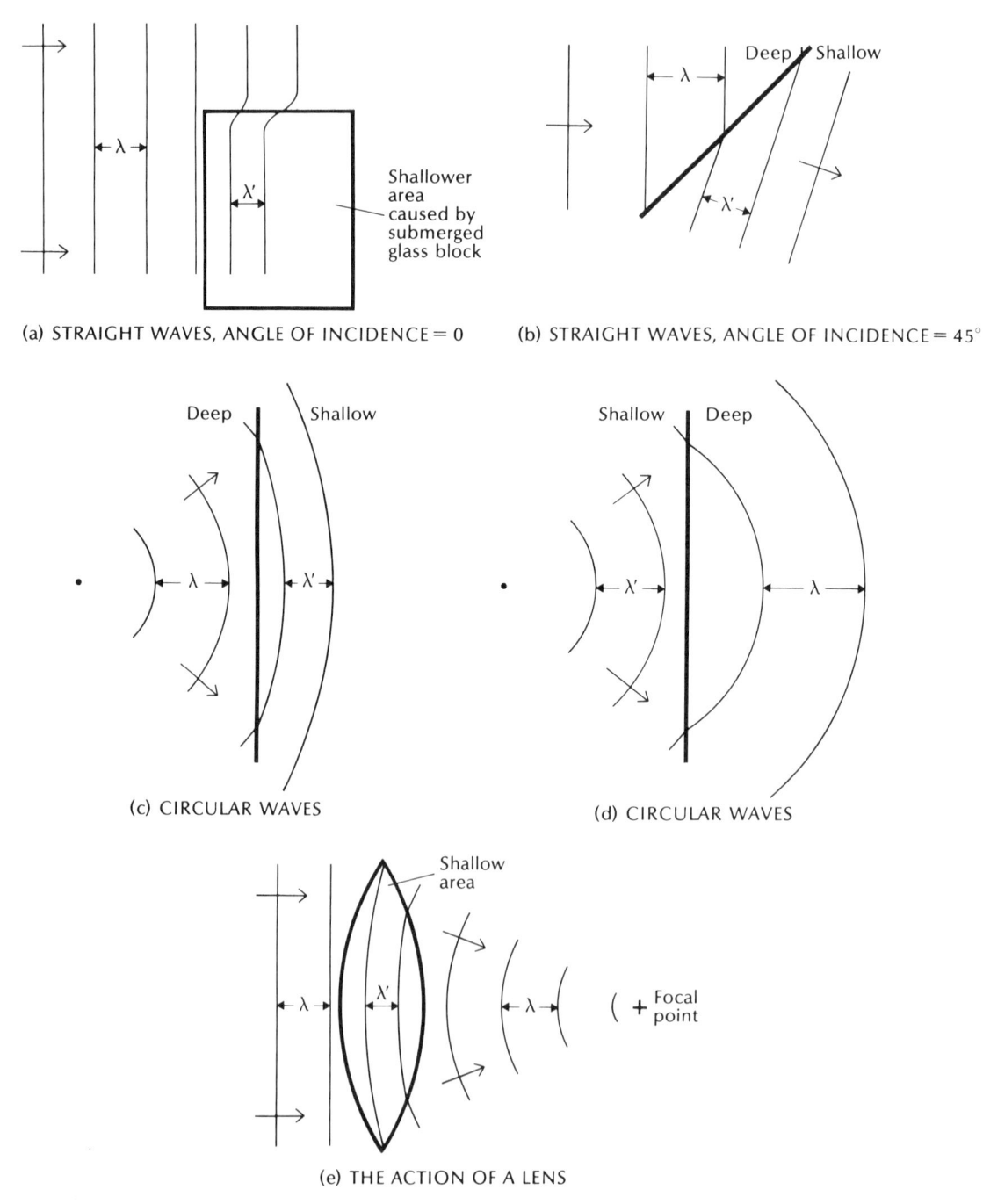

(b) STRAIGHT WAVES, ANGLE OF INCIDENCE = 45°

(c) CIRCULAR WAVES

(d) CIRCULAR WAVES

(e) THE ACTION OF A LENS

Fig. 24.2

Light behaves in a similar way in that it slows down as it passes from air into glass or water, and it is this slowing down which causes the bending of light rays. As light enters a denser medium:

its speed becomes slower,
its wavelength becomes shorter,
its frequency does not change.

Its speed and wavelength return to their previous values when the light emerges into air again.

These changes are related to the refractive index, n, by the equations

$$\frac{v}{v'} = n \quad \text{and} \quad \frac{\lambda}{\lambda'} = n$$

where v and λ are the velocity and wavelength in air,
v' and λ' are their values in water or glass.

Diffraction

Diffraction, shown in Figure 24.3, is the spreading of waves round an obstacle or as they pass through a slit.

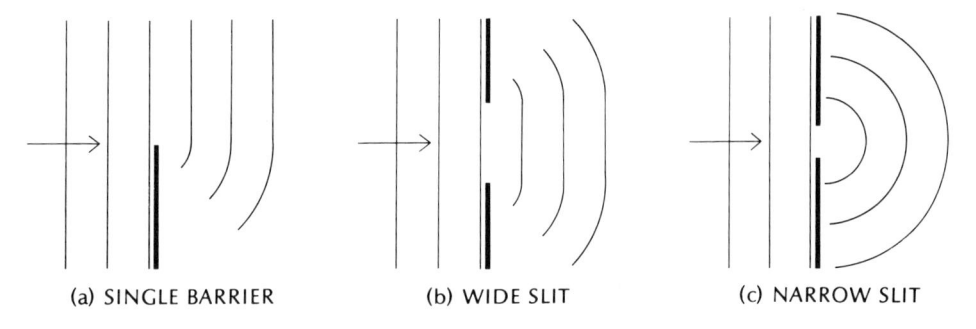

(a) SINGLE BARRIER   (b) WIDE SLIT   (c) NARROW SLIT

Fig. 24.3

Interference

Figure 24.4 shows, at the top, how an **interference pattern** is produced in a ripple tank by two separate paddles dipping into the tank, vibrating together and driven by the same vibrator. At the bottom, it shows the exactly similar pattern produced when waves are diffracted through two narrow slits.

- **Constructive interference** is the production of an extra large amplitude where two waves meeting are in phase with each other.

- **Destructive interference** is the cancelling or partial cancelling which occurs when two waves meeting are out of phase with each other. If the two separate waves have equal amplitudes, the resulting amplitude is zero; otherwise, the resulting amplitude is small.

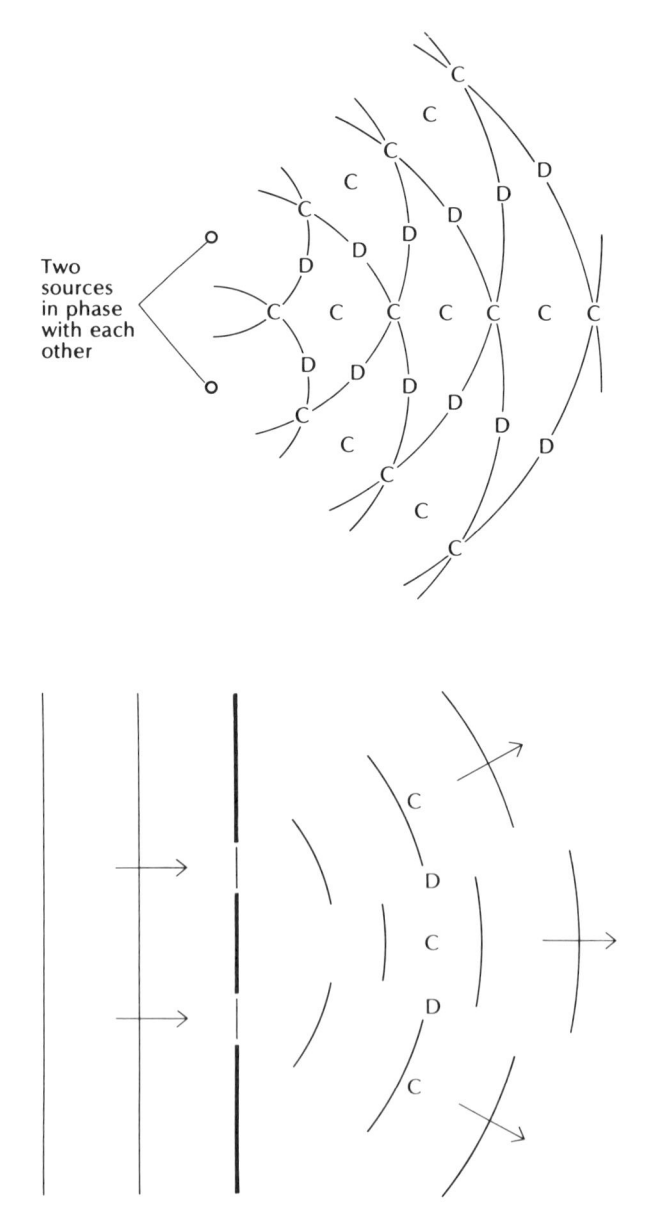

Two sources in phase with each other

Wave-crests are shown; troughs are half-way between them
C: constructive interference — crest on crest or trough on trough
D: destructive interference — crest on trough

Fig. 24.4

Wave Patterns

Beats

A good example of interference is provided by sound. When two sounds of slightly different frequencies are heard simultaneously, the result is **beats** — that is, a sound which is loud and soft alternately because the interference is alternately constructive and destructive. The number of times that the loudness is at a maximum in each second is the 'beat frequency' and is equal to the difference between the two separate frequencies:

$$f_{\text{beat}} = f_1 - f_2 \quad \text{or} \quad f_2 - f_1$$

whichever is positive.

Example 24.1 An accurately calibrated oscillator is set to 440 Hz and connected to a loudspeaker so that a note of this frequency is heard. At the same time an oboe sounds a long note, and 3 beats per second are audible. What is the frequency of the oboe?

Solution
$$f_o = f_{\text{LS}} + f_{\text{beat}} = 440 + 3 = 443\,\text{Hz}$$
or
$$f_o = f_{\text{LS}} - f_{\text{beat}} = 440 - 3 = 437\,\text{Hz}$$

Example 24.2 In the example above, how could you test whether the frequency of the oboe was 437 Hz or 443 Hz?

Solution Alter the oscillator setting slightly to find whether its frequency needs to be increased or decreased in order to reduce the beat frequency. When the beats have been made *slower*, the oscillator has moved *towards* the frequency of the oboe.

Questions on Chapter 24

1. Ripples with a wavelength of 12 mm are produced in a ripple tank. They enter an area of shallow water as shown in Figure 24.2(b), the angle of incidence being 45°, and as a result the wavelength reduces to 8 mm. Find, either by a scale drawing or by calculation, the angle through which the ripples turn as they enter the shallow area.

2. A beam of light enters a glass block as shown in Figure 18.7 on p. 121. The angle of incidence is 54° and the angle of refraction is 31°. Calculate the speed of light in the glass. (Speed of light in air = 3×10^8 m/s)

Chapter 25

Light Waves

Diffraction and interference, which can be observed in water waves in a ripple tank, also happen with light. This shows that light consists of waves. Since the wavelength of light is so short — less than a micrometre — the slits used with light must be much narrower than those used in a ripple tank.

Diffraction of Light

Light spreads out on passing through a slit just like the ripples in Figure 24.3(b). To observe this, hold two pencils, parallel and not quite touching each other, in front of your eye so as to form a slit. Look through the slit at a compact light source such as a 12 volt bulb. If the slit is vertical, the light from the bulb seems to be smeared out horizontally, showing that the light has spread out on passing through the slit. The colour effects that you see can be explained by more advanced wave theory.

Interference of Light

Interference of light may be observed by holding a double slit in front of your eye and looking through it at a compact source of light placed several metres away from you. The double slit may be a glass slide painted with an opaque paint in which two parallel scratches are ruled about half a millimetre apart. You will see the diffraction effect described in the previous paragraph but in addition there are alternate light and dark stripes — usually called 'fringes' — in the centre of the pattern. These correspond to the alternate constructive and destructive interference of Figure 24.4.

By making measurements on the fringes it is possible to measure the wavelength of light. The apparatus is shown diagrammatically in Figure 25.1. For an accurate experiment the lamp should be one which emits one wavelength only, such as a sodium lamp which gives out monochromatic yellow light, but the fringes are easier to see if you use a ray-box bulb with a green filter in front of it.

Light Waves

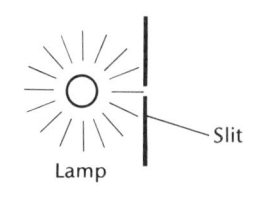

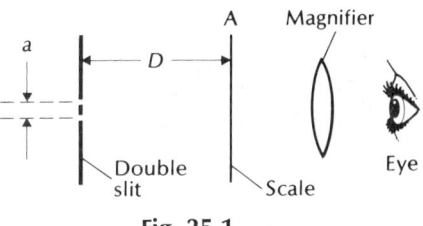

Fig. 25.1

Placing a screen at A would do no good, for the pattern of fringes on it would be too faint to see. Instead, a transparent scale of millimetres, placed at A, is viewed from behind with a magnifier. The number of fringes in each millimetre of the scale is counted — counting either the bright ones or the dark ones — and so the width, x, of each fringe is found. The wavelength is given by:

$$\lambda = \frac{ax}{D}$$

Theory

The central fringe is a bright one. To form the bright fringe next to the central one,* the lengths of the light paths through the two slits must differ by one wavelength. This difference of path length is marked λ in Figure 25.2(b). The two triangles in the two parts of Figure 25.2 are similar — they have equal angles — and so the ratios of their sides are equal. That is:

$$\frac{x}{D} = \frac{\lambda}{a}$$

$$\therefore \quad \lambda = \frac{ax}{D}$$

This would not be true if the rays diverged at a wider angle, because D and a are not corresponding sides of the two triangles, but it is accurately true with the small angles which occur in the two-slit experiment. This theory does not apply to the grating (p. 167) because there we are concerned with quite large values of the angle θ.

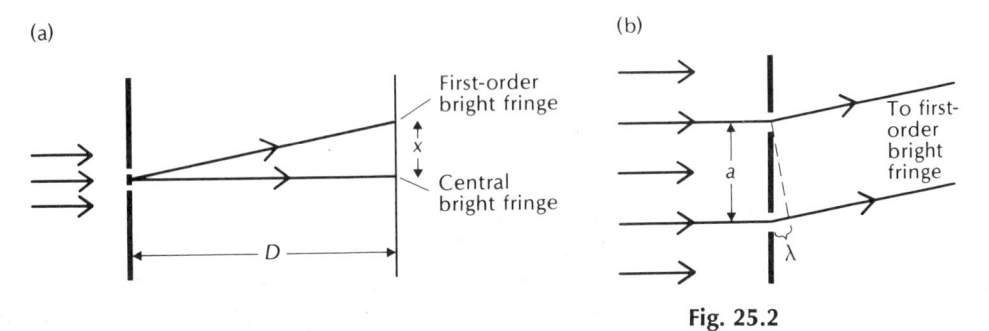

Fig. 25.2

*This is called the 'first-order' fringe as it is formed in the same way as the first-order spectrum that we shall meet on p. 167.

Since red light has the longest wavelength and violet light has the shortest, fringes formed by red light are the furthest apart and those formed by violet light are the closest together, if the distance apart of the slits, a, is the same.

Polarisation

Water waves and light waves are both transverse, but in the case of water waves the displacement of the water can only be vertical whereas light has no such restriction. If a ray of light is travelling horizontally, its displacement may be vertical, or it may be horizontal and at right angles to the ray, or in a slanting direction, but usually it is in all these directions one after the other in quick succession. A light ray which has its displacement confined to one direction, such as vertical, is 'polarised'. (We will consider on p. 169 what the displacement of a light ray means.)

The easiest way to polarise light is to pass it through a sheet of Polaroid, which absorbs the vibrations in one direction and lets through those in the direction at right angles to it. In Figure 25.3(a) both sheets of Polaroid are set so as to let through vertical vibrations, so the first one absorbs half of the light energy but the second transmits all the light that reaches it — or almost all of it. In Figure 25.3(b) the two Polaroids are 'crossed' and no light can go through both.

This provides evidence that light waves are transverse. It has various practical uses, too. For example, light reflected from a horizontal water surface is partly polarised, and so Polaroid sunglasses can cut down the glare of reflected light.

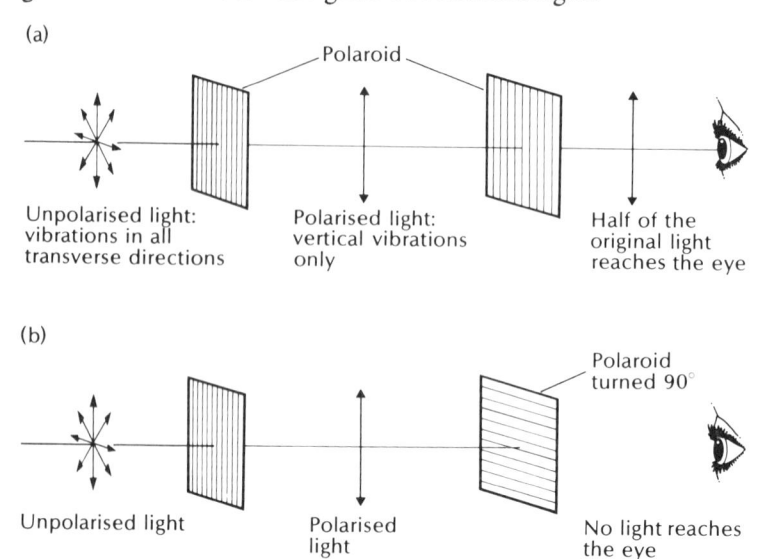

Fig. 25.3

The Diffraction Grating

Although this is called the 'diffraction' grating, it works as much by interference as by diffraction. It is used to produce a spectrum (as an alternative to the use of a prism) and also to measure the wavelengths of individual lines in the spectrum.

One form of grating consists of a regular array of parallel ridges and furrows on a transparent surface at a spacing of several hundred to each millimetre. An easier form of grating to understand consists of alternate opaque and transparent strips, so that the gaps between the opaque strips form slits which are narrow enough to diffract the light. Compare Figure 25.4 with Figure 24.3(c) on p. 161.

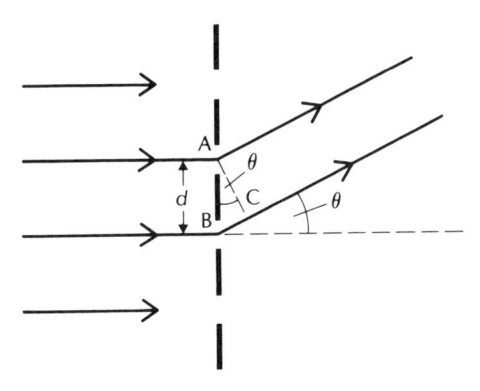

Fig. 25.4

Light is seen only in directions in which the interference is constructive. Since there are so many slits, the interference between any two adjacent slits must be exactly constructive, and so the distance BC in Figure 25.4 must be exactly one wavelength or a whole number of wavelengths. But angle BAC is equal to the angle through which the light has been turned by the grating. Calling this angle θ we see that:

$$BC = AB \sin \theta$$

$$\therefore \quad n\lambda = d \sin \theta$$

where n is a whole number (1 for the first-order spectrum, 2 for the second-order, and so on)
λ is the wavelength of the light
d is the distance apart of adjacent slits in the grating.

The arrangement of the spectra of different orders is shown in Figure 25.5. Notice that the red light is deviated the most; this agrees with the two-slit experiment (p. 164) but it is the opposite of what occurs with a prism (Figure 18.15 on p. 125).

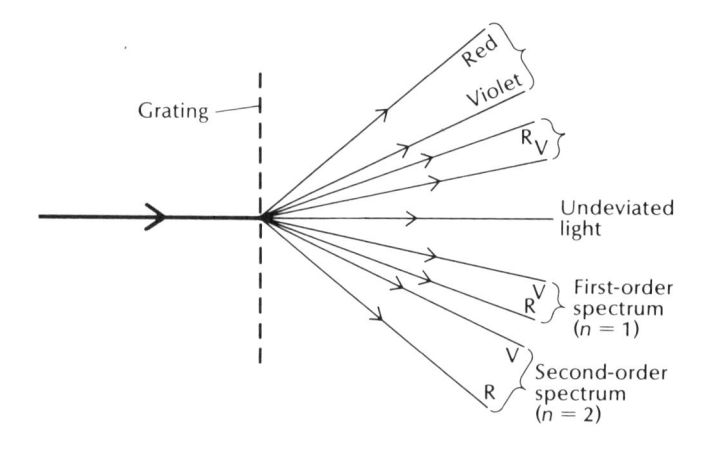

Fig. 25.5

Example 25.1 A grating having 500 lines per millimetre is placed at right angles to a parallel beam of yellow light of wavelength 0.60 µm. Find a) the angle through which the light forming the first-order spectrum is deviated and b) the number of orders that are visible.

Solution a)
$$d = \frac{1}{500} \text{ mm} = 0.002 \text{ mm} = 2 \text{ µm}$$

Working in micrometres:

$$\sin \theta = \frac{n\lambda}{d} = \frac{1 \times 0.6}{2} = 0.3$$

$$\therefore \quad \theta = 17\tfrac{1}{2}°$$

b) Since $\sin \theta$ cannot be greater than 1, the fourth order cannot be seen, for:

$$\frac{n\lambda}{d} = \frac{4 \times 0.60}{2} = 1.2 > 1$$

Thus only three orders are visible.

Note that it is not necessary to change micrometres into decimals of a metre, for if d and λ are both in micrometres their ratio is correct.

The Nature of Light

We have seen that light consists of transverse waves of very short wavelength. Here is a summary of the evidence.

The evidence that light is a wave is:
    that it can interfere (see p. 164),
    that it can be diffracted (see p. 164), and
    that it can be polarised (see p. 166).

The evidence that light is transverse is:
    that it can be polarised.

The evidence that the wavelength of light is very short is:
    that to diffract light appreciably a very narrow slit is needed, and
    that the wavelength can be measured by the two-slit interference method (p. 165) and found to be less than a micrometre.

This does not tell us what a light wave consists of. A water wave is composed of displacements of the water surface; a sound wave is made up of movements of the air or of some other medium, together with the associated pressure changes. But what is light?

The answer is that light, as well as radio waves and the other types listed on p. 170, consists of an electric field and a magnetic field, both of them oscillating at high frequency. These two fields are at right angles to each other and to the direction in which the wave is is travelling. These waves are therefore called 'electromagnetic' waves.

Fluorescence

Some chemical compounds emit light when they absorb waves of shorter wavelength than light, that is, ultra-violet rays or X-rays or gamma rays. This is called **fluorescence**.

To show fluorescence in the laboratory, darken the room and place a clean handkerchief under an ultra-violet lamp. The lamp should shine downwards on to the handkerchief and not into your eyes, because ultra-violet rays are harmful except in small amounts. The handkerchief will probably shine with a bluish light. The reason is that many washing powders contain a fluorescent substance, in order to make clothes washed with them appear as bright as possible when seen by daylight, which contains a small amount of ultra-violet radiation.

The word 'fluorescence' also applies to the emission of light as a result of impact by electrons which happens, for example, in a television tube.

The Complete Spectrum of Electromagnetic Waves

		Approximate wavelength	
RADIO WAVES	Long waves Short waves VHF UHF Microwaves	About a kilometre A few centimetres	↑ Longer wavelength Higher frequency ↓
INFRA-RED RAYS		A millimetre to a micrometre	
LIGHT	Red Orange Yellow Green Blue Violet	A fraction of a micrometre	
ULTRA-VIOLET RAYS		One to a hundred nanometres	
X-RAYS		A fraction of a nanometre	
GAMMA RAYS		Less than $\frac{1}{10}$ nanometre	

How They Are Produced and Detected

	Production	Detection
RADIO WAVES	Aerials connected to electric circuits	
INFRA-RED	Hot bodies such as the Sun or the element of an electric fire	A thermometer with a blackened bulb, or a photo-transistor
LIGHT	Same as infra-red and also same as ultra-violet	The eye or a photographic film
ULTRA-VIOLET	Electric currents in gases (example: fluorescent tube lamp)	Photographic film or fluorescence
X-RAYS	Fast electrons hitting a metal in a vacuum	
GAMMA RAYS	Radioactive nuclei	G–M tube,* etc.

*See p. 237.

Questions on Chapter 25

1. A parallel beam of monochromatic light falls on two narrow parallel slits 0.65 mm apart. The light that passes through the slits falls on a screen 500 mm beyond the slits and forms fringes spaced at two bright fringes per millimetre. Calculate the wavelength of the light.

2. Green light of wavelength 550 nm ($= 550 \times 10^{-9}$ m) is shone on two parallel slits 0.5 mm apart. How far beyond the slits must a screen be placed if the bright fringes formed by interference on the screen are to be 0.5 mm apart?

3. A diffraction grating consists of lines ruled at intervals of 2.0 μm on a glass plate. When monochromatic light falls on it at zero angle of incidence, the light forming the third-order spectrum is deviated through an angle of 64°. What is the wavelength of the light?

4. Light of wavelength 0.50 μm falls at normal incidence on a grating ruled with 800 lines per millimetre. Find the angle of deviation of the light *a*) in the first-order spectrum and *b*) in the second-order spectrum. Also *c*) find whether the third-order spectrum is visible.

Chapter 26

Colour

- The **primary colours** are red, green and blue. The human eye sees other colours as mixtures of these three primary colours. There are many complications in the way the eye works, but it is useful to think of the nerves in the retina as responding in three different ways: red light causes the 'red' response, yellow light causes the 'red' and 'green' responses equally, and so on.

  The 'primary colours' used in painting are different because paints work by subtraction.

- The **secondary colours** are equal mixtures of two primary colours. They are turquoise (or cyan), magenta (or purple), and yellow.

Addition of Colour

The three primary colours may be 'added' on a screen, as shown in Figure 26.1. Secondary colours appear where two primaries overlap, and white appears where all three overlap, provided that the red, green and blue lights are equally strong.

- **Complementary colours** are pairs of colours which produce white light when they are added. Each pair of colours which forms a vertical column in the key to Figure 26.1 is complementary.

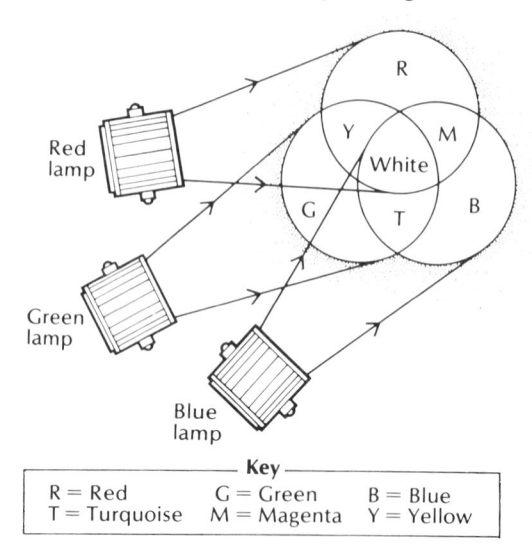

Key:
R = Red   G = Green   B = Blue
T = Turquoise   M = Magenta   Y = Yellow

Fig. 26.1

Subtraction of Colour

A secondary filter (for example, a piece of yellow glass) subtracts one primary colour from white light — or from any other kind of light — which passes through it.

- A turquoise filter stops red light.
- A magenta filter stops green light.
- A yellow filter stops blue light.

The effect of overlapping three secondary filters is shown in Figure 26.2.

Overlapping secondary filters seen against a bright background

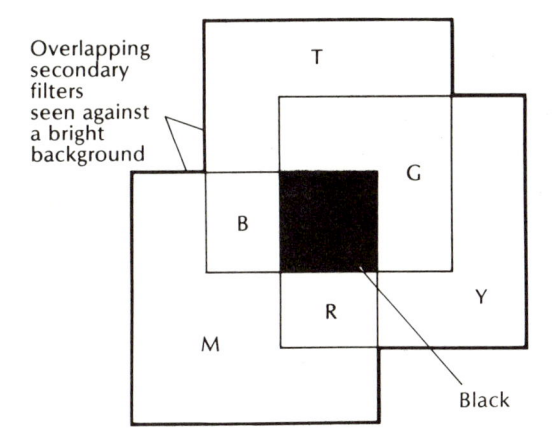

Fig. 26.2

Example 26.1 What colour does an actor's magenta coat appear under yellow stage lighting?

Solution This is a case of subtraction; the magenta dye in the coat stops green light instead of reflecting it. So from the colour subtraction diagram, where magenta and yellow overlap, the answer is red.

Note that the answer to Example 26.1 would have been different if yellow sodium lighting had been used. Yellow stage lighting is white light from which the blue and violet have been removed by a yellow filter, and so it is a mixture of red, orange, yellow and green. Sodium lighting is monochromatic — one wavelength only — and so objects under sodium light can only appear yellow, or dim yellow which is brown, or black.

Section E:
ELECTRICITY AND MAGNETISM

Lightning — a hundred-million volt spark.

Chapter 27

Charge

When you take off a shirt or a pullover it may become sufficiently 'charged' to cling to you. If you rub the barrel of a pen on your sleeve you may be able to pick up little bits of paper with it. To study this effect in the laboratory, use a rod made of an insulator such as Perspex, acetate, glass or polythene. Rub the rod with a cloth and hang it up as shown in Figure 27.1, and then rub another rod and hold it near to the suspended rod. If both rods are clean and dry, they will either attract or repel each other. The drying is especially important if you use a glass rod because glass tends to attract a thin film of moisture which allows the charge to leak away.

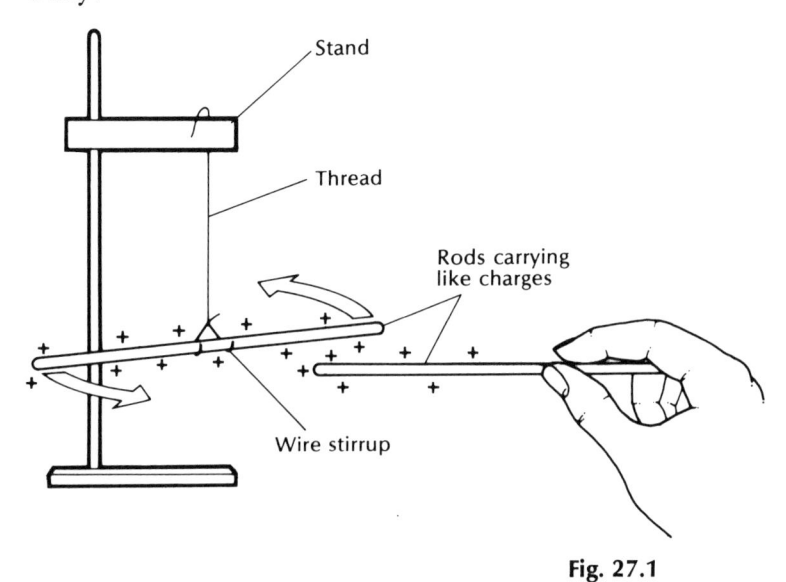

Fig. 27.1

You can find by this method that there are two kinds of charge. They have been given the names *positive* and *negative*. The kinds of charge produced are:

    on Perspex, acetate or glass   positive,
    on polythene   negative,
    on the cloth   opposite from the rod.

The rules for attraction and repulsion are:

    like charges   (both + or both −)   repel,
    unlike charges (one + and one −)   attract.

What Electric Charge Is

When it was first decided which kind of charge to call positive and which to call negative, no one knew what charge was. Later, J. J. Thomson discovered electrons; he did this by means of experiments in which electrons travel through a vacuum as they do in a television tube. We now know that every atom consists of a cloud of electrons surrounding a very small, very dense nucleus. The electrons are negatively charged and the nucleus contains protons which are positively charged; if there are equal numbers of both, the whole atom is uncharged.* When we rub an acetate rod with a cloth, electrons are transferred from the rod to the cloth, but they go the other way if the rod is made of polythene.

A **positive** charge is a **lack** of electrons; a positively charged body contains fewer electrons than protons.

A **negative** charge is a **surplus** of electrons; a negatively charged body contains more electrons than protons.

An uncharged body contains equal numbers of electrons and protons.

Induced Charge

If a charged Perspex rod A is brought near to an uncharged conductor B (Figure 27.2(a)), the electrons in B are attracted towards the Perspex rod. There are then opposite charges on the two sides of B, a surplus of electrons on one side and a lack of electrons on

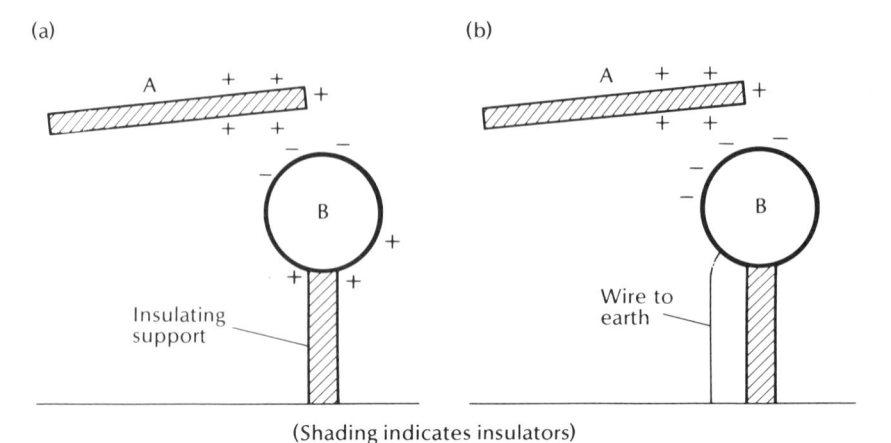

(Shading indicates insulators)

Fig. 27.2

*The nucleus also contains neutrons — except in the case of hydrogen — but these have no charge and so they do not concern us in this chapter.

the other. These are called 'induced charges'. This assumes that B is insulated from earth; if it is earthed (Figure 27.2(b)) the positive induced charge will escape down the earthing wire — that is, electrons will come up the wire from earth.

This explains why a charged body attracts an uncharged one and is attracted by it. The unlike induced charge is nearer and causes a stronger attraction, but the like induced charge, being on the far side of the body, is further away and so causes a weaker repulsion. The total effect is therefore an attraction.

Action of Points

When a conducting body is charged, the charge remains entirely on the surface of the body and is more concentrated on the more convex areas. At a point, such as the pointed end of a rod, it may be so concentrated that some of it is given to the surrounding air, which is then repelled and moves away from the point, carrying away charge and so discharging the body. This is called an 'electric wind'.

This can happen just as well with a positive charge as with a negative one. In this case what happens at the point is that electrons are transferred from the air to the body; this leaves the air positively charged, and it is repelled and moves away, the effect being to reduce the positive charge on the body.

To avoid this effect, bodies which are intended to hold a charge are designed with rounded corners and no points.

■ The **Van de Graaff generator** uses an electric wind. It is a device for producing high voltages, from perhaps 100 kilovolts for a small version up to several megavolts in the case of a large machine. Some of its features are shown in Figure 27.3. The lower roller is charged by contact with the belt by the same process which charges a rod when it is rubbed with a cloth. The charge on the roller causes an induced charge on the lower points, and an electric wind carries this charge from the points on to the belt. The belt carries the charge up to the top of the machine where it is transferred to the top terminal by an electric wind from another set of points. The top terminal is well rounded so that it does not easily lose charge.

Van de Graaff generators can be designed to produce either positive or negative voltages and so the charges may be the opposite of those shown in Figure 27.3. Large generators may use a power pack to charge the lower points, instead of relying on induction.

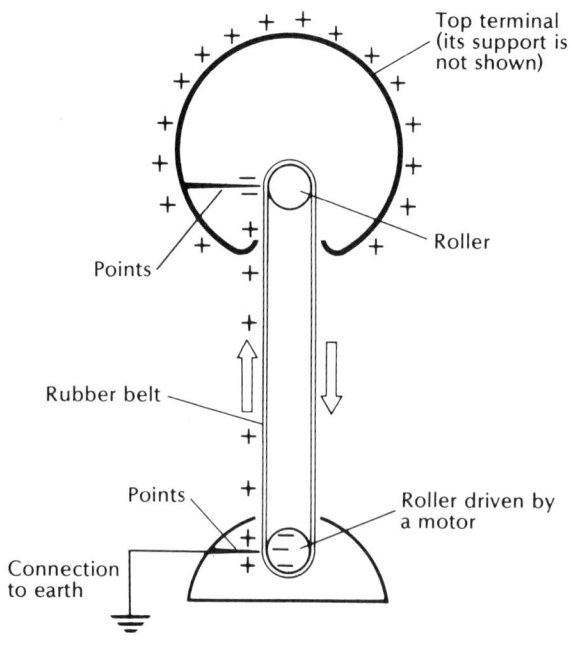

SOME OF THE FEATURES OF A
VAN DE GRAAFF GENERATOR

Fig. 27.3

The Leaf Electroscope

An electroscope is an instrument for indicating an electric charge and the leaf type is probably the best known and one of the simplest. Figure 27.4(a) shows it as it appears when it is charged; when it is uncharged, the leaf hangs vertically, close to the bottom end of the rod.

If you touch a charged conductor on to the top plate of an uncharged electroscope, some of the charge is transferred to the

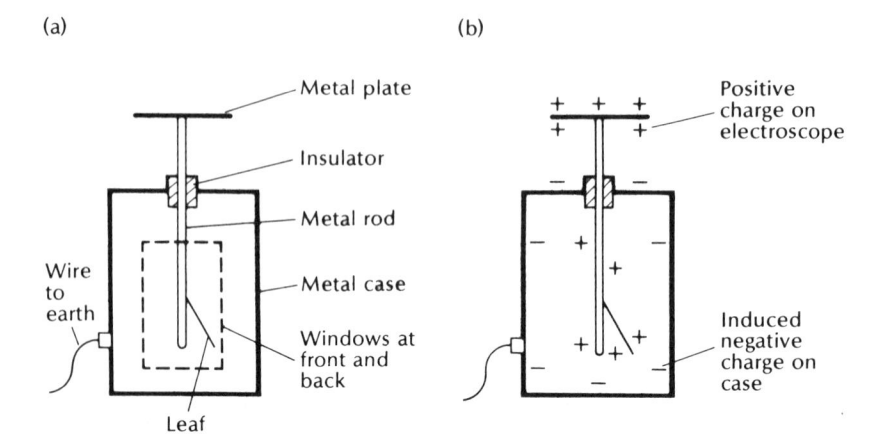

Fig. 27.4

electroscope and some of this flows down to the bottom end of the rod and the leaf (Figure 27.4(b)). The leaf then rises because it is repelled by the rod. Leaves of electroscopes used to be made of gold because it can be beaten thin enough to be very light and flexible, but nowadays an alloy is used as it is cheaper.

When a charged body is brought near to an uncharged electroscope, the leaf rises because of the induced charges (Figure 27.5(a)). This can be used to test the sign of a charge; one method of doing this is described below.

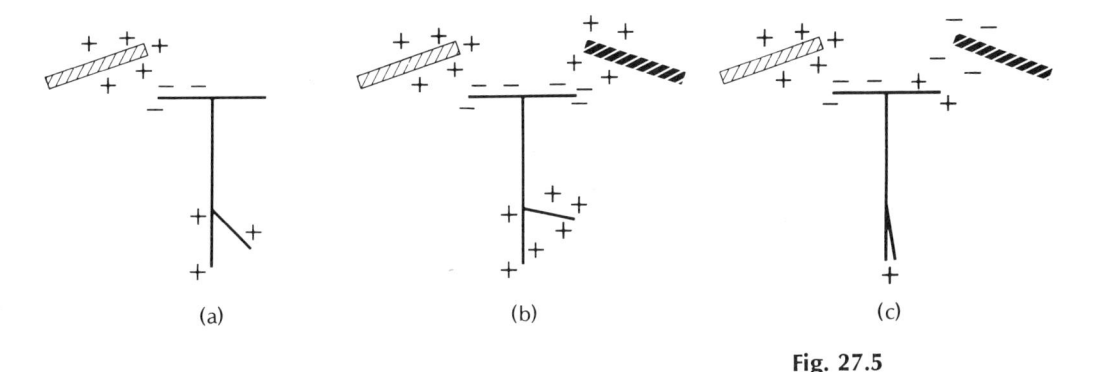

Fig. 27.5

Rub a Perspex rod with a cloth and bring it near to the electroscope. Since the rod is Perspex, its charge is known to be positive and so the charges are as marked on Figure 27.5(a).

Bring the object to be tested near to the electroscope without removing the Perspex rod. If the unknown charge is positive it causes the leaf to rise further, as shown in Figure 27.5(b). If the unknown charge is negative, the effect of it on the electroscope cancels or partly cancels the effect of the Perspex rod. The leaf therefore falls, as in Figure 27.5(c).

Faraday's Ice-pail Experiment

This was an early quantitative experiment in electrostatics which was carried out with a gold leaf electroscope; it proved that an induced charge is equal in magnitude to the charge which induces it.* Faraday first lowered a charged sphere into a bucket which stood on an electroscope, causing a distribution of charges as shown in Figure 27.6. He then found that when he touched the sphere A on the inside of the bucket B the leaf did not move; this

---

*In Figures 27.2, 27.3 and 27.5 the induced charge is shown as being smaller than the inducing charge. This is because there is more induced charge, not shown in the diagrams, on the bench and on the experimenter's body and on the walls of the room, and it is the *total* induced charge which equals the inducing charge.

Fig. 27.6

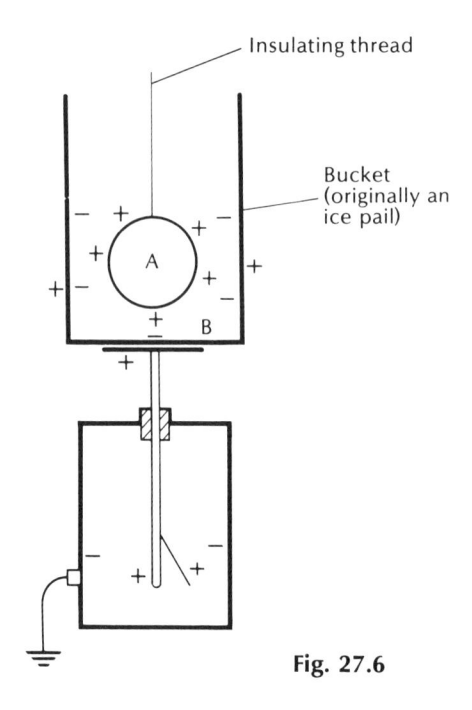

showed that the charge on the outside of the bucket had neither increased nor decreased. Therefore the charges on A and B must have cancelled each other out exactly with no charge left over, and so they must have been equal in magnitude.

SI Unit of Charge

The SI unit of charge is the **coulomb**. This is much bigger than the charges that we have been considering; the charge on a gold leaf electroscope is likely to be only a few nanocoulomb. The coulomb is defined from the ampere, as explained on the next page.

Chapter 28

Current and Voltage

Electric current is a flow of charge. In metals it is a flow of electrons, since they are the only charged particles which are free to move, the protons being fixed in the nuclei. Since electrons are negative charges, the electron flow is in the opposite direction from the current, as shown in Figure 28.1

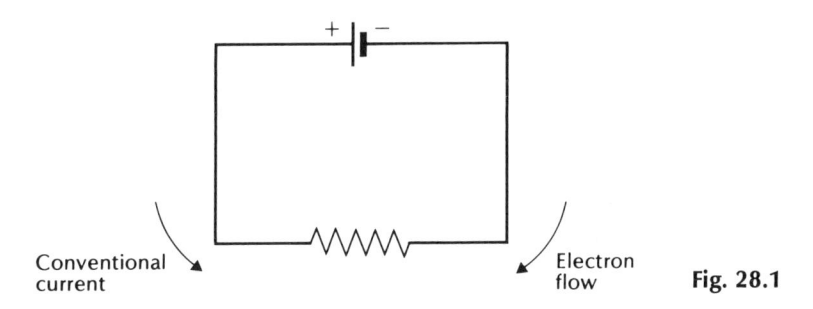

Conventional current　　　　Electron flow　　Fig. 28.1

- The **ampere** (A) is the SI unit of current. The ampere is defined in terms of electromagnetic forces and its definition is given on p. 221, after the section on magnetic fields. The coulomb is defined from the ampere.

- A **coulomb** is the charge which passes *a point* in one second when a current of one ampere is flowing.

$$Q = It$$

where　Q is the charge that passes　　　　(in C)
　　　　I is the current　　　　　　　　　(in A)
　　　　t is the time during which the current flows　(in s)

It may help you to picture what a coulomb is, and how it is related to the ampere, if you remember that:

- a coulomb is a certain number of electrons (or rather, for a positive charge, the lack of them);

- an ampere is a certain number of electrons per second passing a point in a circuit.
  (The number referred to is actually 6.25×10^{18}.)

The current is the same all round a circuit, if the currents in parallel branches are added together. In Figure 28.2:

$$I_1 = I_2 + I_3 = I_4$$

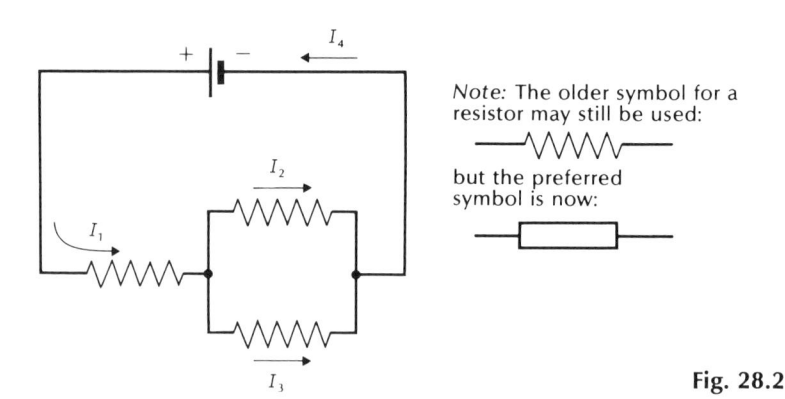

Note: The older symbol for a resistor may still be used:

—⋀⋁⋀⋁—

but the preferred symbol is now:

—▭—

Fig. 28.2

Voltage

Electrons repel each other, and they are attracted by the protons which are fixed in the nuclei. In many cases all the forces acting on an electron will cancel out, giving zero resultant, but in other cases they will not exactly balance and a resultant force will act on the electron. Then if the electron moves, some energy will be released or else energy will be needed to make it move.

■ When a movement of charge from one point to some other point either releases energy or requires it, there is a **potential difference** (p.d.) between the points. For example, in Figure 27.2(b), energy is released if an electron is carried from B to A, but it requires energy to carry an electron from A to B; there is a potential difference between A and B. In Figure 28.3, electrons are passing from A through the battery to B and, to make them do this, energy is being supplied from the chemical energy stored in the battery. This energy is needed to move them towards B against the repulsive forces of the electrons which are already at B. Electrons are also passing from B through the resistor to A and this releases energy, which appears as heat in the resistor.

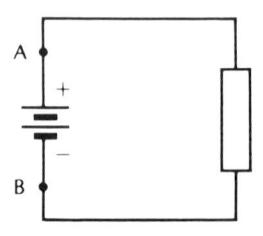

Fig. 28.3

Current and Voltage

■ A **volt** is the potential difference between two points if it needs one joule of energy to move one coulomb of charge from one point to the other.

$$\text{Energy} = \text{p.d.} \times \text{Charge}$$
$$W = V \times Q$$

where W, standing for 'work', is the amount of energy.

Now imagine this movement to take place in exactly one second. Since a joule per second is a watt, and a coulomb per second is an ampere, we get another, equally acceptable definition of the volt:

■ A **volt** is the potential difference between two points if it needs one watt of power to maintain a current of one ampere flowing from one point to the other.

$$\text{Power} = \text{p.d.} \times \text{Current}$$
$$P = V \times I$$

or, less correctly but perhaps easier to remember:

$$\text{Watts equals volts times amps.}$$

Quick Question 36 | What current does a 60 W light bulb take from 240 V mains?

Potential differences add up round a circuit. In Figure 28.4:

$$V_1 + V_2 + V_3 = V_4$$

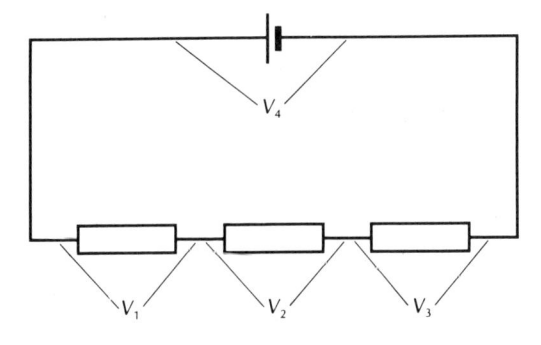

Fig. 28.4

The Potentiometer

Two potential differences may be compared by using a potentiometer. The circuit is shown in Figure 28.5. To compare the p.d. between the terminals of one cell with that of another cell, connect each cell in turn at C. Each time, find the balance point, B, where the resistance wire can be touched with the movable contact without causing any deflection of the galvanometer, and measure the length AB. Then:

$$\frac{V_1}{V_2} = \frac{AB_1}{AB_2}$$

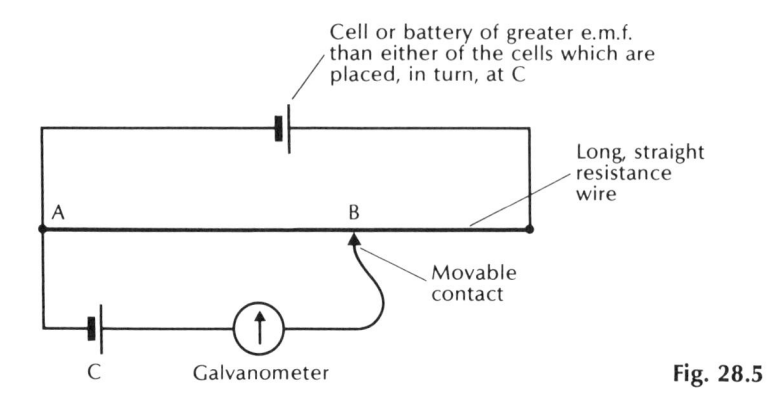

Fig. 28.5

Ohm's Law

Ohm's law states that:

> The current flowing through a conductor is proportional to the potential difference between its ends provided that the temperature does not change.

This can be written:

$$V \propto I \quad (T \text{ constant})$$

Ohm's law is not universally true, though it happens to be true to a high degree of accuracy for most metallic conductors, both pure metals and alloys, and for some non-metallic conductors as well.

The Water Analogy

To grasp the ideas of current and voltage it is helpful to compare electric circuits with water circuits (see Figure 28.6). An example of a water circuit is a central heating system. If it is in a large, single-storey building the circulation may be caused by a pump, instead of by natural convection, and then the circuit corresponds more closely to an electric circuit containing a battery.

The water current might be measured in litres per second, or for a small laboratory model it could be in cm^3 per second; this corresponds to the electric current in amperes, which are coulombs per second.

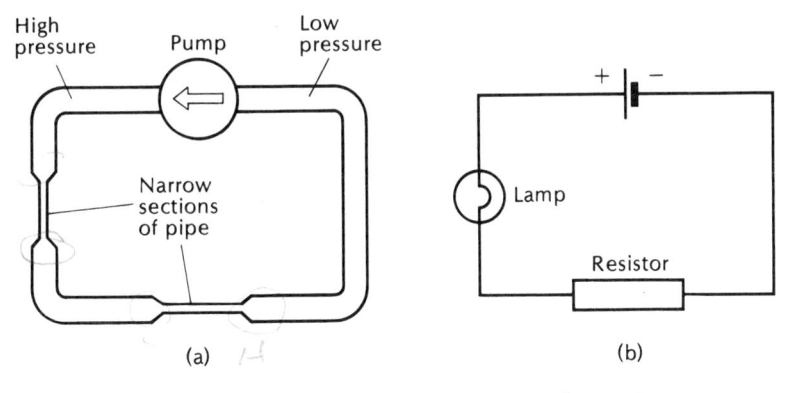

Fig. 28.6

The narrow sections of the water pipe do not let water pass through so easily as the wider pipes of the rest of the circuit. These narrow sections represent parts of the electric circuit which impede the flow of electric current; these are called 'resistors'. Lamps and electric heating elements are special kinds of resistor.

The potential difference between the two ends of a resistor is represented by the pressure difference between the two ends of the narrow section of pipe. To measure this pressure difference a gauge similar to the type shown in Figure 28.7(a) would be suitable; notice two things about it:

- it needs to be connected to both sides of the narrow section of tube, and
- it lets hardly any water current pass through itself.

These facts are both true in the electrical case.

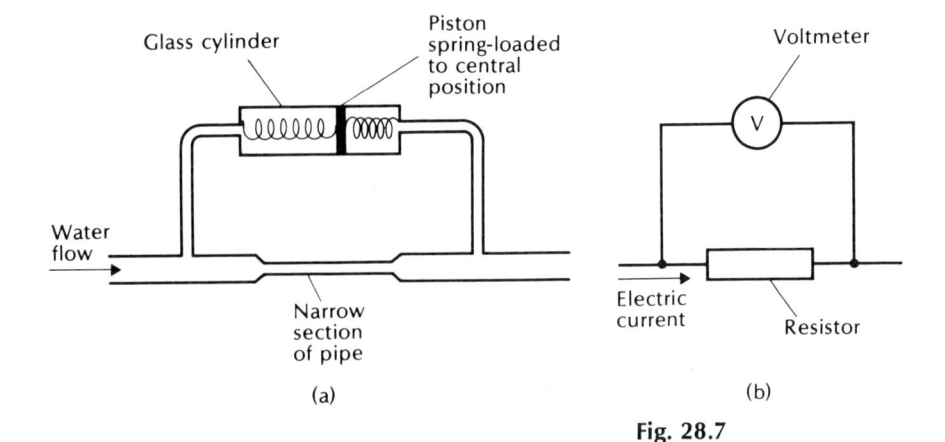

Fig. 28.7

The water analogy can be extended to many other types of circuit. For example, the diodes that we will meet on p. 204 correspond to non-return valves for water, like the valves shown in Figure 8.6 on p. 61.

Questions on Chapter 28

1. The charge on one electron is (minus) 1.6×10^{-19} C. How many electrons pass each point in a wire when a current of one microampere flows for 1 s? (For the meaning of 'micro' see p. 248.)

2. A torch bulb takes a current of 0.3 A. What charge passes through it when it is turned on for 5 s?

3. What is the power of a torch bulb rated at 3 V, 0.3 A?

4. The work done in moving an electric charge of one coulomb from one point P on a wire to another point Q on the same wire is 2.5 J.
   a) What is the potential difference between points P and Q?
   b) Calculate the work done in transferring a charge of 300 C from P to Q.
   c) 300 C flow from P to Q as a steady current of 0.5 A, calculate
      (i) the time taken for 300 C to move from P to Q,
      (ii) the rate at which work is done. (C)

5. A light bulb is marked '240 V 60 W', meaning that it is designed to take a power of 60 W from 240 V mains. What current does it take?

6. An electric fire works on 240 V mains and has three bars, each bar being rated at a power of 1 kW. What current does the fire use when all three bars are switched on?

7. A typical lightning flash carries a charge of 20 C across a potential difference of 10^8 V. Neglecting any change of p.d. that may take place during the flash, calculate the amount of energy expended. If all this energy could be stored and used to run a 1 kW electric fire, for how long would it last?

8. A Van de Graaff generator produces sparks between its top terminal and an earthed sphere. Each spark carries a charge of $2 \, \mu C$. Assuming that the potential difference between the top terminal and earth remains constant at 200 kV, find the amount of energy transformed in each spark.

9. The balance point of a potentiometer is 900 mm from the end A of the wire (as marked in Figure 28.5) when a dry cell of voltage 1.50 V is connected as the cell under test. When a Daniell cell is put in place of the dry cell, the new balance point is 660 mm from A. What is the voltage of the Daniell cell?

Chapter 29

Resistance

In cases where Ohm's law is true we have:

$$V \propto I$$

or $\qquad V = IR$

where R is constant
$\qquad V$ is the potential difference $\qquad$ (in V)
$\qquad I$ is the current $\qquad$ (in A)

R is called the 'resistance' and is measured in ohms.

■ An **ohm** is the resistance of a conductor which has a potential difference of one volt between its ends when a current of one ampere is flowing through it. The symbol for an ohm is Ω (the Greek capital letter 'omega').

Quick Question 37

a) What is the resistance of a resistor which lets through a current of 4 A when a p.d. of 240 V is applied to it?
b) A high-value resistor passes a current of 1 mA when the voltage applied to it is 1 kV. What is its resistance? (For the prefixes on the units, see p. 247.)

The obvious method of measuring resistance is by taking readings of p.d. and current. That method is given next, and it is followed by a different method which is more suitable for measuring higher values of resistance.

Measurement of Resistance by Ammeter and Voltmeter

The circuit for this is shown in Figure 29.1. Before the battery is connected into the circuit, the variable resistor should be set to maximum resistance to make sure that there will not be a large current which might damage the ammeter; this resistor setting should not be reduced without keeping an eye on the ammeter reading to see that the current does not become excessive.

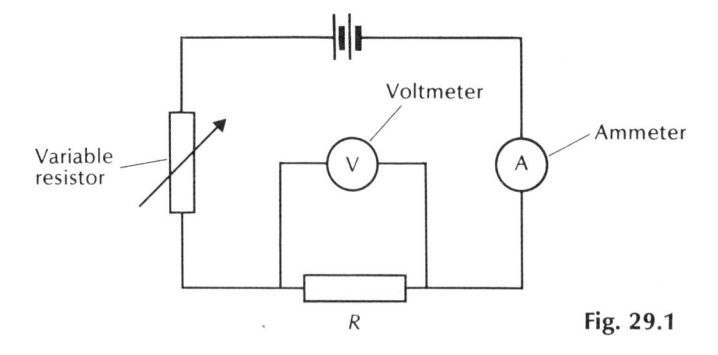

Fig. 29.1

To use the circuit, alter the setting of the variable resistor several times, taking readings from the voltmeter and ammeter each time. This is a suitable form of table heading:

V/V	I/A	$\dfrac{V}{I} = R/\Omega$

The values of R in the last column should then be averaged.*

An alternative way of using the readings is to plot a graph of V against I (Figure 29.2). This would give a straight line through the origin if there were no errors. Draw the straight line through the origin which most nearly fits all the points; the gradient of this line is the resistance.

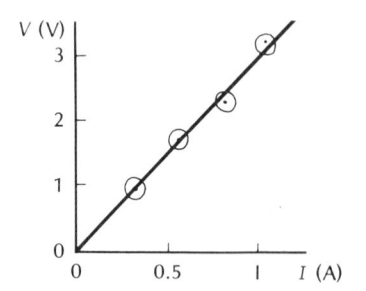

Fig. 29.2

If you measure the resistance of a lamp by this method, the values of R in the third column of the table will all be different and if you plot a graph it will be curved. This is because the resistance of a lamp filament is greater when it is hotter. To find the resistance of the lamp under its normal working conditions, set the variable resistor until the voltmeter indicates the correct working voltage of the lamp.

---

*Note that 'V/V' means 'V measured in volts', 'I/A' means 'I measured in amperes', and so on. The older notation 'V(V)' and 'I(A)' may still be met.

Measurement of Resistance by Substitution

The circuit is shown in Figure 29.3. The outline of the method is this:

(i) With the unknown resistor at R, read the meter.

(ii) Remove the unknown resistor and put a dial-type resistance box in its place at R.

(iii) Adjust the resistance box until the meter reading is the same as before.

(iv) Read the setting of the resistance box, which is equal to the value of the unknown resistor.

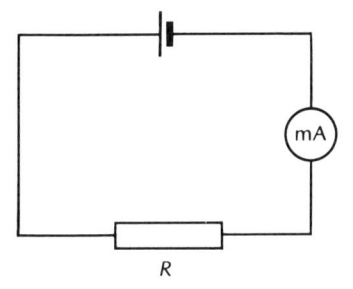

Fig. 29.3

This method is suitable for rather larger resistances than the previous experiment and that is why a milliammeter is likely to be suitable, rather than an ammeter. This makes it all the more necessary to ensure that the current is not large enough to damage the meter. These precautions should be taken:

- At the beginning of the experiment, connect the resistance box in series in the circuit, ensuring that it is already set to maximum resistance, and then reduce its setting to zero by stages while watching the meter.
- Set the resistance box to its maximum resistance again before removing the unknown resistance.

Resistors in Series and in Parallel

To find the effective resistance of a combination of resistors, if they are **in series**, add the separate values to find the resistance of the combination. For example, in Figure 29.4 the combined resistance is 6 Ω.

Fig. 29.4

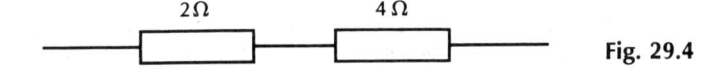

If the resistors are in parallel, add the values of $\frac{1}{R}$ to find $\frac{1}{\text{Combined resistance}}$. In Figure 29.5:

$$\frac{1}{2} + \frac{1}{4} = \frac{3}{4} = \frac{1}{\text{Combined resistance}}$$

∴ Combined resistance $= \frac{4}{3}\,\Omega = 1\tfrac{1}{3}\,\Omega$

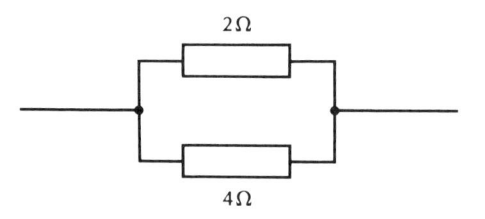

Fig. 29.5

Quick Question 38

Three resistors have values of 20 Ω, 20 Ω and 40 Ω respectively. What is the resistance of the combination when all three are connected a) in series and b) in parallel?

Ammeters and Voltmeters

The instrument which forms the basis of most electrical measurements is the **galvanometer**; we will see how it works on p. 218. A typical galvanometer may need a few milliamperes of current to move the pointer to full-scale deflection.

■ To convert the meter into an **ammeter** to measure bigger currents, add a *shunt*, that is, a low resistance connected in parallel. The resulting combination has a low resistance and for many purposes we can assume that an ammeter has zero resistance.

Example 29.1 A galvanometer has a resistance of 20 Ω and reads up to 10 mA. How can it be changed into an ammeter reading to 1 A?

Solution When the pointer is at full-scale deflection:

10 mA goes through the meter,

∴ 990 mA goes through the shunt. (See Fig. 29.6)

So the shunt takes a 99 times greater current and therefore has a 99 times smaller resistance.

$$\therefore \quad \text{Resistance of required shunt} = \frac{20}{99} \Omega = 0.202 \, \Omega$$

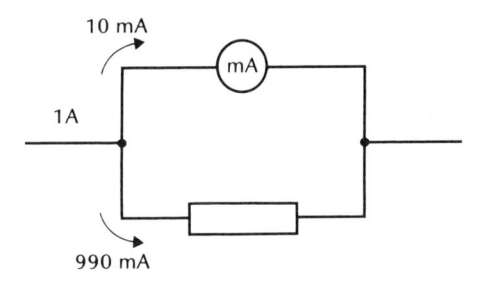

Fig. 29.6

■ To convert the galvanometer into a **voltmeter**, add a *series resistor* (sometimes called a 'multiplier') of fairly high resistance. The resulting combination has a high resistance and for many purposes we can assume that a voltmeter has an infinite resistance and that no current flows through it.

Example 29.2 How can the galvanometer mentioned in the last example be turned into a voltmeter reading to 10 V?

Solution Applying $V = IR$ to the whole meter including the series resistor (see Fig. 29.7) gives:

$$10 = \frac{10}{1000} \times R$$

$$\therefore \quad R = 1000 \, \Omega$$

This includes the resistance of the galvanometer. Subtracting that gives the required resistance, which is:

$$1000 - 20 = 980 \, \Omega$$

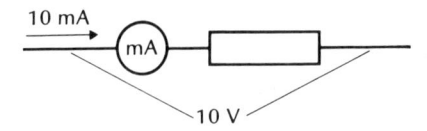

Fig. 29.7

Quick Question 39 A galvanometer gives full-scale deflection when a current of 100 µA passes through it, and its resistance is 100 Ω. How can it be converted into a) a voltmeter reading up to 1 V, and b) an ammeter reading up to 1 A?

Resistivity

The resistance of a wire depends on its length and thickness as well as on the material it is made of. To compare different materials, leaving out the effects of length and thickness, we use their resistivities.

■ The **resistivity** of a material is the resistance which a sample of it would have if its length was 1 m and its area of cross-section was 1 m². The resistance of a wire is related to its resistivity by the equation:

$$R = \frac{\rho l}{A}$$

where R is the resistance of the wire   (in Ω)
ρ is the resistivity of the material   (in $\Omega\,m$)
l is the length   (in m)
A is the area of cross-section   (in m²)

Quick Question 40

If a metal wire is stretched so that its length is doubled and its area of cross-section is halved, what happens to its resistance? Assume that straining the wire does not alter its resistivity.

Conductors are materials with low resistivities, such as metals.

Semiconductors, such as silicon, have considerably higher resistivities.

Insulators are materials with extremely high resistivities, such as glass, rubber and most plastics.

The resistivity of a metal increases if the temperature rises. This means, for example, that the filament of a lamp has a much higher resistance when the lamp is on than it has when the filament is cold. Semiconductors behave in the opposite way; their resistivities decrease if the temperature rises. A **thermistor** is a resistor which is made of a semiconductor material so that its resistance will be lower when it is hot.

Questions on Chapter 29

1 What is the resistance of:
a) a low-voltage heater which takes a current of 4 A from a 20 V supply,

Resistance

    b) a light bulb which takes a current of 0.5 A from 240 V mains,
    c) a resistor which, when connected to a p.d. of 2 kV, lets through a current of 100 mA?

2 What current will pass through:
    a) a 5 Ω resistor which is connected to a 12 V supply,
    b) a heating coil with a resistance of 2 Ω when the p.d. across it is 15 V,
    c) a 1 MΩ resistor when a voltage of 1 kV is applied to it?

3 A 12 V 24 W lamp and a thermistor and an ammeter are connected in series. Voltmeters are connected across the lamp and the thermistor as shown in the circuit diagram (Figure 29.8). Two different currents are passed round the circuit in turn and these readings are taken.

	Ammeter reading/A	Reading of V_1/V	Reading of V_2/V
First time	0.1	0.15	1.0
Second time	2.0	12.0	2.0

    a) By what factor did the resistance of the lamp increase from the first time to the second time?
    b) By what factor did the resistance of the thermistor decrease?

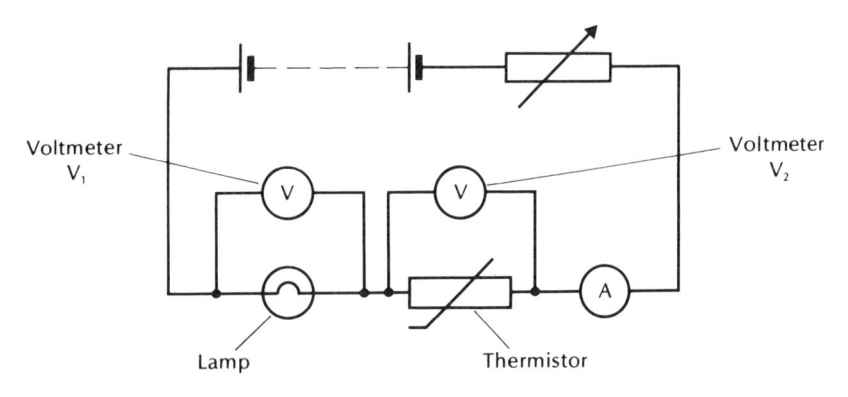

Fig. 29.8

4 What is the combined resistance of a 2 Ω resistor and a 3 Ω resistor connected a) in series with each other, b) in parallel?

5 What is the combined resistance of a 500 Ω resistor and a 1 kΩ resistor a) in series and b) in parallel?

6 What is the combined resistance of three resistors of values 100 Ω, 200 Ω and 300 Ω a) all in series and b) all in parallel?

7 If three 10 Ω resistors are available, by using combinations of two or all three of them it is possible to make up six other resistance values in addition to 10 Ω. What are the six values?

8 How can a galvanometer of resistance 10 Ω which reads up to 5 mA be converted into *a)* a voltmeter reading to 5 V, *b)* an ammeter reading to 2 A?

9 A galvanometer reads up to 1 mA and has a resistance of 40 Ω. How can it be turned into *a)* a voltmeter reading to 10 V and *b)* a milliammeter reading to 500 mA?

10 An ammeter reads up to 2 A and has a resistance of 0.10 Ω. How can it be converted into a 4 A meter?

11 Calculate the resistance of a 10 m length of wire of cross-sectional area 1 mm² made of constantan, which has a resistivity of 0.50 $\mu\Omega$ m (or 5.0×10^{-7} Ω m).

12 The resistivity of aluminium is 2.5×10^{-8} Ω m. If some aluminium strip is 10 mm wide and 0.10 mm thick, find *a)* the resistance of one metre of this strip and *b)* the length of this strip which has a resistance of one ohm.

13 An electric filament lamp is marked '240 V 120 W'. Calculate the lamp resistance when in normal use. How many such lamps could be used in parallel across a source of 240 V which is protected by a 2 A fuse? (SUJB)

Chapter 30

Cells, Circuits and Energy

Cells

A cell converts chemical energy into electrical energy. Two or more cells connected together are called a battery. A *primary cell* is one which cannot have its supply of energy renewed except by

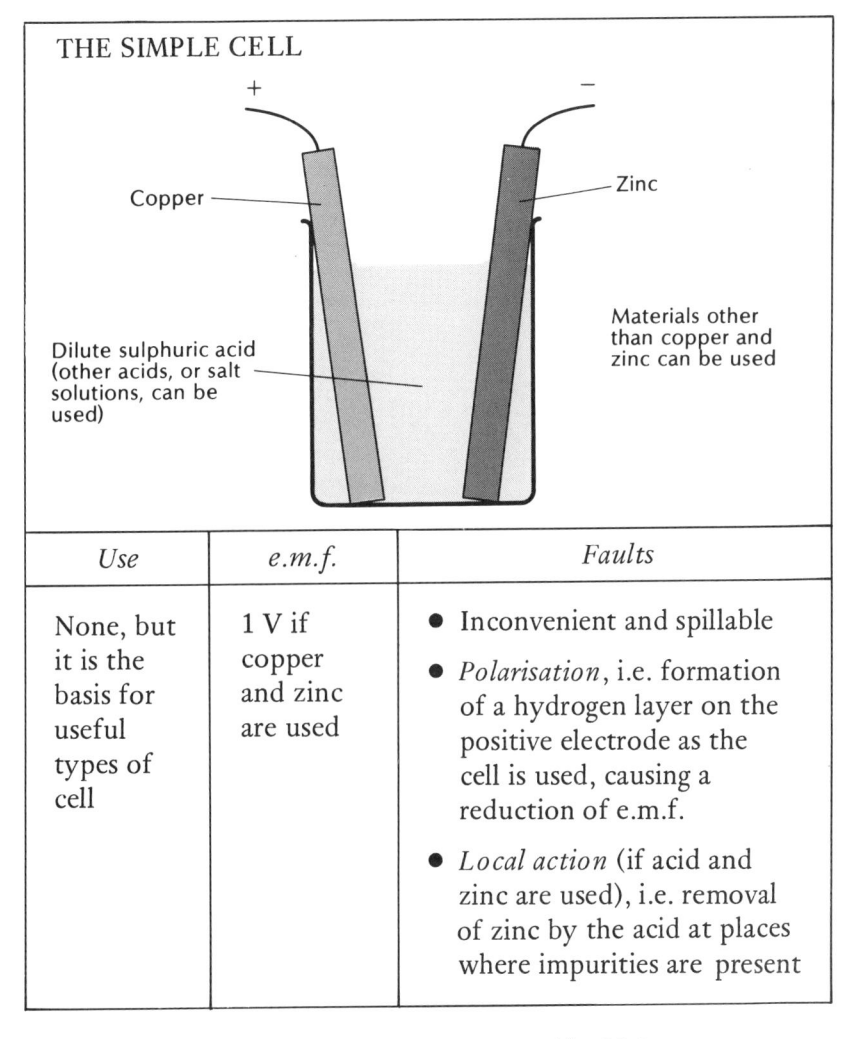

	THE SIMPLE CELL	
Use	*e.m.f.*	*Faults*
None, but it is the basis for useful types of cell	1 V if copper and zinc are used	• Inconvenient and spillable • *Polarisation*, i.e. formation of a hydrogen layer on the positive electrode as the cell is used, causing a reduction of e.m.f. • *Local action* (if acid and zinc are used), i.e. removal of zinc by the acid at places where impurities are present

Fig. 30.1

THE DRY CELL (Dry Leclanché cell)

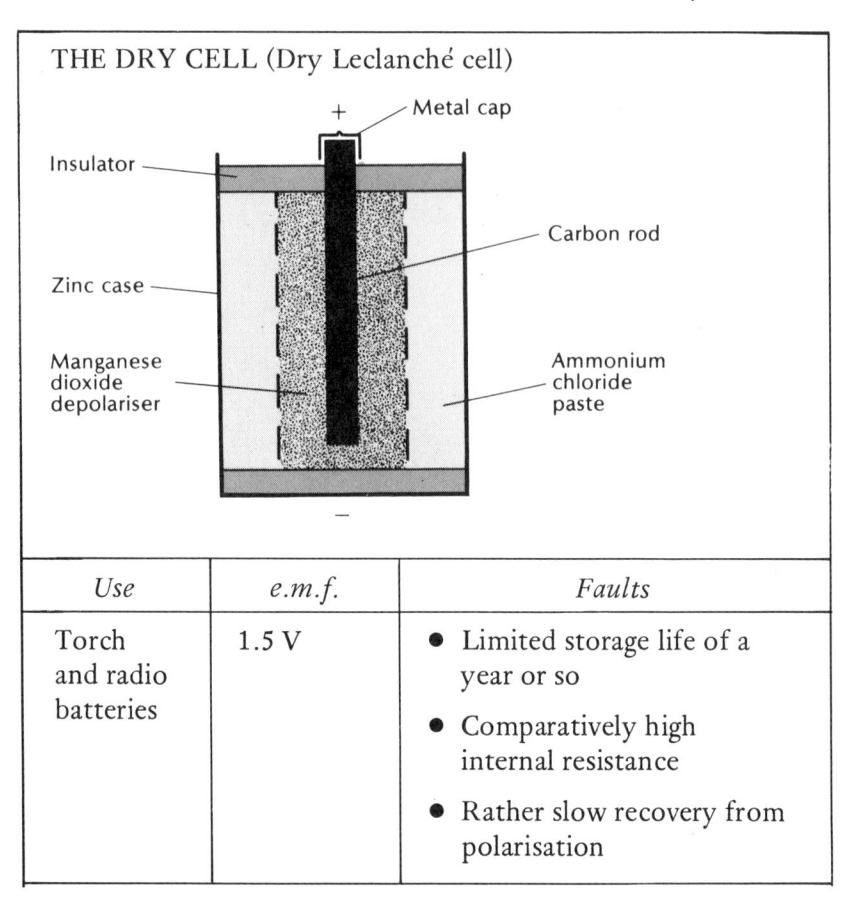

Labels: Metal cap (+), Insulator, Carbon rod, Zinc case, Manganese dioxide depolariser, Ammonium chloride paste

Use	e.m.f.	Faults
Torch and radio batteries	1.5 V	• Limited storage life of a year or so • Comparatively high internal resistance • Rather slow recovery from polarisation

Fig. 30.2

renewing the chemical ingredients. The first two types of cell given in Figures 30.1 and 30.2 are primary cells. A *secondary cell* on the other hand can be re-charged by passing a current through it in the reverse direction. A circuit to do this is shown in Figure 31.9. A secondary cell is also called an 'accumulator', and a common type is the lead–acid accumulator shown in Figure 30.3.

The **care of accumulators** consists of:

- charging after use;
- charging at intervals of a few weeks if they have not been used;
- ensuring that the charging current agrees with the manufacturer's directions;
- topping up the liquid level as necessary with distilled water to replace losses due to evaporation and electrolysis.

In the case of a car battery, the charging and the regulation of the charging current to the correct value are done automatically when the engine is running.

THE LEAD–ACID ACCUMULATOR

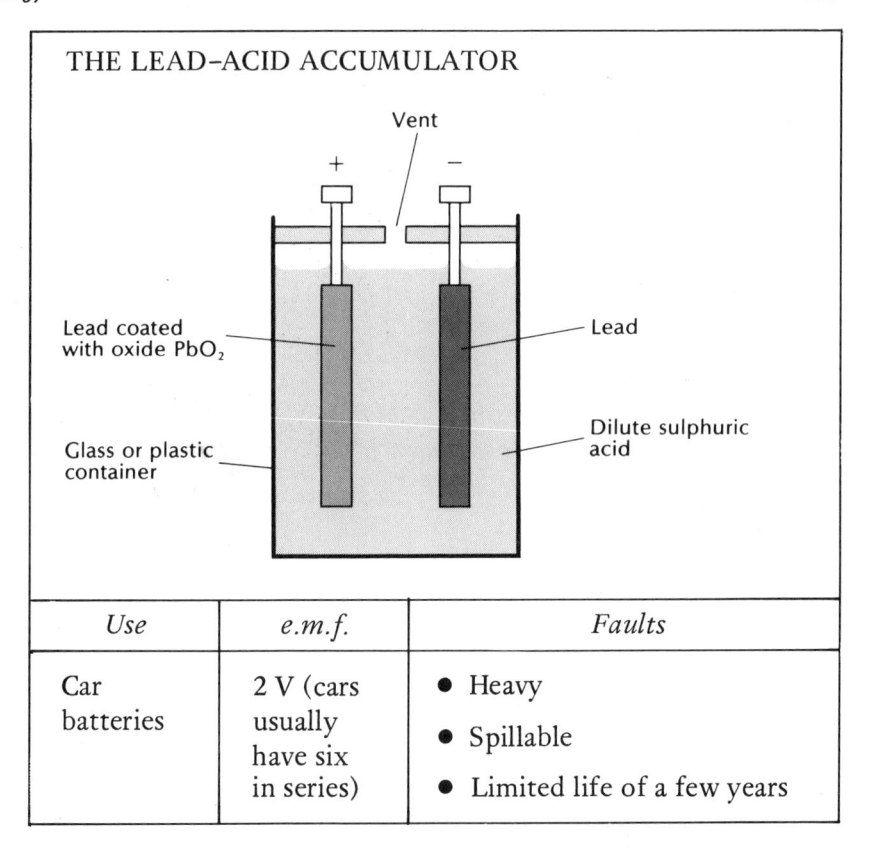

Labels: Vent; +; −; Lead coated with oxide PbO_2; Lead; Glass or plastic container; Dilute sulphuric acid

Use	e.m.f.	Faults
Car batteries	2 V (cars usually have six in series)	• Heavy • Spillable • Limited life of a few years

Fig. 30.3

The size of an accumulator is given as an 'ampere-hour capacity'. For example, a 30 ampere-hour accumulator can deliver a current of 1 A for 30 hours or 3 A for 10 hours, if it is fully charged at the start. If it is re-charged at 3 A, it will need more than 10 hours to become fully charged again because some energy is lost as heat; its efficiency is less than 1.

Electromotive Force

The potential difference between the terminals of a cell or battery when no current is flowing through it is called its 'electromotive force' (e.m.f.). When the battery is supplying a current, the p.d. is decreased — think of a car's lights dimming while the starter takes a big current. If a current is sent through the battery in the other direction, as when charging an accumulator, the p.d. is greater than the e.m.f.

The accepted definition of e.m.f. is this: the electromotive force in a circuit is the amount of energy transformed when unit charge (one coulomb) moves right round the circuit. For example, if a battery with an e.m.f. of 6 V drives a lamp, then for each coulomb that goes round the circuit 6 J of chemical energy in the battery is transformed into internal energy, mostly in the bulb but also partly in the connecting wires and in the battery itself.

Circuit Calculations

To apply the equation $V = IR$ to a complete circuit:
(i) use the e.m.f., E, instead of the p.d., and
(ii) use the total resistance of the circuit, which includes the internal resistance, r, of the battery.

The equation can then be written:

$$E = I(R + r)$$

where E is the e.m.f.   (in V)
       I is the current   (in A)
       R is the total resistance of the external circuit   (in Ω)
       r is the internal resistance of the battery   (in Ω)

The 'external circuit' means the whole circuit except for the battery.

Quick Question 41 What current does a 6 V battery with an internal resistance of 1 Ω send through a 3 Ω resistor?

Example 30.1 A battery of two cells, each having an e.m.f. of 1.5 V and an internal resistance of 0.5 Ω, is connected to a 2 Ω resistor and a 3 Ω resistor in series. What is the p.d. across the 2 Ω resistor?

Solution Applying $E = I(R + r)$ to the whole circuit gives:

$$3.0 = I(2 + 3 + 1)$$

$$\therefore \quad I = 0.5 \text{ A}$$

Applying $V = IR$ to the 2 Ω resistor gives:

$$V = 0.5 \times 2$$
$$= 1.0 \text{ V}$$

Power and Energy

On p. 185 we had:
$$\text{Power} = VI$$
and on p. 189 we had:
$$V = IR$$
Putting these together gives:
$$\text{Power} = I^2R$$
Since:
$$\text{Power} = \frac{\text{Energy used}}{\text{Time taken}}$$
we can multiply either of these expressions for power by the time, t, in seconds to obtain an expression for the amount of energy. So we have:
$$\text{Power supplied by a current} = VI = I^2R$$
$$\text{Energy supplied by a current} = VIt = I^2Rt$$

Note that the power supplied to an electric motor or a transformer is *not* given by I^2R, because motors and transformers have e.m.f.s and the equation $V = IR$ is not true of them. So:

- for heaters and resistors, use any of the four expressions;
- for motors and transformers, use the VI expressions and not the I^2R ones.

These equations all apply to alternating current as well as to direct current.

Example 30.2 An immersion heater takes a current of 4.0 A from 240 V mains. How much heat does it produce in half an hour?

Solution Heat $= VIt = 240 \times 4.0 \times (30 \times 60) = 1\,728\,000\,\text{J} = 1.73\,\text{MJ}$

■ The **kilowatt hour** (kW h) is the unit of energy most used in connection with the supply of mains electricity; on electricity bills it is just called a 'unit'. It is the energy supplied if a power of one kilowatt continues for one hour.

$$1\,\text{h} = 3600\,\text{s} \quad \text{and} \quad 1\,\text{kW} = 1000\,\text{W}$$
$$\therefore \quad 1\,\text{kW h} = 3\,600\,000\,\text{J} = 3.6\,\text{MJ}$$

Example 30.3 What is the cost of running a two-bar electric fire for six hours a day for a whole week, if each bar is rated at 1 kW and the price of electricity is 5p per unit?

Solution

$$\text{Power} = 2\,\text{kW}$$
$$\text{Time} = 6 \times 7 = 42\,\text{h}$$
$$\therefore \quad \text{Energy} = 2 \times 42 = 84\,\text{kWh}$$
$$\therefore \quad \text{Cost} = 84 \times 5\text{p} = 420\text{p} = £4.20$$

Questions on Chapter 30

1. A battery of e.m.f. 6 V and internal resistance 2 Ω is connected to two 5 Ω resistors in series. Find a) the current which flows and b) the potential difference across one of the resistors.

2. A cell has an e.m.f. of 1.5 V. When a 5 Ω resistor is connected to it a current of 0.20 A flows. What is the internal resistance of the cell?

3. The output of a high-voltage power pack has an e.m.f. of 2 kV and an internal resistance of 1 MΩ. A 1 MΩ resistor is connected across the output terminals. Find a) the current which flows and b) the p.d. across the external resistor. Also c) find the current which flows if the external resistor is removed and the output terminals are short-circuited by connecting them together with a short, thick piece of wire.

4. A 1.5 V dry cell of internal resistance 2 Ω and two 4 Ω resistors are connected in two different ways.

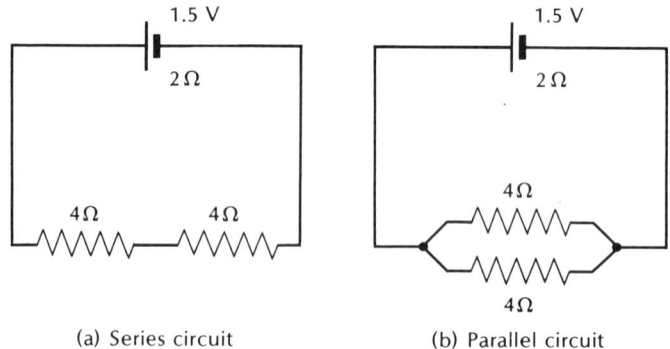

(a) Series circuit   (b) Parallel circuit   **Fig. 30.4**

  a) For the series circuit (Figure 30.4(a)):
      (i) what is the current through the cell?
      (ii) what is the p.d. between the cell terminals?
  b) For the parallel circuit (Figure 30.4(b)):
      (i) what is the current through the cell?
      (ii) what is the current through each resistor? (O)

5 What is the cost of electricity to run a three kilowatt fan heater for four hours a day, six days a week for three weeks if the price of electricity is 5 p a unit?

6 What is the cost of running a 100 W lamp all day and all night for a week if the price of electricity is 6p a unit?

7 An electric fire is rated 2 kW, 240 V and consists of two identical elements connected in parallel. Calculate for *each* element, when the fire is connected to a 240 V supply,
(i) the current taken,
(ii) the resistance, and
(iii) the energy consumed in 5 hours.
If both elements are used for 5 hours, calculate the total cost if the Electricity Board charges 5p for each 'unit'.
(A 'unit' is 1 kW h.) (L)

8 A car has 12 V lighting and the capacity of its battery is 30 ampere hours. It is parked with its lights on and the battery is fully charged to begin with. How long will it take for the battery to become discharged:
a) if the front parking lights and the rear lights are on, four bulbs each rated at 6 W,
b) if the two headlamps are on as well, each headlamp being rated at 48 W?

9 *a)* A wire was connected to a battery and it was found that the energy converted into heat was 30 joules when 20 coulombs of charge flowed through the wire in 5 seconds. Calculate:
(i) the potential difference between the ends of the wire;
(ii) the current flowing through the wire;
(iii) the resistance of the wire;
(iv) the average power developed in the wire.
b) If the current in the wire were doubled and all the energy were released as heat in the wire, how much heat would be produced in the wire in 5 seconds? (JMB)

10 An electric heating element immersed in a large beaker of water has a potential difference of 240 V applied across it. The current through the element is 10.0 A.

In 80.0 s the temperature of the beaker and water rises from 15.0 °C to 65.0 °C. Calculate the total heat capacity of the beaker and its contents; assume that no heat is lost from the beaker. (C)

Chapter 31

AC, Rectifiers and Oscilloscopes

■ **Direct current** (DC) is current that flows in one direction the whole time.

■ **Alternating current** (AC) flows in both directions alternately.

Mains electricity is alternating, and in this case the frequency is 50 Hz, so that the period is 0.02 s. The current reverses every hundredth of a second. This is shown in Figure 31.1, where one direction of current is counted as being positive and the other direction negative. The maximum value of the current, marked I_{max} in the figure, is usually called the 'peak' current.

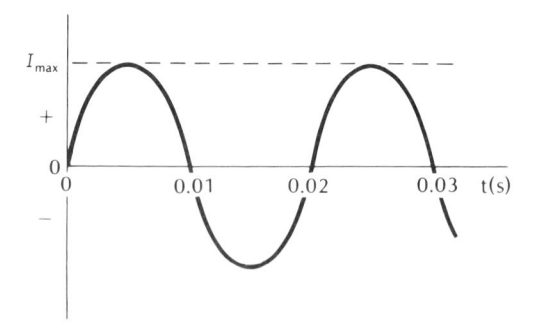

Fig. 31.1

It is sometimes necessary to change AC into DC, and a device which does this is called a **rectifier**. Here are two examples of the need for a rectifier.

- In a radio or television set the AC Mains supply must be turned into DC to work the amplifiers and the picture tube;

- Many cars have alternators instead of DC dynamos, as they produce a greater output at low engine speeds than dynamos do. The AC produced by the alternator must be turned into DC to charge the battery.

■ A **diode** is a device which conducts electricity in one direction only. Rectifiers are composed of one or more diodes. The conventional symbol for a diode is shown in Figure 31.2.

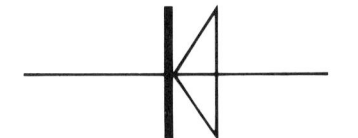

Fig. 31.2

- A **semiconductor diode** is a silicon or germanium crystal containing very small and carefully controlled amounts of impurities. It does not obey Ohm's law. The I-V graph, called the 'characteristic', of a typical diode is shown in Figure 31.3.

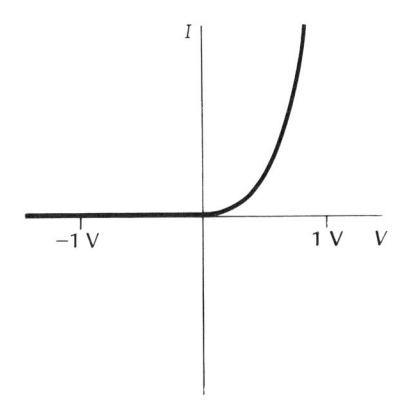

Fig. 31.3

- A **vacuum diode** (Figure 31.4) has a filament heated by a current passing through it. Electrons can leave this filament because it is hot (this is **thermionic emission**), but none can flow from the

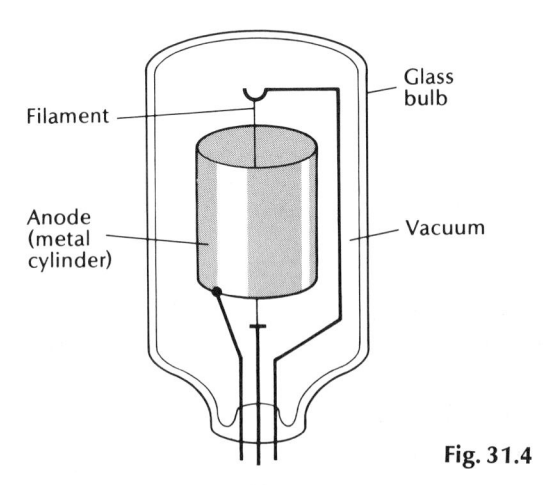

Fig. 31.4

anode to the filament. The characteristic (the I-V graph) is drawn in Figure 31.5; it shows 'saturation' when the p.d. is high enough to ensure that all the electrons that leave the filament are able to reach the anode.

- A **half-wave rectifier** is a single diode connected in series in a circuit. It produces direct current from an alternating supply, but the current is intermittent as shown in Figure 31.6 because only half of the wave-form of the alternating current is used.

- A **full-wave rectifier** uses both halves of the AC wave-form. A common version of it is made up of four diodes connected as shown in Figure 31.7; this is called a 'bridge rectifier'. If its input current is as shown in Figure 31.8(a), then the output current has a graph like Figure 31.8(b) if it has no smoothing capacitor. But if a smoothing capacitor is connected across the output terminals it produces a much more constant current as shown in Figure 31.8(c).

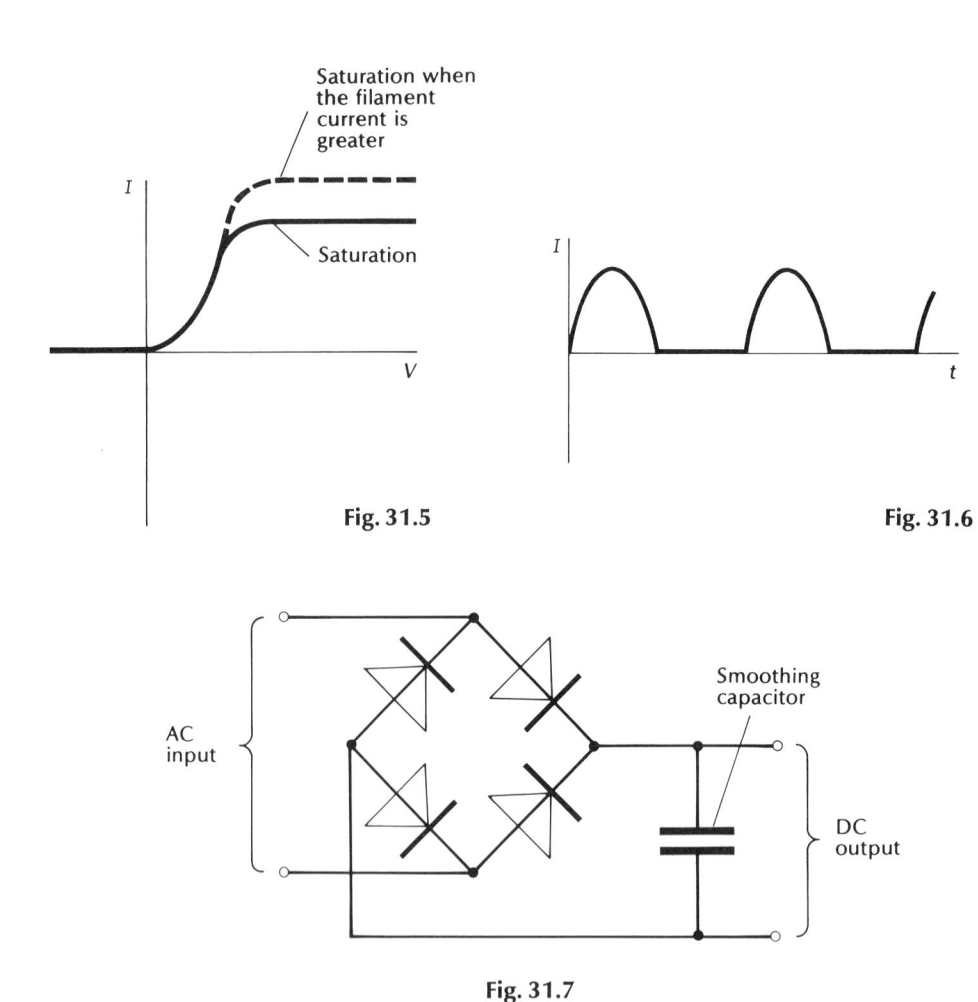

Fig. 31.5

Fig. 31.6

Fig. 31.7

The circuit of a **battery charger** is shown in Figure 31.9. This uses a transformer to reduce mains voltage to a voltage a little greater than that of the battery. It also uses a full-wave rectifier, but not a smoothing capacitor.

(a) AC INPUT

(b) OUTPUT WITHOUT SMOOTHING CAPACITOR

Graph of AC for comparison

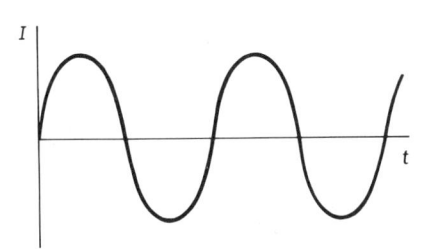

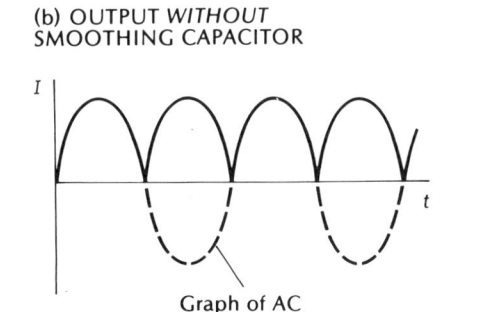

(c) OUTPUT WITH SMOOTHING CAPACITOR

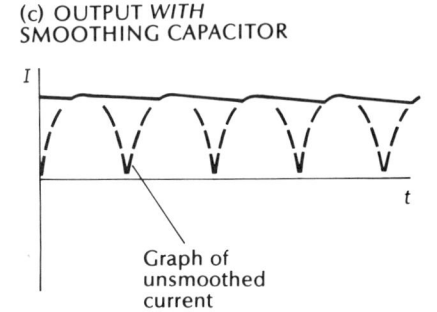

Graph of unsmoothed current for comparison

Fig. 31.8

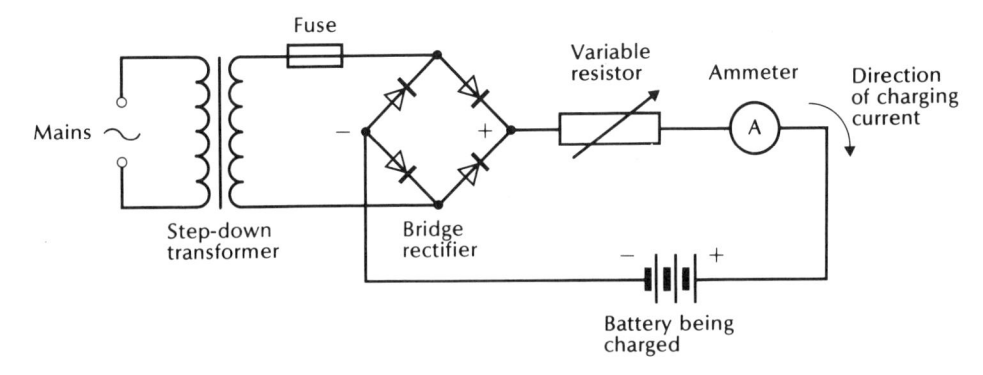

Fig. 31.9

Capacitors

A capacitor is a device for storing two equal and opposite charges. It consists of two conducting plates, very close to each other and separated by a thin layer of insulator. The charge on each plate, Q, is proportional to the potential difference, V, between the plates:

$$Q = VC$$

where C is the capacitance of the capacitor in farads (F), though capacitances are more often given in microfarads (μF). The conventional symbol for a capacitor is shown in Figure 31.7.

Oscilloscopes

■ In a **cathode ray tube** (Figure 31.10) a fluorescent coating on the inside of the screen gives out light when electrons hit it. If a potential difference is applied to the *y* deflector plates, the upper one being positive and the lower one negative, the electrons will be deflected upwards and the spot of light will appear higher up on the screen. The result is the same if the upper plate is made positive and the lower one is connected to earth, or if the upper one is earthed and the lower one made negative. In a similar way, voltages on the *x* plates cause horizontal deflections, and so graphs can be made to appear on the screen.

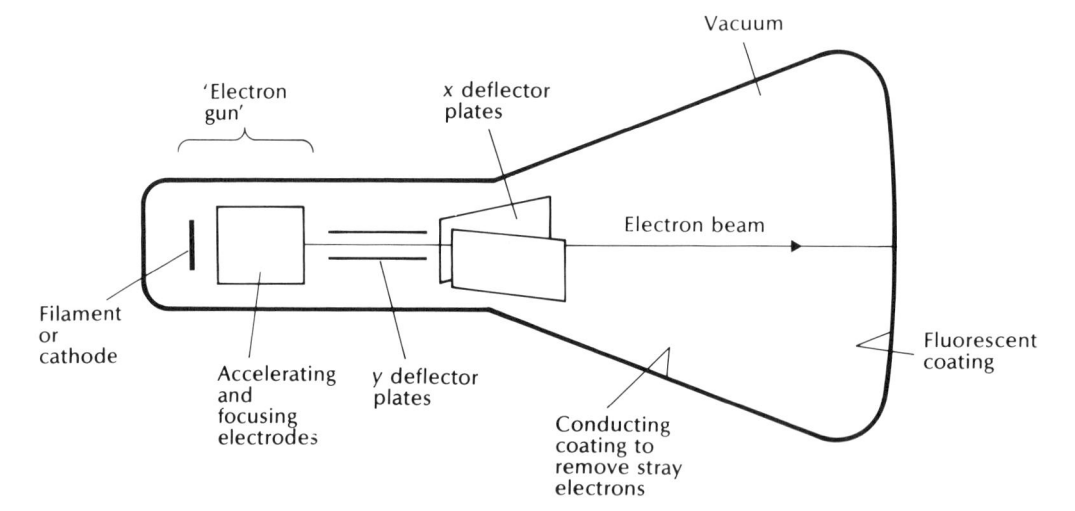

CATHODE RAY TUBE

Fig. 31.10

■ A **cathode ray oscilloscope** consists of a cathode ray tube, amplifiers, a power supply unit, and a time base.

■ The **time base** is a circuit which produces a 'saw-tooth' voltage (Figure 31.11) which can be applied to the *x* plates. When this is done, the spot of light moves across the screen at a steady rate at regular intervals, enabling a graph of potential difference against time to be displayed. Figure 31.12 shows four such graphs. In all four cases the time base is in operation; the voltages applied to the *y* plates are:

    a) zero,

    b) direct, positive to the upper plate,

    c) and *d*) alternating.

In *d*), either the applied voltage has double the frequency of *c*), or else the frequency of the time base has been halved.

TIME BASE OUTPUT VOLTAGE Fig. 31.11

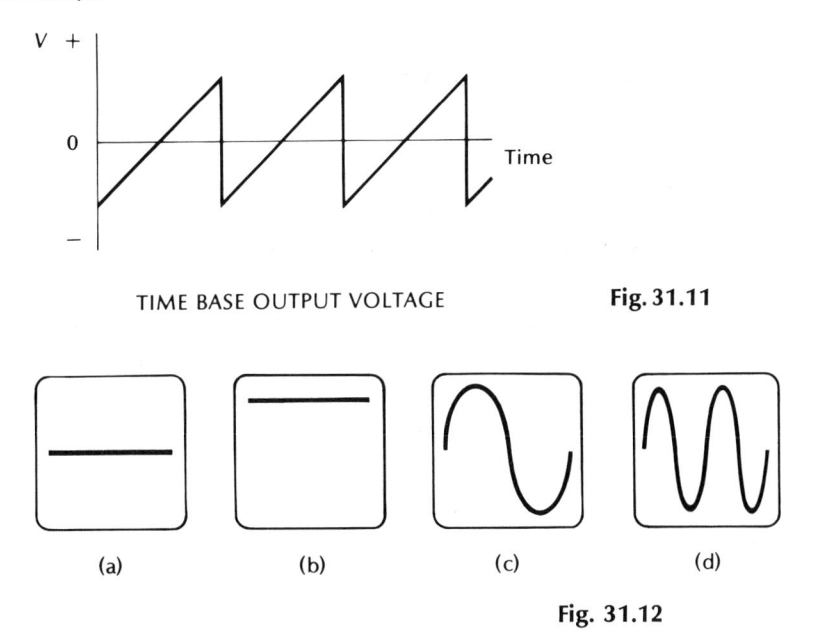

(a)   (b)   (c)   (d)

Fig. 31.12

■ **Television tubes** differ from the tubes of oscilloscopes in that they use magnetic deflection; the electrons are deflected by magnetic fields produced by currents flowing in coils. This will be explained on p. 218.

Questions on Chapter 31

1. The time base of an oscilloscope is set to a frequency of 50 Hz. What pattern would you see on the screen if the plates were connected as indicated below?

    a) x plates to the time base
       y plates to 50 Hz AC
    b) x plates to the time base
       y plates to 100 Hz AC
    c) x plates to the time base
       y plates to full-wave rectified 50 Hz AC
    d) x plates to 50 Hz AC
       y plates to full-wave rectified 50 Hz AC

2. What pattern will be observed on the screen of an oscilloscope if both pairs of plates are connected to alternating voltages of equal frequencies and equal amplitudes:

    a) if the two voltages are in phase with each other,
    b) if they are 90° out of phase, so that each one is at a maximum when the other is momentarily zero?

Chapter 32

Magnetism

If you place a bar magnet where it can turn freely, it will swing until it points roughly north–south. The end that points roughly north is called the north pole of the magnet and the other is the south pole. A good way of allowing the magnet to turn freely is to float it on water by putting it on a saucer or on a suitably shaped piece of plastic foam.

The rules for attraction and repulsion between two magnets are:

like poles (both N or both S)   *repel*,

unlike poles (one N and one S)   *attract*.

(Compare this with the forces between electric charges, p. 177.) The magnets may be suspended, like the rods in Figure 27.1 on p. 177, but floating the magnets on water is easier.

■ A **permanent magnet** — one that keeps its magnetism once it has been magnetised — must be made of steel or of a hard alloy. Soft iron and soft alloys retain little of their magnetism but may be made into induced magnets.

■ An **induced magnet** (or 'temporary magnet') is a piece of soft iron or soft alloy which is kept magnetised by being in a magnetic field caused, perhaps, by an electric current flowing in a coil or by the presence of another magnet nearby. In Figure 32.1 the soft iron bar is an induced magnet because of the permanent magnet

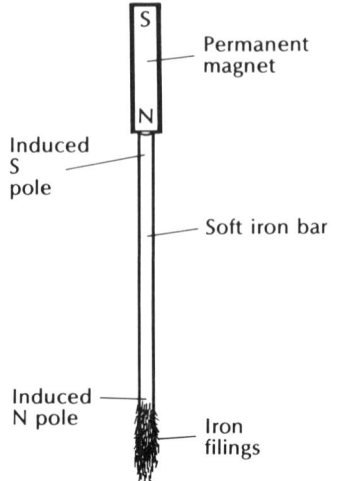

Fig. 32.1

above it; most of the iron filings will drop off when the permanent magnet is removed. (Compare this with induced electric charges, p. 178.)

■ Soft iron or soft alloys can be used for **magnetic screening** (or 'magnetic shielding') so that a magnet on one side of the screen produces very little field on the other side. One of the best materials for this purpose is a soft alloy called Mumetal (pronounced 'mew-metal'). A screen made of Mumetal is often placed around the tube of a cathode ray oscilloscope to prevent the electron beam from being deflected by the fields of nearby magnets or of electric currents or by the Earth's field.

■ **Magnetic materials** are materials that can be made into magnets; they are iron, nickel and cobalt, many alloys which contain one or more of these three elements, and also some alloys which do not. Of these materials, the soft ones cannot be made into permanent magnets but only into induced magnets or electromagnets. Materials like copper and glass which can neither be magnetised nor attracted by a magnet are called 'non-magnetic'.

Methods of Magnetising and Demagnetising

Here is a summary of methods which may be used to magnetise a bar of a hard magnetic material such as steel.

- **Stroking** with a magnet: single touch (Figure 32.2) and double touch (Figure 32.3).

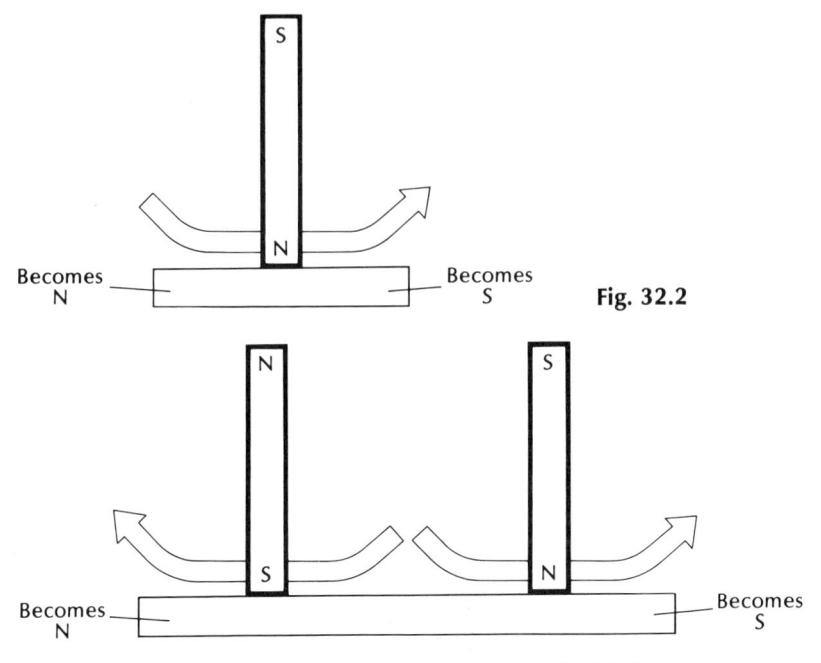

Fig. 32.2

Fig. 32.3

- **Hammering** a bar which is lined up with the Earth's field. (This only makes weak magnets, and it weakens strong ones.)
- **DC solenoid** carrying a large current. A solenoid is a long-shaped coil and the bar must be placed inside it while the direct current flows; it only needs to flow for a fraction of a second.
- **AC solenoid** which may be driven from the electric mains if it is correctly designed and properly insulated. It has the disadvantage that the direction of magnetisation — which end is north and which is south — cannot be predicted, because of the continual reversal of the current. It has the advantage that the same apparatus can be used for demagnetising.

  To magnetise: switch off while the bar is inside.

  To demagnetise: remove the bar while the current is on.

Magnetic Fields

A **magnetic field** is a region in which a freely pivoted compass needle will point in a definite direction. If the field is fairly strong, it can be 'mapped' with iron filings instead of a compass. A field can be represented by **lines of flux** (also called 'lines of force'); these are curves which show at each point the direction in which the north pole of a freely suspended compass needle would point. Where they are closer together the field is stronger.

If the field is caused by an electric current, each flux line is a closed curve.

If the field is caused by a magnet, each flux line starts at the north pole of the magnet and finishes at the south pole.

Some magnetic field patterns are shown in Figure 32.4.

■ The **right-hand grip rule** (Figure 32.5) can be used to predict the direction of the flux produced by a current. It can be used in two ways:
  - if the current is in a straight wire,
    point the thumb along the current and the fingers show the flux direction;
  - if the current is in a coil,
    point the fingers along the current and the thumb shows the flux direction along the straight central flux line.

■ The **corkscrew rule** does the same job as the right-hand grip rule: think of the direction of rotation and the direction of movement of an ordinary screw when it is being screwed either in or out.

Magnetism

(a) STRAIGHT WIRE

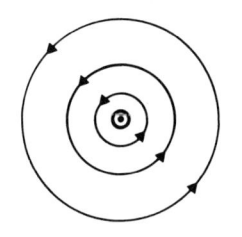

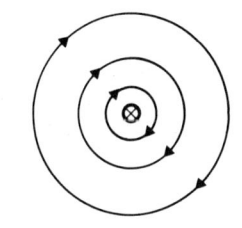

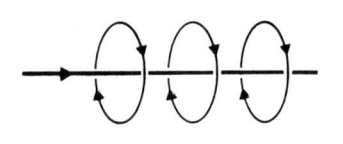

(b) TWO PARALLEL STRAIGHT WIRES

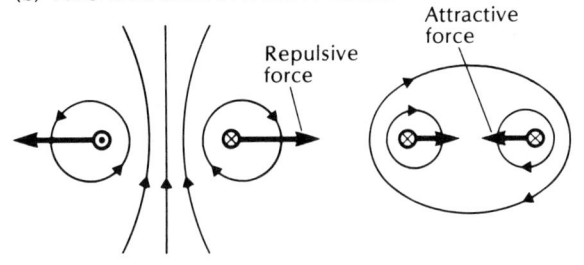

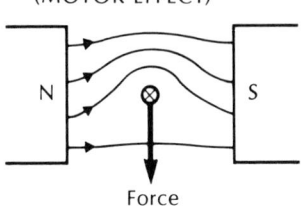

Repulsive force

Attractive force

(c) STRAIGHT WIRE IN A MAGNETIC FIELD (MOTOR EFFECT)

Force

(d) CIRCULAR COIL

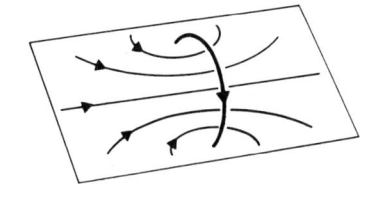

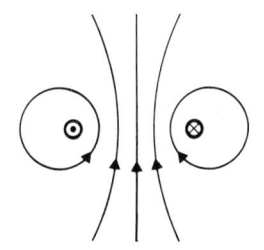

(e) SOLENOID

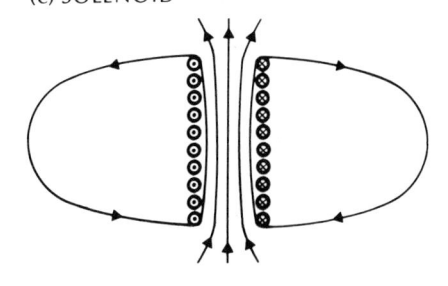

Key
⊙ Current coming out of paper (point of arrow)
⊗ Current going into paper (feathers of arrow)

(f) TOROIDAL COIL

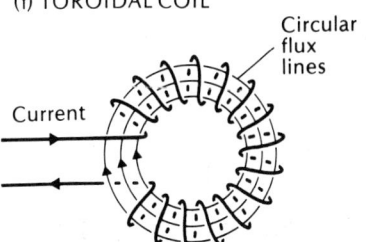

Circular flux lines

Current

(g) BAR MAGNET

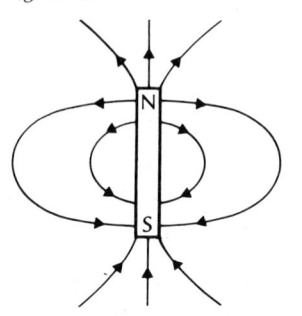

Fig. 32.4

THE RIGHT-HAND GRIP RULE

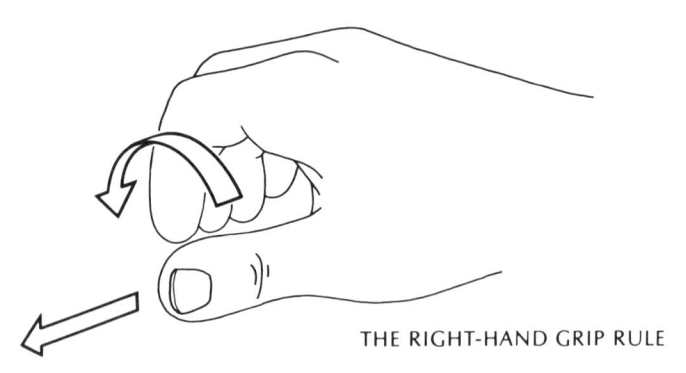

Fig. 32.5

Electromagnets

The field of a solenoid can be made very much stronger by putting a piece of soft iron inside it, so making an **electromagnet**. The soft iron retains hardly any magnetism after the current is switched off.

- An **electric bell** makes use of an electromagnet. One version of a bell is shown in Figure 32.6.

- A **relay** is a switch operated by an electromagnet. A simple type is shown in Figure 32.7. When a current flows in the solenoid the armature is pulled further into the solenoid and the bar on the right of the diagram completes the switch circuit. When the current in the solenoid stops, the spring pulls the armature back again.

ELECTRIC BELL

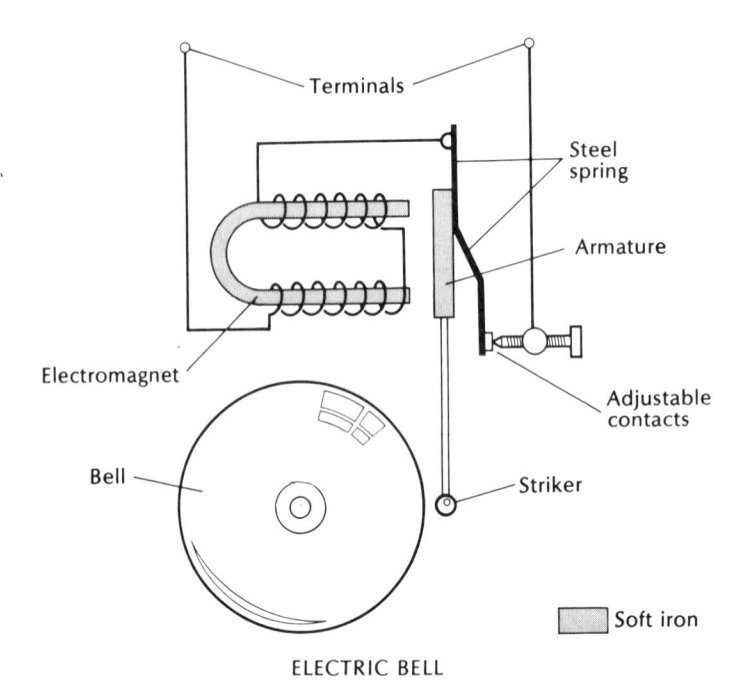

Fig. 32.6

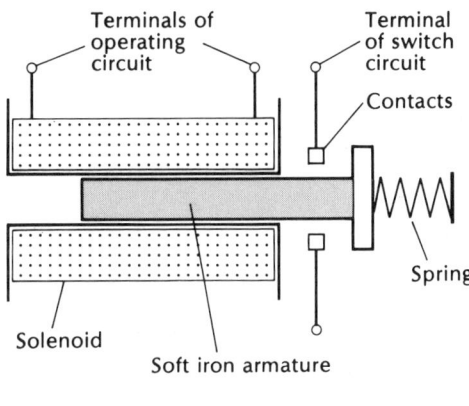

Magnetism 215

Fig. 32.7 — RELAY (Terminals of operating circuit, Terminal of switch circuit, Contacts, Spring, Solenoid, Soft iron armature)

■ **A moving-iron ammeter** works on the principle of an electromagnet. When a current flows in the coil (Figure 32.8) both the iron bars become temporary magnets with the same direction of magnetisation, so that they repel each other. This instrument is suitable for measuring AC as well as DC.

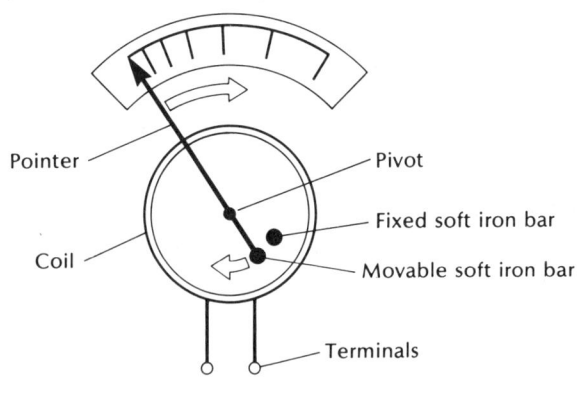

Fig. 32.8 — MOVING-IRON AMMETER (Pointer, Pivot, Fixed soft iron bar, Coil, Movable soft iron bar, Terminals)

The Domain Theory of Magnetism

A single atom of iron behaves as a magnet. This is because two of its electrons are circulating in the electron cloud so as to have the effect of an electric current flowing in a very small circular coil. This is not true of a carbon atom, to take one example, because in that case the electrons circulating in different directions cancel out each other's effects.

In a piece of iron, each atom is lined up with its neighbours, so that they all have their north poles pointing in the same direction, throughout a region called a 'domain'. If the iron is unmagnetised, adjacent domains have their atoms lined up in the opposite direction, or in some other direction, so that the total effect is zero (Figure 32.9).

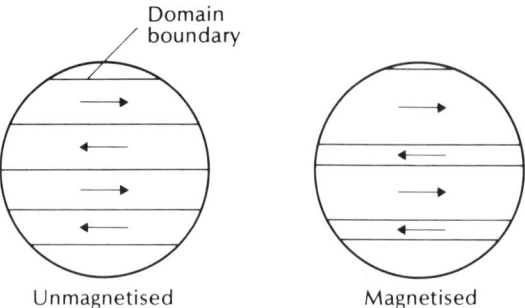

Domain boundary

Unmagnetised   Magnetised   **Fig. 32.9**

If you now magnetise the piece of iron, atoms at the domain boundaries turn round so that some domains grow while others become smaller and the total effect is no longer zero.

Steel is composed of iron with other elements, often carbon, included in it. Carbon inclusions in the iron act as barriers to the movement of the domain boundaries. That is why steel is harder to magnetise than pure iron, but, once it is magnetised, it keeps its magnetism better.

Chapter 33

Motors and Dynamos

The Motor Effect

When a wire carries a current in a magnetic field, a force acts on the wire, provided that the wire crosses the flux lines and does not lie along them. This is called the 'motor effect'. Figure 33.1 shows how it can be demonstrated. In that case, the wire moves upwards when the switch is closed, but if either the magnet or the battery is reversed the wire moves downwards instead.

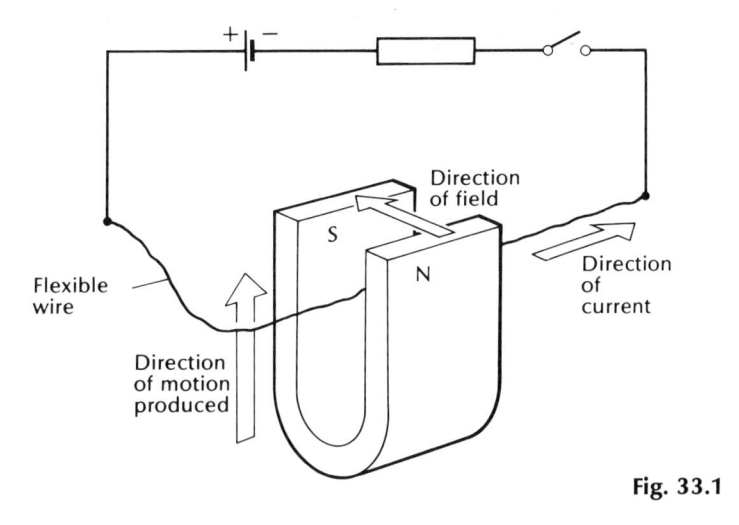

Fig. 33.1

- **Fleming's left-hand rule** can be used to predict the direction of the motion produced: put the thumb and the first two fingers at right angles to each other as shown in Figure 33.2. Then:
  - the First finger shows the Field (or magnetic Flux),
  - the seCond finger shows the Current,
  - the thuMb shows the Motion produced.

- **Electron beams** can be deflected by magnetic fields, and this is an example of the motor effect. This happens in television picture tubes, where electrons travel through a vacuum to hit the screen. Magnetic fields are produced by currents flowing in coils, and these deflect the electron beam so that it hits all parts of the screen in turn.

Fig. 33.2

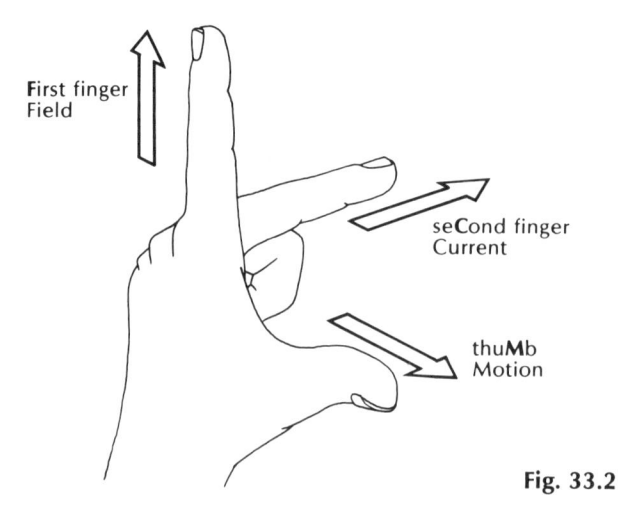

When Fleming's left-hand rule is applied to an electron beam, the thumb shows the deflection of the beam. For example, to consider the moment when the electrons are hitting the top of the screen, the thumb should point upwards. Since the current is in the opposite direction from the electron flow, as we saw on p. 183, the second finger must point in the direction opposite to the velocity of the electrons, that is, towards the back of the tube.

■ The **forces on a coil** carrying a current in a magnetic field are opposite on the two sides of the coil, forming a couple, as shown in Figure 33.3. This principle is used in the moving-coil galvanometer and in the motor.

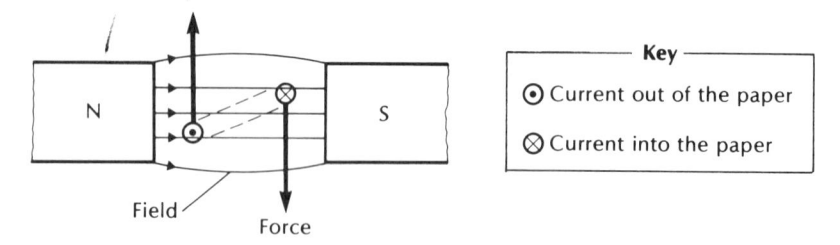

Fig. 33.3

■ In the moving-coil galvanometer (Figure 33.4) the couple acting on the coil causes a limited amount of rotation against the opposing couple due to the hair springs. The current reaches the coil through one hair spring and returns through the other one. So the hair springs have two purposes:

- to carry the current, and
- to provide the opposing couple.

A soft iron cylinder inside the coil increases the strength of the magnetic field by reducing the total width of air gap. This cylinder is fixed and does not rotate. The soft iron cylinder also shapes the field, making it radial. This is necessary if the scale is to be linear, that is, if the scale divisions are to be all equal in length.

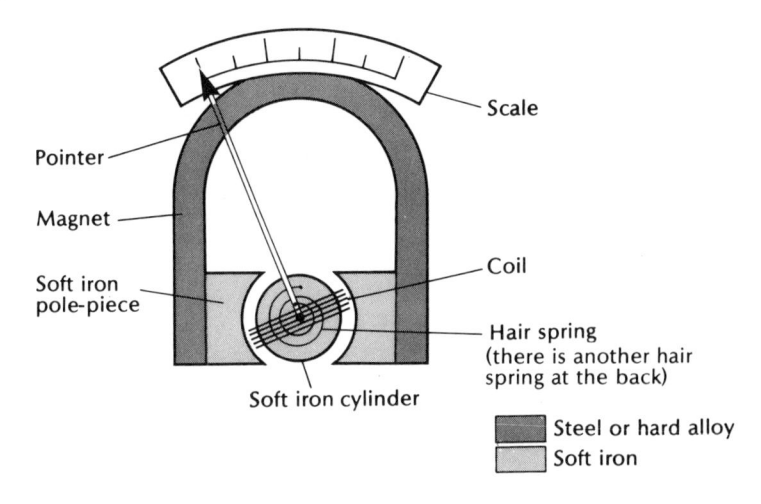

Fig. 33.4

To increase the sensitivity, that is, to make the end of the pointer move further for a given current:

(i) make the field stronger by means of a stronger magnet or a narrower air gap,
(ii) increase the number of turns of the coil,
(iii) make the hair springs weaker,
(iv) make the pointer longer.

■ In the **direct current motor** (Figure 33.5) the couple acting on the coil causes a continuous rotation. This requires that the current in the coil reverses at every half-turn.

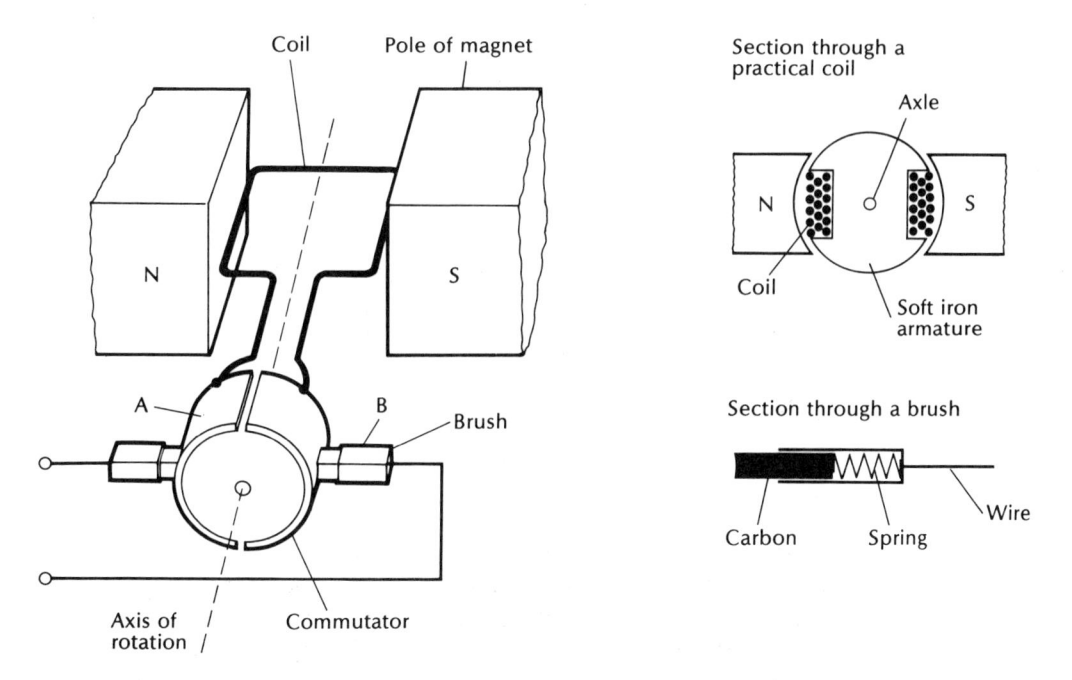

Fig. 33.5

The current reaches the coil through the brushes and commutator. The commutator reverses the current when commutator segment A moves round to touch brush B, and so on every 180°.

A soft iron armature inside the coil increases the strength of the magnetic field by reducing the total width of air gap. The armature rotates, and the coil is wound on it.

To increase the couple exerted by the motor for a given current:
(i) make the field stronger by means of a stronger magnet or a narrower air gap,
(ii) increase the number of turns of the coil.

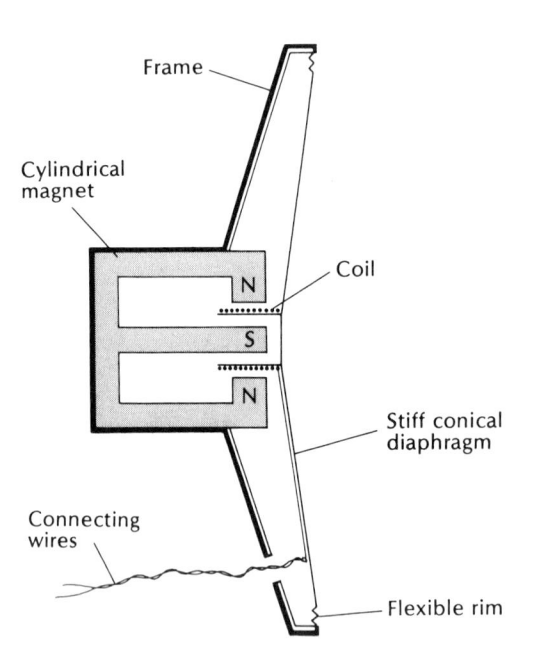

Fig. 33.6

■ The **loudspeaker** (Figure 33.6) is a good example of the motor effect. A varying current is sent through the coil, and since the coil is between the poles of the permanent magnet, this produces a varying force. The coil therefore moves, carrying the conical diaphragm with it and sending out sound waves.

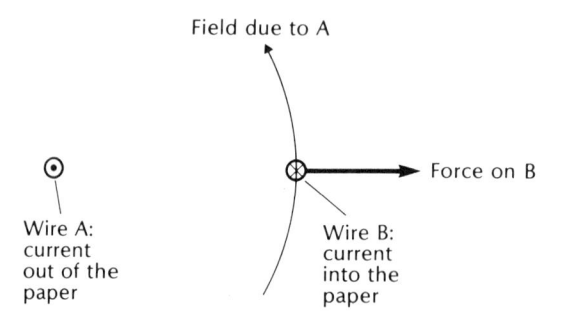

Fig. 33.7

■ The **force between parallel wires** carrying currents can be explained by the motor effect. In Figure 33.7 the direction of the field due to the current in wire A can be found by the right-hand grip rule or the corkscrew rule; then Fleming's left-hand rule shows that the force between the wires is a repulsion. If the two currents were in the same direction, instead of in opposite directions, the force would be an attraction – compare Figure 32.4(b). This force between parallel current-carrying wires is the basis of the definition of the ampere:*

An ampere is the current which, when flowing along two straight, parallel and infinitely long conductors of negligible cross-section placed one metre apart in a vacuum, causes them to exert a force of 2×10^{-7} N on each other for each metre of their length.

Electromagnetic Induction

This is also called the 'dynamo effect' and it is the reverse of the motor effect.

When a wire moves in a magnetic field an electromotive force is produced in the wire, provided that the movement cuts across the flux lines and does not go along them. If the wire is part of a complete circuit, a current will flow as a result. Figure 33.8 shows how this can be demonstrated. The galvanometer shows a current while the wire is being moved up or down, but not if the wire is still or moving horizontally.

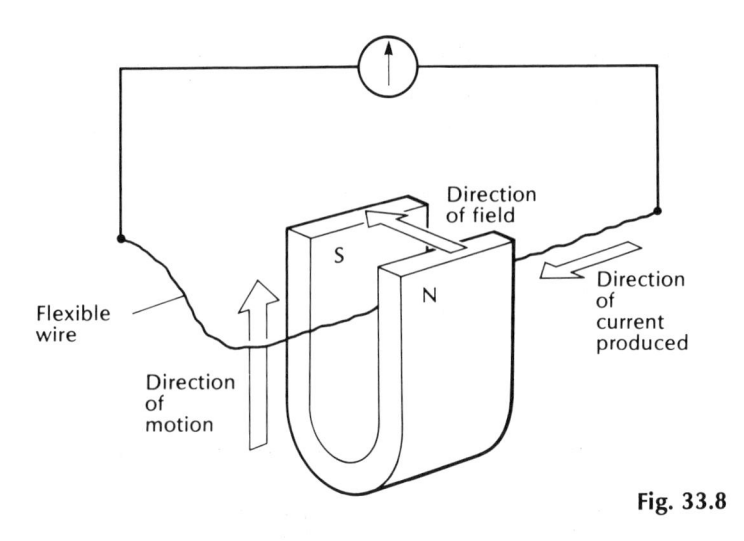

Fig. 33.8

*Only required by one examination board.

- **Fleming's right-hand rule** can be used to predict the direction of the current produced. This rule is shown in Figure 33.9 and the meanings of the thumb and the two fingers are the same as in the case of the left-hand rule given on p. 217, except that it is the current which is produced and the motion is one of the causes.

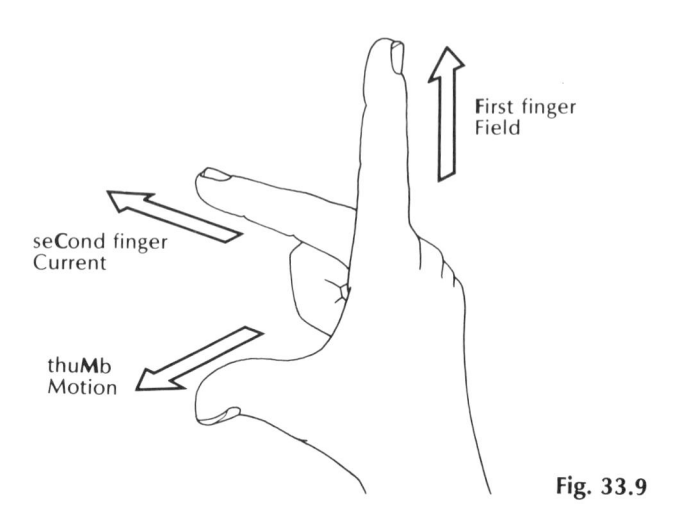

First finger
Field

seCond finger
Current

thuMb
Motion

Fig. 33.9

- The two laws of electromagnetic induction are Faraday's law and Lenz's law. **Faraday's law** states:

  > The induced e.m.f. is proportional to the rate at which the circuit cuts across magnetic flux.

  Note that the law refers to e.m.f. The current depends also on the resistance of the circuit.

  If there is no movement, or if a wire moves along the lines of flux without cutting across them, then there is no e.m.f.

  The e.m.f. is doubled if:
  - the speed of the motion doubles,
  - the field is doubled in strength,
  - twice as long a conductor moves across the field,
  - twice as many strands of conductor are used in series, like the turns of a coil.

- **Lenz's law** states:

  > The direction of the induced current is such that it opposes the change which caused it.

  For example, the current produced in Figure 33.8 causes a force opposing the upward movement of the wire; this force is like the force in Figure 33.1 with the current reversed.

  Another example: if a magnet is moved towards a copper plate an 'eddy current' flows as shown in Figure 33.10. Like a current in a

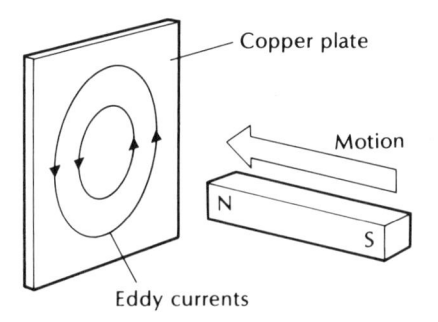

Fig. 33.10

coil, this acts as a magnet. By Lenz's law the near side of the plate acts as a like pole to the one approaching it, thus repelling it and opposing the motion. If the magnet moves away, the current reverses and there is an attraction.

Applications of Electromagnetic Induction

■ A simple **alternating current generator**, or alternator, is shown in Figure 33.11. Since each side of the coil moves alternately upwards and downwards across the magnetic flux as the whole coil rotates, the induced e.m.f. continually reverses and so does the current produced. The current is therefore alternating. This AC output may be turned into DC by a rectifier — see p. 206.

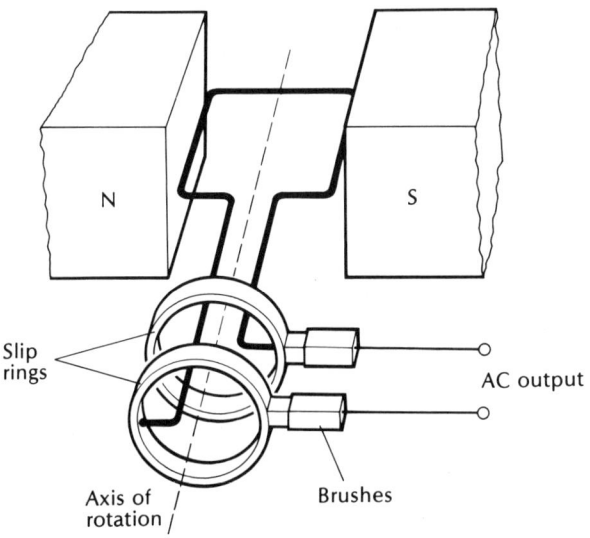

Fig. 33.11

■ A simple **DC generator**, or dynamo, differs from Figure 33.11 in having a commutator instead of slip rings. It is the same as a simple form of DC motor and Figure 33.5 serves for both.

Because motors and dynamos are essentially the same it follows that a motor, when it is running, produces an electromotive force like a dynamo. This is in the opposite direction from the e.m.f. which causes the current that drives the motor, and so it is called the **back e.m.f.** Sample values are given in Figure 33.12 which shows a DC motor with a resistance of $\frac{1}{2}\Omega$ running off a 6 V battery of negligible resistance. The back e.m.f. of the motor is 5 V. In this case, the current is:

$$I = \frac{\text{Total e.m.f.}}{R} = \frac{6-5}{\frac{1}{2}} = 2\,\text{A}$$

The power given out by the battery is:

$$\text{e.m.f. of battery} \times I = 6 \times 2 = 12\,\text{W}$$

The power developed by the motor is:

$$\text{Back e.m.f.} \times I = 5 \times 2 = 10\,\text{W}$$

The power wasted as heat in the resistance of the motor is:

$$I^2 R = 2^2 \times \tfrac{1}{2} = 2\,\text{W}$$

Now consider what happens when the motor is started. When the switch is first closed the motor has not yet begun to turn and so it has no back e.m.f. The current is therefore:

$$I = \frac{\text{e.m.f.}}{R} = \frac{6}{\frac{1}{2}} = 12\,\text{A}$$

which is much larger than the current taken by the motor when it is running. It is sometimes necessary to include an extra resistor, the 'starting resistor', in the circuit until the speed has built up sufficiently, in order to prevent this large starting current from flowing and damaging the motor.

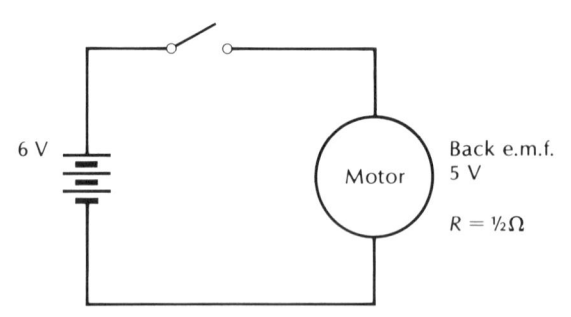

Fig. 33.12

■ **Electromagnetic damping** of a moving-coil galvanometer is another example of electromagnetic induction. If the coil is moving, a current is induced in the coil in addition to any current which the galvanometer may be measuring. In accordance with Lenz's law,

Motors and Dynamos

this additional current opposes the motion that produced it and so the movement of the coil and pointer is damped. (For damping, see p. 145.)

■ The **moving-coil microphone** is the same as a moving-coil loudspeaker (Figure 33.6 on p. 220) except that it is smaller and has a smaller and flatter diaphragm. Sound causes the diaphragm to move, carrying the coil with it, and the coil therefore cuts across the flux of the magnet, producing a varying current.

Transformers work by electromagnetic induction; we will meet them in the next chapter.

A Comparison

The Motor Effect

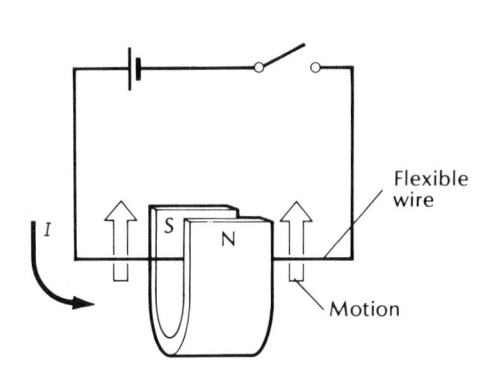

Fig. 33.13

When the switch is closed, a current starts in the direction shown and the wire moves upwards.

Field ⎫
Current ⎭ ... are causes

Motion ... is the result

To predict the direction of the motion use Fleming's left-hand rule.

Electromagnetic Induction
(the dynamo effect)

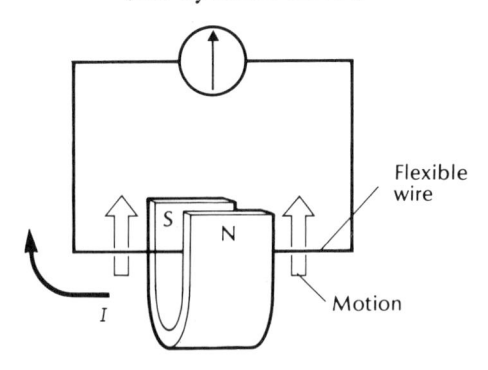

Fig. 33.14

When the wire is moved upwards, the galvanometer indicates a current in the direction shown, but only while the wire is moving.

Field ⎫
Motion ⎭ ... are causes

Current ... is the result

To predict the direction of the current use Fleming's right-hand rule.

Questions on Chapter 33

1 An electric motor with a resistance of 1.5 Ω takes a current of 3 A from a 24 V supply. Find:
   a) the power input into the motor,
   b) the power wasted as heat due to resistance,
   c) the power output.

2 What is the maximum starting current of the motor in Question 1?

3 What is the back e.m.f. of the motor of Question 1 when it is running normally?

Chapter 34

Transformers

A simple type of transformer is shown in Figure 34.1. When a current flows in the primary coil, the flux which it causes passes through the secondary coil because of the shape of the iron core. Whenever this flux is changing, there is an induced e.m.f. in the secondary coil. Therefore a secondary e.m.f. is produced whenever the primary current is changing.

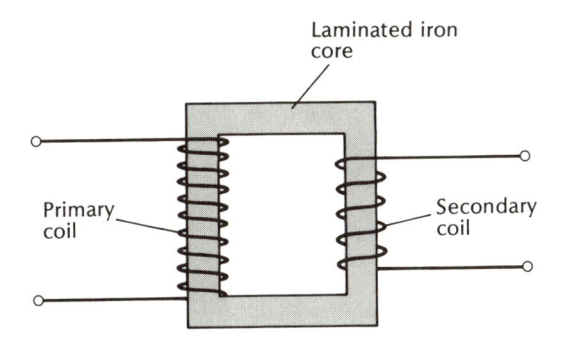

Fig. 34.1

Since alternating current is changing all the time, a transformer can work continuously on AC. Its main purpose is to increase or decrease the voltage of an AC. An AC flowing through the primary coil at one voltage causes an AC to flow in the secondary coil at a higher or lower voltage. Whether it is higher or lower depends on the 'turns ratio'.

■ The **turns ratio** of a transformer is the number of turns of the secondary coil divided by the number of turns of the primary coil. This equals the ratio by which the transformer changes the voltage of an AC.

$$\frac{V_s}{V_p} = \frac{N_s}{N_p}$$

where N means number of turns and the subscripts mean 'primary' and 'secondary'

If Turns ratio > 1
then $V_s > V_p$ and it is a 'step-up' transformer.

If Turns ratio < 1
then $V_s < V_p$ and it is a 'step-down' transformer.

The power output of a transformer is equal to the power input (apart from some power losses mentioned below), and so:

$$V_s I_s = V_p I_p$$

From this it follows that if a transformer steps the voltage up it steps the current down, but it is still called a 'step-up' transformer.

$$\frac{V_s}{V_p} = \frac{N_s}{N_p} = \frac{I_p}{I_s} \quad \text{apart from power losses}$$

Quick Question 42 | A transformer works on 240 V mains and has 1000 turns in its primary coil and 100 turns in its secondary coil. What is its output voltage?

The lost energy turns into heat by three methods:

(i) the coils are heated by the current flowing through their resistance;

(ii) the iron core is heated by eddy currents (compare Figure 33.10 on p. 223) but this is kept to a minimum by 'laminating' the core, that is, building it up of thin plates;

(iii) the iron core is also heated by being repeatedly magnetised and demagnetised. This is called 'hysteresis loss'.

■ **High-voltage transmission** of electric power makes use of transformers. The AC supply is stepped up to a high voltage at the power station and stepped down again near to where it is to be used. Using a high voltage means that a relatively small current flows through the transmission wires (since $\frac{V_s}{V_p} = \frac{I_p}{I_s}$) and this minimises the power loss, which is given by $I^2 R$, R being the resistance of the transmission wires.

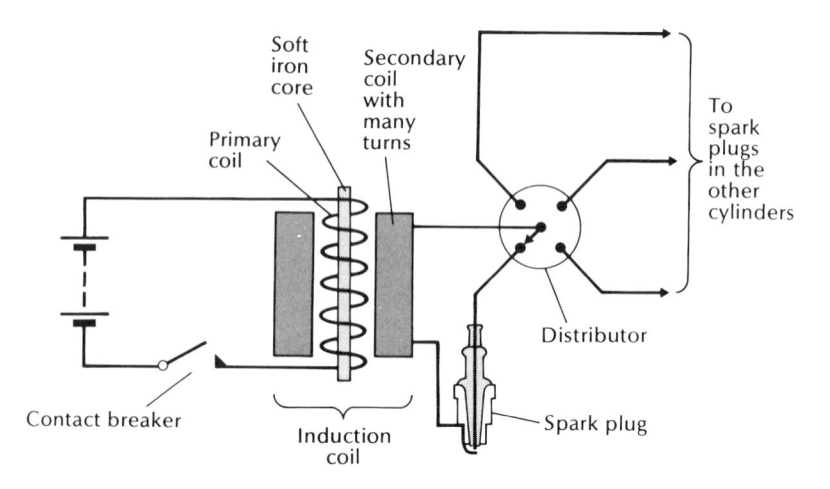

CAR IGNITION SYSTEM   Fig. 34.2

■ An **induction coil** is a step-up transformer designed to be used not with AC but with a direct current which changes suddenly by being switched off. An example of this is a car ignition system shown in Figure 34.2.

Questions on Chapter 34

1 A mains transformer drives a 12 V ray-box. Its secondary coil has 100 turns. How many turns has its primary coil? (Mains voltage = 240 V)

2 A ray-box lamp rated at 12 V 24 W is lit by a transformer from 240 V mains. Find a) the current flowing through the lamp and b) the current taken from the mains. Ignore energy losses in the transformer.

3 A transformer with a turns ratio of 5 works from 240 V mains and supplies a current of 2 A. What are a) its output voltage and b) its input current?

4 A power of 12 kW is to be carried by overhead wires of total resistance 2 Ω. The power can be fed into the wires either a) at 240 V or b) at 24 kV. In each case find (i) the current through the wires and (ii) the power wasted in the resistance of the wires.

5 a) With all the domestic appliances in use, a house takes 20 kW at 240 V. Supposing that this came direct from a generator through cables of total resistance 0.5 Ω, what would be the 'lost' volts in the cables and the power wasted as heat in the cables?

b) Supposing that the same power of 20 kW were transmitted at 120 000 volts from a generator through cables of total resistance 0.5 Ω, and then the voltage were transformed down to 240 V using perfectly efficient transformers, what would be the 'lost' volts in the cables, and the power wasted as heat in the cables?

(O)

Chapter 35

Electrical Safety and Domestic Wiring

Fuses

A fuse is a piece of wire which melts if a current greater than its 'rated current' flows through it. This breaks the circuit before the large current can do any damage.

The rated value of the fuse must be higher than the current it is expected to carry but it should not be a lot higher.

Example 35.1 If fuses are available marked 1 A, 2 A, 5 A, 10 A and 13 A, which should be used for a 2 kW 240 V electric fire?

Solution

$$\text{Power} = V \times I$$
$$2000 = 240 \times I$$
$$\therefore \quad I = 8.3 \text{ A}$$

So the 10 A fuse should be used. The 13 A one would also work though with less safety.

Earthing

Metal frames of mains appliances like cookers and electric fires are connected, through the third wire of the flex, the largest pin of the three-pin plug and the conduit or metal tube through which the supply wires run, to a metal spike driven into the ground. If a fault allows the 'live' (high-voltage) wire of the mains supply to touch the metal frame, a current flows through this fault and down the earthing wire. This current is enough to melt the fuse in the live wire. So the metal frame is cut off from the mains supply before it can give anyone a shock.

Domestic Wiring

Figure 35.1 shows the principles of the electric wiring of a house.*

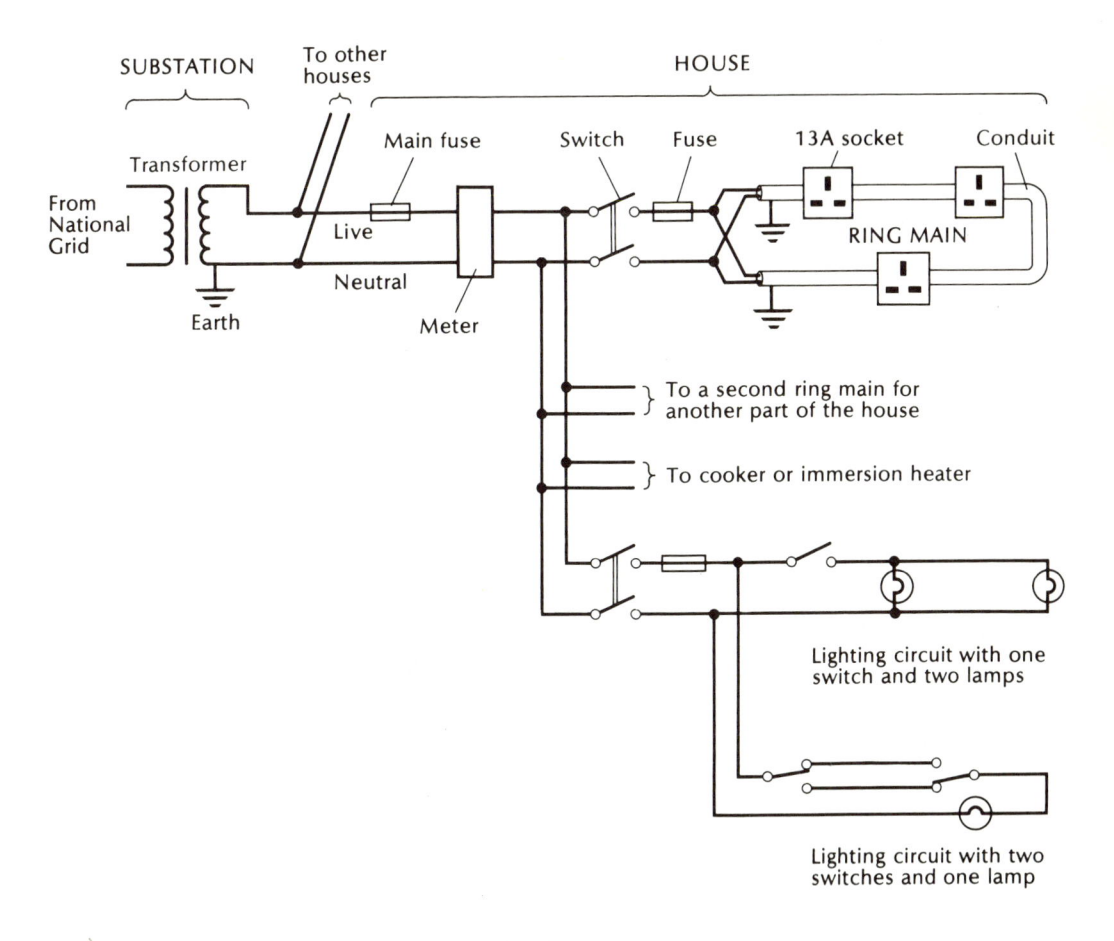

Fig. 35.1

The potential difference between the 'live' wire and earth is about 240 V (in the United Kingdom); the 'neutral' wire on the other hand is connected to earth at the substation, and although it may have a slight p.d. to earth when measured at the house, on account of its resistance between the house and the substation, this will only be a few volts.

The 'ring main' is a loop of wires, connected to the supply at both ends, feeding a number of 13 A sockets. Ring mains are not used for lighting circuits.

---

*The transformer at the substation is shown in the figure as an ordinary one with two coils. In practice it will be a more complicated type having six coils and it will be driven by 'three-phase' current.

The colour code for wiring a 13 A plug is shown in Figure 35.2.

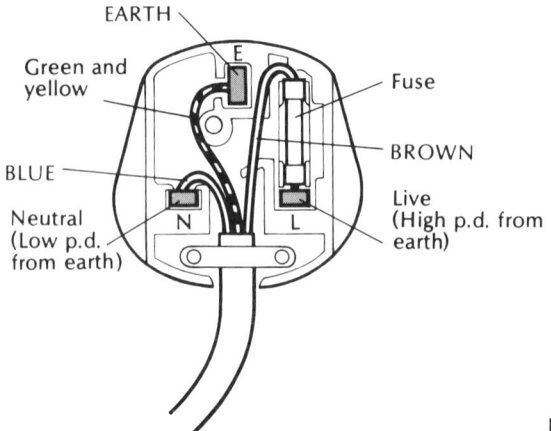

Fig. 35.2

Questions on Chapter 35

1. Suggest a suitable rating for a fuse in a 12 V circuit which supplies the two 36 W headlamp bulbs of a car.

2. Which of the fuse ratings listed in Example 35.1 would be the most suitable for a 60 W mains bulb?

Section F:
NUCLEAR PHYSICS

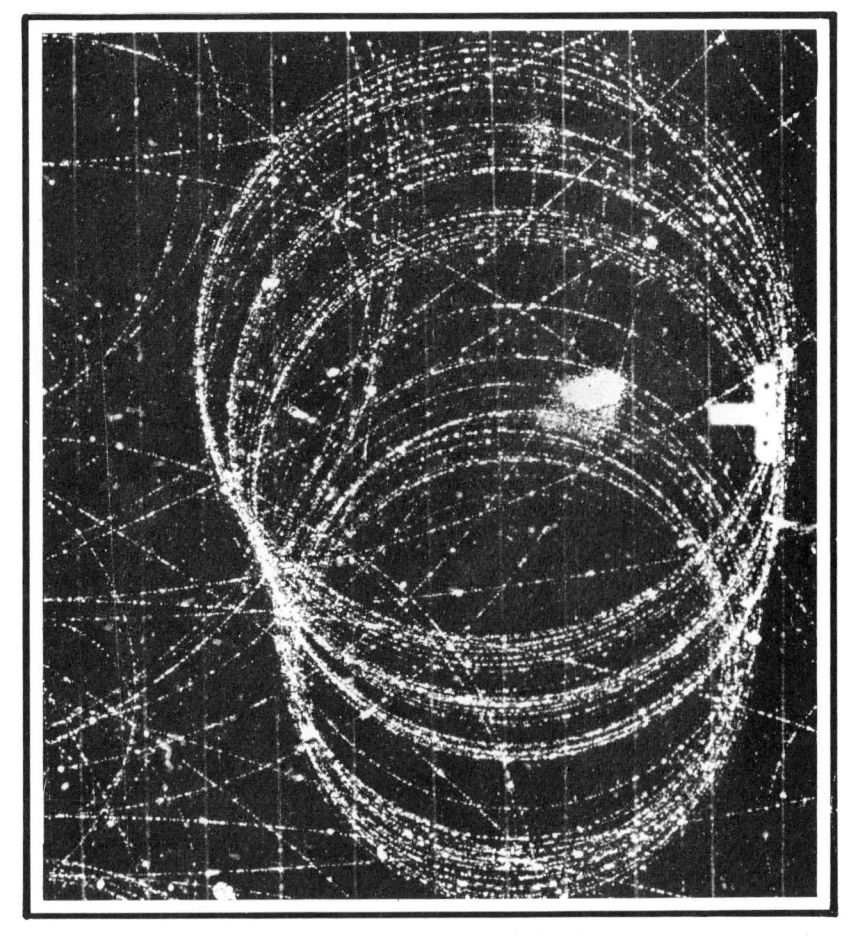

The track of a high-speed electron in a cloud chamber.

The path of the electron is curved because a magnetic field is present. The electron circles round many times.

The straight lines are not tracks of particles; they are part of the apparatus.

Chapter 36

Atoms and Nuclei

In round numbers, an atom is about 10^{-10} m in diameter and its nucleus is about 10^{-15} m in diameter, and yet the nucleus contains all except about one four-thousandth of the mass of the atom. The nucleus is made up of protons and neutrons, and the outer part of the atom is made up of electrons which can be pictured as circling round the nucleus in orbits. Neutrons have no electric charge, and the charge of a proton is equal to that of an electron in magnitude, but opposite in sign. The table summarises the properties of these particles.

	Charge	Approximate comparative mass
Proton	+	2000
Neutron	0	2000
Electron	−	1

The number of protons in the nucleus is called the **atomic number**, Z, and this indicates the element: $Z = 1$ for hydrogen, $Z = 2$ for helium, and so on. The atomic number is:

- the number of protons in the nucleus,
- the charge on the nucleus, in units equal to the charge of an electron, but positive,
- the number of electrons in the atom, if it is not ionised.

The total number of protons and neutrons added together is the **mass number**, A. Atoms with equal atomic numbers but different mass numbers are called **isotopes**.

A type of atom specified by its atomic number and mass number is called a **nuclide**, though it may loosely be referred to as an isotope. The symbol for a nuclide is:

$$^{A}_{Z}X$$

Mass no. — A
Atomic no. — Z
Chemical symbol — X

For example:

$^{12}_{6}C$ is the common isotope of carbon, with 6 protons and 6 neutrons in each nucleus;

$^{14}_{6}C$ is a less common, radioactive isotope of carbon, with 6 protons and 8 neutrons.

The lower figure may be left out and the two isotopes referred to as ^{12}C and ^{14}C (usually called 'carbon twelve' and 'carbon fourteen') since the reader may be expected to know that the atomic number of carbon is 6.

Alpha Particle Scattering

The first evidence that the nucleus is so small — only one hundred-thousandth of the diameter of an atom — came from the scattering of α particles by thin gold foil. Alpha particles (as we shall see in the next chapter) are helium nuclei which are emitted at high speed from certain radioactive substances. Most of the α particles which hit the gold foil are undeviated but a few are turned through big angles, even bouncing straight back. Figure 36.1 illustrates this.

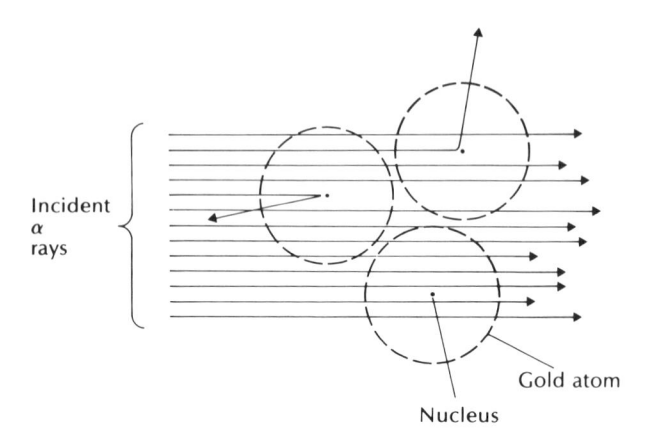

Fig. 36.1

Chapter 37
Radioactivity

Radioactivity means the emission of rays from the nuclei of certain nuclides. Nuclides that do this are called 'radioactive'. Apart from some rarer types that do not concern us, three types of ray may be emitted. They are named, in order of increasing power of penetration, α, β and γ rays — these are the Greek letters alpha, beta and gamma.

When these rays pass through matter they may cause some of the electrons in the matter to be expelled from the atoms to which they belong, leaving these atoms positively charged. In most cases the expelled electron will then join another atom so that that atom becomes negatively charged. An electrically charged atom is called an 'ion' and so this process is called **ionisation**. Radioactivity may be detected by the ionisation which the rays cause.

■ The **cloud chamber** (Figure 37.1) is one of the many types of radiation detector. In it, vapour condenses along the track of a particle because of the ionisation which the particle has caused. This forms a visible condensation trail.

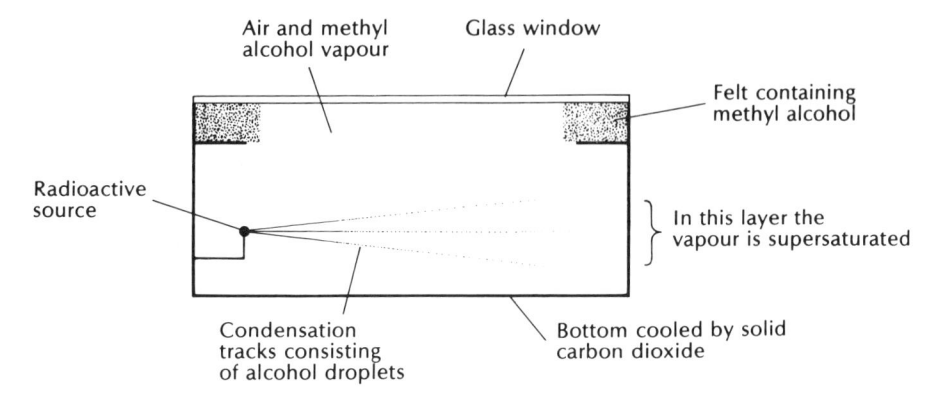

CLOUD CHAMBER (DIFFUSION TYPE)

Fig. 37.1

■ The **Geiger–Müller tube** (shortened to G–M tube, or Geiger tube) is another radiation detector; this is shown in Figure 37.2. Ions produced in the gas inside the tube are accelerated by the high voltage and start an avalanche of ions, so that the gas becomes an electric conductor for a moment. The number of times this happens is counted electrically.

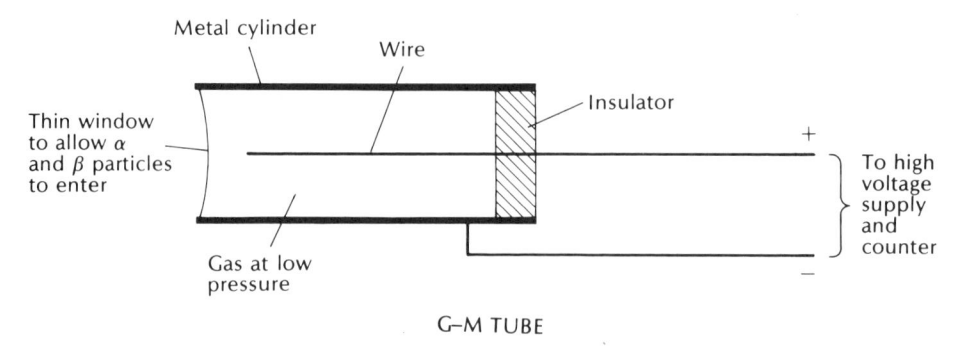

```
                    Metal cylinder
                      \      Wire
                       \      /           Insulator
Thin window             \    /           /
to allow α        ┌──────────────────┐                +  ┐
and β particles ──┤                  │╳╳                 │ To high
to enter          │                  │╳╳                 │ voltage
                  │                  │╳╳                 ├ supply
                  │                  │                   │ and
                  └──────────┬───────┘                   │ counter
                            /        └──────────────────┘
                           /                          ─
                    Gas at low
                    pressure
                         G-M TUBE
```

Fig. 37.2

The three types of ray emitted by radioactive substances are compared in the table.

	α rays	β rays	γ rays
Nature	Nuclei of ^{4}He each composed of 2 protons and 2 neutrons	Electrons	Electromagnetic waves of shorter wavelength than X-rays
Charge	+2	−1	0
Comparative mass	About 4000	1	0
Ability to penetrate	Stopped by thin paper or several cm of air	Stopped by 1 or 2 mm of plastic or $\frac{1}{2}$ mm of aluminium	Only partly stopped by several cm of lead
Deflection by electric and magnetic fields	In the opposite direction to cathode rays	In the same direction as cathode rays	None
Effect on the nucleus when ray is emitted	A decreases by 4 Z decreases by 2	A unchanged Z increases by 1	Loss of energy but no change of A or Z

To distinguish between the three types of ray by experiment, the easiest way is to use the differences between their abilities to penetrate. To do this, use the apparatus shown in Figure 37.3 and place 'absorbers' of aluminium or lead sheet between the source and the G–M tube. Another way is to observe how the rays are deflected by an electric or magnetic field. γ rays are undeflected; β rays are deflected more than α rays and in the opposite direction. To find their directions of deflection, compare the table with p. 218.

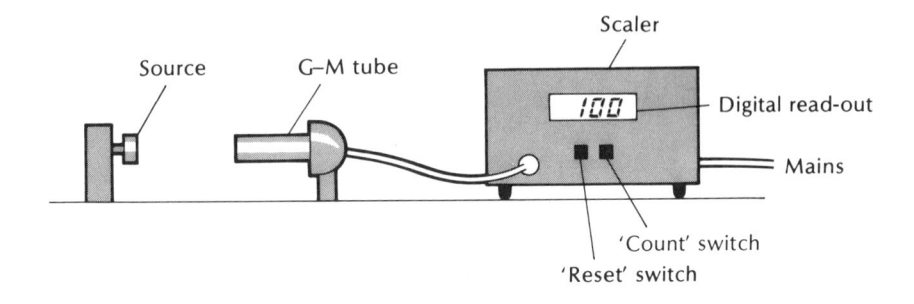

Fig. 37.3

α rays are emitted from nuclei of high atomic number which have too much mass to be stable.

β rays are emitted from nuclei which have too many neutrons compared with the number of protons; one neutron in the nucleus turns into a proton and an electron.* The electron cannot remain in the nucleus and is shot out.

γ rays are emitted from nuclei which have extra energy to get rid of after they have emitted an α or β particle.

Example 37.1 Radium 206 is an alpha emitter. What is its daughter nuclide?

Solution The 'daughter' means the product remaining after the emission. From the Periodic Table (assuming you have access to one) you find that, for radium, $Z = 88$.

Z decreases by 2 from 88 to 86, and

A decreases by 4 from 206 to 202.

From the Periodic Table, element 86 is seen to be radon, Rn. So the answer is radon 202, or $^{202}_{86}$Rn.

*and an antineutrino, which is not important at O-level.

Equations

The α emission of the last example can be represented by the equation:

$$^{206}_{88}\text{Ra} \rightarrow\ ^{202}_{86}\text{Rn} + ^{4}_{2}\alpha$$

Notice that the total values of A and of Z agree on the two sides of the equation:

$$206 = 202 + 4 \quad \text{and} \quad 88 = 86 + 2$$

An example of β emission is the decay of carbon 14 to nitrogen; the equation can be written:

$$^{14}_{6}\text{C} \rightarrow\ ^{14}_{7}\text{N} + ^{0}_{-1}\beta$$

The figure '−1' attached to the letter β is not an atomic number, as the other subscripts are, but it is the charge of the β particle and it is useful to write it there as it makes the numbers agree on the two sides of the equation as before.

Equations are of little use for γ emission because the daughter nuclide is identical with the original nuclide except that it has less energy.

Half-life

The half-life, $T_{\frac{1}{2}}$, of a radioactive nuclide is the time taken for half of the atoms in a sample of it to decay. For example, the half-life of $^{14}_{6}\text{C}$ is 6000 years (approximately) and so in 6000 years half of the atoms of $^{14}_{6}\text{C}$ will decay into $^{14}_{7}\text{N}$, the common isotope of nitrogen, by emitting β particles. In another 6000 years half of the remainder will decay, and so on. So the fractions of the original sample which remain after successive half-lives are $\frac{1}{2}, \frac{1}{4}, \frac{1}{8}, \frac{1}{16}$ and so on. The rate of decay, which can be measured by finding the number of counts per minute of a G–M tube, decreases in the same way.

Each radioactive material has its own half-life and the values range from a small fraction of a second to thousands of millions of years.

Example 37.2 The activity of a freshly prepared radioactive sample is tested by a Geiger tube which records 4000 counts per minute. On repeating the test 8 days later the result is 500 counts per minute. What is the half-life of the sample?

Radioactivity

Solution The activity decreases in the ratio

$$\frac{500}{4000} = \frac{1}{8} = \frac{1}{2} \times \frac{1}{2} \times \frac{1}{2}$$

Therefore the time is three half-lives.

$$\therefore \quad T_{\frac{1}{2}} = \frac{8 \text{ days}}{3} = 2\tfrac{2}{3} \text{ days}$$

■ This example ignores **background radiation** caused by cosmic rays and by radioactivity of the Earth. The 'background count' should be measured separately, by using a Geiger tube with the radioactive source removed, and should then be subtracted from each count that is done with the source in position.

Randomness

In considering half-life, we assumed that very large numbers of atoms were present and that the count rates were fairly high. With smaller numbers it is more noticeable that the decay is random.

The random nature of radioactive decay can be shown by taking a succession of counts with a G–M tube, using a source which has a long half-life and therefore does not change appreciably during the experiment. The various readings will differ from each other but a true count rate can be found by:
- counting for a long time, or
- averaging a number of shorter counts.

Uses of Radioactivity

Among the many uses of radioactive substances are:
- **Chemical labelling.** Carbon dioxide 'labelled' by containing a small amount of the radioactive isotope ^{14}C may be used in a reaction. A G–M tube can then be used to find out which reaction product contains the labelled carbon.
- **Sterilising.** Plastic hypodermic syringes are sterilised after manufacture not by heat, which would melt them, but by γ radiation from a radioactive isotope of cobalt.

Safety

Radiation causes damage to the human body. To guard against this, precautions must be taken, including:

- **Small quantity** — use as small a mass of the radioactive substance as possible for the experiment or task to be done.
- **Distance** — keep away from the source of radiation, using long-handled forceps and remote-reading instruments.
- **Screening** — work behind a shield; for γ rays the shield should be made of lead.
- **Short exposure** — don't remain near to the source for a longer time than necessary.

Fission

Fission is the splitting of a heavy nucleus such as the uranium isotope ^{235}U into two parts. These two 'fission fragments' fly apart at high speed; their kinetic energy is shared with neighbouring atoms with which they collide, and so heat is produced. Two or three separate neutrons are also emitted when fission takes place and these may hit other nuclei and cause them to undergo fission too. This kind of 'chain reaction' happens at a controlled rate in a nuclear reactor.

Although energy is accurately conserved in ordinary cases, it is not conserved when very high speeds are involved, such as the speeds with which the fragments fly apart in nuclear fission. In this case some mass is turned into energy. The amounts of mass and energy involved are related by the equation:

$$E = mc^2$$

where E is the energy which appears   (in J)
          m is the decrease of total mass   (in kg)
          c is the speed of light   (3×10^8 m/s)

Questions on Chapter 37

1. Write the equation expressing the α decay of uranium 238 (symbol U, atomic number 92) into an isotope of thorium (symbol Th).

2. Write the equation expressing the β decay of strontium 90 (symbol Sr, atomic number 38) into an isotope of yttrium (symbol Y).

3 'Tritium' is the name given to a particular isotope whose nucleus consists of one proton and two neutrons. It emits β particles. What is its daughter product? Write the equation for the decay. The first three elements in the table of the elements are:

    hydrogen   H   atomic number = 1
    helium   He   atomic number = 2
    lithium   Li   atomic number = 3

4 The following symbols represent five nuclides (nuclei):

$$^{58}_{29}A;\ ^{54}_{27}B;\ ^{59}_{29}C;\ ^{58}_{30}D;\ ^{59}_{30}E.$$

(i) Which nuclides are isotopes of each other?
(ii) Which nuclide could be produced from which other by the emission of an α particle?
(iii) Which nuclide could be produced from which other by the emission of a β particle?
(iv) Which nuclide possesses most neutrons?   (L)

5 What is the half-life of a radioactive sample which decreases its activity, measured with a G–M tube, from 4800 counts per minute to 300 counts per minute in 24 hours? (Ignore background radiation.)

6 A sodium chloride sample containing the radioactive isotope ^{24}Na is placed in front of a G–M tube which registers 100 counts/minute. If the background count rate is 20 counts/minute, what count rate would you expect the G–M tube to give 30 hours later? (^{24}Na is β active and has a half-life of 15 hours.)

Chapter 38

Waves and Particles

We naturally think of α and β rays as streams of particles, and of γ rays as waves, and to our minds those seem to be entirely different things. In the early years of this century scientists discovered that the distinction is not as clear as it seems.

γ rays have particle-like properties as well as wave-like ones. An example of γ rays behaving as particles is their effect on a G–M tube: they trigger off the tube at random intervals of time just as α and β rays do.

A particle of γ radiation or of any other type of electromagnetic radiation is called a **photon**. As you go up the spectrum (see p. 170) towards longer wavelengths the particle-like properties of the radiation become less and less noticeable in comparison with the wave-like properties, but in some ways light and even infra-red rays behave as particles.

Line Spectra

The emission of a line spectrum by a gas — for example, the monochromatic yellow light given out by a sodium lamp, or the mixture of monochromatic red and monochromatic blue light produced by sending an electric current through hydrogen — can only be explained in terms of photons. Each atom of the gas can only exist with certain amounts of energy; it has definite *energy levels*. If it jumps from one energy level to a lower one it gives out its surplus energy in the form of a photon. Since all the atoms doing this particular jump produce photons with equal energies, the light given out is monochromatic, because a definite energy corresponds to a definite wavelength.

APPENDIX/INDEX

Appendix: SI Units

The Basic Units from which all the others are Derived

Mass	*kilogram*	kg	See p.	3
Length	*metre*	m	p.	3
Time	*second*	s	p.	3
Current	*ampere*	A	p.	221
Temperature	*kelvin*	K		73

Other Named Units

Force	*newton*	N	See p.	23
Energy / Work	*joule*	J	p.	48
Power	*watt*	W	p.	50
Pressure	*pascal*	Pa	p.	57
Frequency	*hertz*	Hz	p.	144
Charge	*coulomb*	C	p.	183
p.d. / e.m.f.	*volt*	V	p.	185
Resistance	*ohm*	Ω	p.	189

A Selection of Units without Separate Names

Velocity	m/s	See p.	3
Acceleration	m/s^2	p.	15
Momentum	kg m/s	p.	41
Density	kg/m^3	p.	6
Expansivity	/K (or /°C)	p.	76
Specific heat capacity	J/kg K	p.	92
Specific latent heat	J/kg	p.	98
Resistivity	Ω m	p.	194

Non-SI Units which are used with the SI System

Energy	*kilowatt hour*	kW h	See p. 201
Pressure	*millimetre of mercury*	mmHg	p. 57
Temperature	*degree Celsius*	°C	p. 73

Prefixes

Example

✗ G	giga	10^9	1 GW (gigawatt) = 1 000 000 000 W
M	mega	10^6	1 MJ (megajoule) = 1 000 000 J
k	kilo	10^3	1 kHz (kilohertz) = 1000 Hz
m	milli	10^{-3}	1 mV (millivolt) = $\frac{1}{1000}$ V
μ	micro	10^{-6}	1 μA (microampere) = $\frac{1}{1\,000\,000}$ A
n	nano	10^{-9}	1 nm (nanometre) = $\frac{1}{1\,000\,000\,000}$ m

Two other prefixes do not go in steps of 1000 and should, strictly speaking, only be used in their cubed forms as units of volume. They are:

- deci, used in $1 \text{ dm} = \frac{1}{10} \text{ m}$

    A cubic decimetre (dm³) equals $\frac{1}{1000}$ m³; it is also called a *litre* (ℓ).

- centi, used in $1 \text{ cm} = \frac{1}{100} \text{ m}$

    A cubic centimetre (cm³) equals $\frac{1}{1\,000\,000}$ m³.

The only multiple of the kilogram which is used is 10^3 kg; this is not called a 'megagram' but a *tonne* (t).

Index

absolute zero 73, 85
AC 201, 204, 227
AC generator 223
AC meter 215
acceleration 15-24
accumulator 198, 199
air column 146, 155-7
alpha particle scattering 236
alpha rays 238, 239
alternating current 201, 204, 227
alternator 223
ammeter 192, 215
ampere 183, 221
amplitude 143, 149
aneroid barometer 59
apparent depth 122
Archimedes' principle 65
atmosphere 57
atom 88, 105, 215, 235

back e.m.f. 224
background radiation 241
barometer 59
battery 197-9
beats 163
bell 214
beta rays 238-42
bicycle pump 61
bi-metal strip 78
boiling 101
Boyle's law 80, 82, 89
brake, hydraulic 58
bridge rectifier 206, 207
Brownian motion 91

camera 136
camera, pinhole 115
capacitor 47, 206, 207
cathode ray tube 208
cells 197-9
Celsius (centigrade) scale 73
central heating 107
centre of gravity 36, 38
charge 177-83
charging 198, 206, 207
Charles' law 80 83
circular motion 32
cloud chamber 233, 237
collision 41
colour 124-5, 172
component 28

conduction of heat 105, 106
conservation of energy 46
conservation of momentum 41
constant flow method 95
convection 106, 107
cooling by evaporation 90
corkscrew rule 212
coulomb 183
couple 35
critical angle 123, 124
current 183, 186

damping 145, 224
DC generator 223
decay, nuclear 240, 241
demagnetising 212
density 6-9, 66
deviation 121
Dewar vessel 109
diffraction 161, 164 169
diffraction grating 167
diffusion 90
diode 187, 204, 205
dioptre 129
displacement 8, 65
domain 215, 216
dynamo 223

earthing 230
echo 150, 151
eddy current 223
efficiency 54
elasticity 25
electric wind 179
electromagnet 214
electromagnetic induction 221-7
electromotive force 199, 200
electron 105, 178, 235
electron flow 183, 218
electroscope 180
e.m.f. 199, 200
energy 46-9, 92, 201, 242
energy levels 244
equilibrant 28
equilibrium 31, 36, 37
evaporation 89, 90, 101
expansion 76-9
expansion of water 107
expansivity 76
explosion 42
eye 137, 172

falling body   15, 17, 47, 49, 62
farad   207
Faraday's law   222
fission   242
fixed point   71
Fleming's rules   217, 222
flotation   66
fluorescence   113, 169, 208
flux lines   212, 213
focal length   119, 129-31
focal point   119, 128
focusing   136, 137
force   23-32, 42, 48
forced and free vibrations   145
freezing   101, 102
frequency   144, 147, 149, 204
friction   30-2
friction compensation   23
fuse   230

galvanometer   192, 218
gamma rays   170, 238-42
gas   80-5
gas thermometer   71, 84
gears   56
Geiger (G-M) tube   237, 238
generator   223
gradient of graph   15, 20, 190
grating   167
gravitational acceleration   15, 18, 25
gravitational field strength   25
greenhouse effect   108

half-life   240
harmonic   154-6
heat capacity   92-5
hertz   144
Hooke's law   25
hydraulic brake   58
hydraulic jack   57
hydrometer   67
hypsometer   72
hysteresis   228

ice pail experiment   181
ice point   71
ideal gas equation   81
image   117, 118, 131-5
impulse   43
inclined plane   55
induced charge   178, 181, 182
induced magnet   210
induction coil   228, 229
infra-red   108, 170
interference   161-6
isotope   235

jack, hydraulic   57
jack, screw   55
joule   48

kelvin   73
kilogram   3
kilowatt-hour   201
kinetic theory   88

latent heat   98
left-hand rule   217, 218
lens   111, 128-34, 160
Lenz's law   222
light, production   113
light, propagation   114
lines of force (flux)   212, 213
litre   7, 248
longitudinal wave   148, 149
loudness   149
loudspeaker   220

machine   53-6
magnet   210-14
magnetic field   212, 213
magnetising   211, 212
magnetism, theory   215, 216
magnification   133
magnifying glass   138
monometer   60
mass   24
mass-energy relation   242
mechanical advantage   53
melting   101
metre   3
micrometer   5
microphone   225
microscope   138, 140
mirror, plane   117, 118
mirror, spherical   118-9, 130, 134
mixtures, method of   95
molecule   88-91
moment   35, 36
momentum   41-3
monochromatic light   164, 173
motor   219, 220, 224
motor effect   213, 217-21, 225
moving coil meter   218
moving iron meter   215

neutron   235
newton   23
Newton's laws   42
node   154-7
normal   117
nucleus   235, 236

Index

ohm 189
Ohm's law 186
oscillation 143–5
oscilloscope 208

parallelogram 26
pascal 57
p.d. 184
period 143, 147
periscope 124, 125
phase 144
photon 244
pinhole camera 115
pipes, open and closed 155–7
pitch 149
plug, 3-pin 232
polarisation 166
potential difference 184, 185
potentiometer 185
power 50, 185, 201
power of a lens 129
prefixes 248
pressure 57–61, 89
pressure, effect on m.p. and b.p. 102
pressures, law of 80, 84
prism 124
projector 137
proton 235
pulley 55
pump 61

quality of sound 150

radiation 108, 242
radio waves 147, 170
radioactivity 237–42
radio telescope 139
reaction 36
real and apparent depth 122
rectifier 206
reflection of light 117–9
reflection of ripples 159
reflection of sound 151
refraction of light 120
refraction of ripples 160
refractive index 120
relay 214
resistance 189–91
resistivity 194
resistor 184, 187
resistors in series and parallel 192
resolving 28
resonance 145, 156
resultant 25, 26
right-hand grip rule 212, 214
right-hand rule 222
ring main 231
ripples 159–62
rocket 43

safety, electrical 230
safety, nuclear 242
saturated vapour pressure 90, 102
scalar 27
scale drawing 133
scattering 236
screw gauge 5
screw jack 55
second 3
semiconductor 194, 205
shadow 114
shunt 192
SI 3, 247, 248
smoothing 206
Snell's law 120
solenoid 212, 213
sound 149–51
specific heat capacity 92–5
specific latent heat 98–100
spectrum 124, 167, 244
speed 12
speed of light 115, 242
speed of sound 150
stability 37
standing (stationary) waves 154
steam point 71
strings, stretched 154, 155
stroboscope 144
sublimation 101
surface tension 62

telescope 138
television tube 209, 217, 218
temperature 71–4, 89
terminal velocity 62
thermionic emission 205
thermistor 194
thermocouple 74
thermometer 71, 74, 78
ticker timer 1, 19, 23
time base 208
tonne 248
total internal reflection 123
transformers 227, 228, 231
transverse waves 148
triangle of forces 27

ultra-violet 170
units 3, 247–8
upthrust 65
U-tube 9, 60

vacuum flask 109
Van de Graaff generator 179, 180
vapour 102
vector 26
velocity 12
velocity ratio 53

vernier　4
vibrations　145
virtual image　118, 132, 133
viscosity　62
volt　185
voltage　184, 186
voltmeter　193

water analogy　186
water, expansion　107

watt　50, 185
wave　143, 146–70, 244
wave, stationary　154
wave-form　144, 150
wavelength　146, 147
wavelength of light　164, 167–9
weight　24, 25
wiring, domestic　231
work　48

X-rays　170